Reviewer Praise for Other Bes
Books by Douglas Gra

D1284246

THE COMPLETE CANADIAN SMALL BUSINESS GUIDE (with Diana Gray)

"This guide is truly a gold mine ... taps into the authors' extensive experience ... an encyclopedic compendium ... the bible of Canadian small business."   *Profit Magazine*

"Thorough and wide-ranging ... bursts with practical tips and explanations."   *Vancouver Sun*

"The ultimate in small-biz aid – if I ever quit my day job this is one of the first books I'd rush out and buy."
    Linda A. Fox, the Toronto Sun

HOME INC.: THE CANADIAN HOME-BASED BUSINESS GUIDE (with Diana Gray)

"Should be required reading for all potential home-basers ... authoritative, current and comprehensive."
    Edmonton Journal

"An absolute necessity for your bookshelf ... crammed with useful information ... will pay for itself in short order."
    Victoria Times – Colonist

THE CANADIAN SMALL BUSINESS LEGAL ADVISOR

"Small business and the law ... who better than Doug Gray to provide the insight Canadian small business owners need on this always complicated topic."
    Hayden Bradshaw, Publisher/Managing Editor,
    Small Business Canada Magazine

"Like all of Doug Gray's reference books, *The Canadian Small Business Legal Advisor* oozes thoroughness. Gray, a lawyer and small business owner as well as a best-selling author, delivers the how-to goods in a pithy package."
    John Caspar, Business in Vancouver

THE CANADIAN SNOWBIRD GUIDE

"An invaluable guide to worry-free part-time living in the U.S. ... by one of Canada's best-selling authors of business and personal finance books."
Globe & Mail

THE CANADIAN GUIDE TO WILL AND ESTATE PLANNING (with John Budd)

"A bargain for its price, it should be part of every family's library."
Globe & Mail

"This is an informative, practical guide to some of the issues, challenges and vocabulary of estate planning. The authors – a lawyer and a chartered accountant – cover all the bases, from the importance of preparing a will, to powers of attorney, trusts, tax planning and funerals."
The National Post

Reviewer Praise for Other Best-Selling Books by Norman Friend

THE COMPLETE CANADIAN FRANCHISE GUIDE (with Doug Gray)

"I am greatly impressed with this book. It is a goldmine of information. Well-organized, practical, and presented in a candid and easily understood manner. A must read, not only for anyone buying a franchise, but also for the neophyte franchisor. An invaluable guide."
John L. Henry
Senior Vice President,
Uniglobe Travel (International) Inc.
and Board of Directors,
Century 21 Real Estate (Canada) Ltd.

"This book tells it like it is ... a realistic look at franchising and what it takes to be successful. The information provided is clear, concise, practical and easy to apply."
Richard B. Cunningham, President
Canadian Franchise Association and
Co-Chair, World Franchise Council

Be Your Own Boss

DOUGLAS GRAY & NORMAN FRIEND

McGraw-Hill
Ryerson

Toronto   Montréal   Boston   Burr Ridge, IL   Dubuque, IA   Madison, WI   New York
San Francisco   St. Louis   Bangkok   Bogotá   Caracas   Kuala Lumpur   Lisbon   London   Madrid
Mexico City   Milan   New Delhi   Santiago   Seoul   Singapore   Sydney   Taipei

McGraw-Hill
Ryerson Limited
A Subsidiary of The McGraw·Hill Companies

ISBN: 0-07-091551-2

1234567890 MP 098765432
Printed and bound in Canada.

_____

National Library of Canada Cataloguing in Publication

Gray, Douglas A.
    Be your own boss : the insider's guide to buying a small business
or franchise in Canada / Douglas Gray, Norman Friend.

Includes index.
ISBN 0-07-091551-2

    1. Small business — Purchasing — Canada. 2. Franchises (Retail trade) —
Purchasing — Canada I. Friend, Norman P. II. Title.

HD62.7.G728 2002   658.1'141   C2002-904175-9

_____

Publisher: **Julia Woods**
Editorial Co-ordinator: **Catherine Leek**
Production Co-ordinator: **Sandra Deak**
Editor: **Katherine Coy**
Electronic Page Design and Composition: **Heidy Lawrance Associates**
Cover Design: **Sharon Lucas**

To my beloved mother, Eleanor Gray.
Your spirit is alway there.
                              Douglas Gray

To my son Bradley Rex
— you are my best friend.
                              Norman Friend

TABLE OF CONTENTS

Chapter 1

Do You Have What It Takes to Be an Entrepreneur?   **1**

Responding to the Call of Entrepreneurism   1

Not Everyone is Cut Out to Be an Entrepreneur   1

Family Support   2

Acceptable Level of Risk   2

Take a Personal Inventory   3

Qualifying as A Business Immigrant   7

How to Assess Your Financial Comfort Level   8

Chapter 2

Selecting Professional Advisors   **17**

Locating Professional Advisors   18

Chapter 3

Choosing the Right Legal Structure   **23**

Types of Legal Structure   23

The Importance of Agreements   28

Chapter 4

Determining the Right Business Fit for You   **35**

Advantages of Going into Business   35

Disadvantages of Going into Business   36

Why Buy a Business Instead of Starting One?   36

What Type of Business Should You be Looking to Acquire?   38

Chapter 5

Selecting the Right Business   47
The Buying Process   47
Where to Look for a Business   48

Chapter 6

Buying a Franchise   53
What is Franchising?   53
Franchise Legislation   54
Investigate Before You Invest   55
Pros of Franchising   59
Cons of Franchising   60
The Franchise Agreement   62

Chapter 7

Understanding Financial Statements   71
What are Financial Statements?   71
How to Evaluate the Financials   73
The Importance of Ratios   75
How Reliable are the Financials?   79

Chapter 8

Methods of Buying a Business   87
The Issue of Taxes   87
Why Sellers Prefer to Sell Shares   88
Why Buyers Prefer to Buy Assets   89
Allocation of the Purchase Price   89

Chapter 9

Establishing a Value   91
Seller's and Buyer's Objectives   91
Fair Market Value   91
Estimating the Value of a Business   92
Methods for Valuing a Business   94

Chapter 10

The Investigation Process   99
The Importance of Due Diligence   99
Components   100
Executing a Confidentiality/Non-Disclosure Agreement   104

Chapter 11

The Negotiation Process   109
The Art of Negotiation //109
Motivation of Both Parties   110
Getting to a Win-Win Deal   111
Using an Intermediary   112
The Sequence of Events   112
Letter of Intent (LOI)   112

Chapter 12

Raising Financing   117
Deciding Between Debt and Equity Financing   117
Source of Financing   118
Developing a Loan Proposal   122

Chapter 13

Location and Leases   145
The Importance of Location   145
Leasing   147
Types of Leases   149
Legal Aspects of a Lease   151
Impact of Government Legislation   155
Key Terms of a Lease   156
Minimizing Personal and Business Risk   162
Negotiating a Lease   166

Chapter 14

Closing the Sale   169
Drafting the Purchase and Sale Agreement   169
Structure of the Purchase and Sale Agreement   170
The Closing   171

Chapter 15

Under New Ownership   179
What Do You Do Now?   179
If It Ain't Broke — Don't Fix It   179
Focus on the Critical Factors   180
Strategic Planning   180
Employees are Your Biggest Asset   181
Customers   181
Suppliers   181
Retaining the Previous Owner through the Transition   182

Chapter 16

Selling Your Business   189
Look Within   189
Forced Sale of a Business   190
Other Reasons   190
Alternatives to Selling   190
Consider the Impact on Your Business   190
Tax Considerations   191
Providing Vendor Financing   193
Preparing to Sell Your Business   195
Packaging the Business   196
Preparing Yourself for After the Sale   196
Finding Buyers   197
Negotiating the Sale   199
Executing a Confidentiality/Non-Disclosure Agreement   199

Glossary   201

Sources of Further Information   211

Web Sites of Interest   220

Index   223

About the Authors   227

DO YOU HAVE WHAT IT TAKES TO BE AN ENTREPRENEUR?

Responding to the Call of Entrepreneurism

Every year, thousands of Canadians from all walks of life respond to the call of entrepreneurism. Young people fresh out of college or university, mature executives who have been set adrift by their corporations, parents who are raising children at home and new immigrants are part of this growing force of independent business people.

The majority of these people have no experience in buying a business. This book has been written to guide prospective business owners through all the phases of buying a business and to provide them with the information necessary — including numerous checklists and sample documents — that will enable them to purchase and operate a profitable and rewarding business.

Not Everyone is Cut Out to be an Entrepreneur

Not everyone is cut out to be an entrepreneur and it is better to find out now rather than later. Many people romanticize about going into business and believe they could run the show. But when the time comes to cash in their equity, mortgage their home, and write a cheque for a relatively large investment, their confidence often disappears. It is not unusual for first-time buyers to lose confidence in themselves at any stage of the buying process, particularly in the final stages of closing. Before you go any further, ask yourself:

- Should I even consider buying a business?
- Am I doing this for the right reasons?
- Do I have realistic expectations?

Although it is important to be optimistic, you must also have realistic expectations. Do not go into this with blinkers on by overestimating the potential rewards and overlooking the demands of running your own business. It is possible that you will earn far less from a business than you think and find yourself working a lot harder than you have ever done before. Realistic buyers understand that the rewards are achievable, but for a price.

Family Support

This is the time to be totally honest with yourself. If you think that going into business for yourself will allow you to spend more time with your family, then you should reconsider your decision. Buying a business and running it during the first couple of years can place a real strain on your marriage because of the time and emotional commitment. If you are going into business for yourself, it is critical to have the support of your family. It is extremely important to discuss everything openly with your spouse as once you have purchased the business financial concerns and lifestyle changes become a family affair whether you like it or not. Your spouse may have different goals and a lower tolerance for risk than you. The following guidelines should help in this area:

1. Explain to your spouse your reasons for wanting to go into business.
2. If your spouse has any objections, try to zero in on exactly what the objections are.
3. Don't try to overcome your spouse's objections until you are sure you fully understand them. Your spouse may actually share some of your concerns but these concerns may be a bigger obstacle for your spouse.
4. Be prepared for some give and take in a few areas, for example, the level of financial risk or the amount of time you wish to commit to the business.
5. Invite your spouse to participate in the search and negotiation process. Have your spouse attend and participate in meetings with lenders and professional advisors.
6. Seriously consider if you have the full support of your family and ask yourself what pressure will this place on your relationship before you proceed.

Acceptable Level of Risk

As the failure rate for businesses is high, there is a degree of risk inherent in the purchase of any business. What level of risk are you prepared to accept? Contrary to the stereotype that entrepreneurs are gamblers; the risks involved in business are often moderate due to the amount of planning and due diligence required. Yet many people who want to go into business take a look at the high failure rate of independent businesses and decide that the risk is unacceptable. Although the statistics vary among the various government agencies and private companies that track the performance rate of businesses, it is generally accepted that 30% of new businesses fail in the first six months of operation and 75% fail within five years. The good news is that buyers of established healthy businesses

> Contrary to the stereotype that entrepreneurs are gamblers; the risks involved in business are often moderate due to the amount of planning and due diligence required.

have far better odds, as four out of five businesses that are still in business after five years succeed.

The Untouchables

Having a clear understanding of what you could lose and coming to grips with how much you are willing to risk for a business can reduce your stress level considerably. The following four tips will help you to achieve this.

1. Divide your personal assets into "touchables" and "untouchables." Put assets such as your home, automobile and approximately 50% of your personal savings (including RRSPs) into the "untouchables" group. Place the remainder into the "touchable" group, which are the assets you are willing to risk on a business. You might wish to modify these groups and percentages to suit your own situation but it is important to do the exercise.

2. How much personal liability are you prepared to expose yourself to? Assume the worst situation possible and stick to that limit. Wherever possible, limit your personal liability on any loans or lease agreements necessary to buy or operate the business. In some instances, you may have no alternative but to provide a personal guarantee if you wish to buy a business; however, it may be possible to either limit the guarantee amount or have an agreement that the guarantee is removed or reduced after a certain period or upon the occurrence of other events (for example, a certain amount of the loan has been repaid).

3. Consider the situation from a risk-benefit perspective. The prospective benefits must far outweigh the financial risk.

4. Talk to your accountant and lawyer about how you might shield some of your personal assets from potential business liabilities. Any actions to protect your personal assets must take place before you incur any debt.

Take a Personal Inventory

Surprisingly, there are a lot of people who invest their life savings into a business and give little consideration as to whether they have the skills to run the business. Most people start a business without ever completing an honest, thorough personal assessment or inventory. Without this self-appraisal, your personal success in business could be limited.

This section is intended to assist you in focusing on your strong points, identifying your weaknesses and dealing with the areas that need improvement. This will enable you to clarify your personal and business goals. To get the most out of your self-assessment, you should be free from distractions and take as much time as necessary.

Your personal inventory is divided into three parts:

- knowledge,
- skills, and
- traits.

Knowledge

In addition to being profitable and providing a good return on your investment, a successful business must be something that you enjoy doing. Generally, what we enjoy doing goes hand-in-hand with what we are good at. Conversely, we are not usually good at doing things we do not enjoy. However, there is a difference between aptitude and knowledge. You should eliminate most businesses for which you truly have no aptitude.

Knowledge can be obtained through study, whereas skill is something you actually do and comes from practice. While it is reasonable to assume that most people can obtain a reasonable amount of knowledge by studying a subject, there is no guarantee that a person can become competent in something merely through practice or repetition. For example, you could study and gain a fair knowledge of art but you may never have the skill to become an artist regardless of how much you practise. It is fair to say that over time you may improve with practice, however your level of skill may only improve marginally. Understanding the distinction between knowledge and skill is very important when you consider the necessary requirements to run a business successfully. For example, if you are lacking in product knowledge, you could most likely overcome it, however, if you are deficient in mechanical skills, it may be difficult — if not impossible — to overcome it.

> In addition to being profitable and providing a good return on your investment, a successful business must be something that you enjoy doing. Generally, what we enjoy doing goes hand-in-hand with what we are good at.

1. Write down and rank in order the five things about which you feel you know the most. Do not limit this list to your work experience as you may have education or specialized training that is not readily apparent from your work experience. Include hobbies, sports and other recreational pastimes as they may point you in a direction you have never considered but one where you might be successful and enjoy what you are doing.
2. Write down the five things about which you feel you have the least knowledge. Most people find this list easier to develop.

Skills

The next step is to do the same exercise with your skill set. Whereas knowledge relates to things that you know, skill relates to things that you can do.
1. Write down the five things you feel you can do better than most other people.
2. Write down the five things that you feel you do poorly.
   This exercise will help you to identify your skills as well as your deficiencies.

Traits

Traits are things you are, rather than things you know or can do. Traits can be described as personality characteristics. Numerous studies have demonstrated that successful entrepreneurs tend to have several traits in common. A number of these traits are described below under "Mental Traits." You have no doubt seen or heard various entrepreneurial traits described in clichés such as risk takers, self-starters, highly motivated, positive thinkers, team builders and people oriented. Generally, the traits of an entrepreneur are remarkably similar to the traits of any good businessperson: good work habits, creative, focused and an ability to take risks. Conversely, successful entrepreneurs can also be outgoing or shy, workaholics or absolutely lazy, introverts or extroverts, people oriented or totally arrogant.

It is also important to note that the term "entrepreneur" used to be exclusively applied to someone who actually created a new enterprise business. Recently, it has tended to be used to describe anyone who runs his or her own business. There are no tests or checklists that can guarantee your success or disqualify you from owning your own business. There appears to be one common denominator, however, which is a driving passion for the business. Nothing was ever achieved without desire. So, do not be overly concerned if you do not possess all, or even the majority, of these qualities. The key question is how *significant* the missing traits are to the type of business you are considering and to your business goals. Understanding your personal strengths and weaknesses will allow you to compensate for them by hiring employees, bringing in partners or taking additional training.

Traits can be subdivided into two categories: physical and mental.

> There are no tests or checklists that can guarantee your success or disqualify you from owning your own business. There appears to be one common denominator, however, which is a driving passion for the business.

Physical Traits

The majority of traits are mental, however, you will obviously need a high level of stamina and energy to meet the intense demands and ongoing pressure of running your own business, especially during the first few years. In addition, you must be able to handle any specific physical demands that the business requires.

Mental traits

- **Total commitment, determination and persistence.** A strong determination to succeed and achieve your personal and business goals regardless of personal sacrifices can overcome many obstacles. It can also compensate for weakness in other areas. This requires your total dedication and commitment to the success of the business

- **Ability to deal with setbacks.** Even though you might feel disappointed at times, you do not allow yourself to be discouraged by minor setbacks. You need to have the ability to treat failures as learning experiences so that similar problems can be avoided in the future. Successful entrepreneurs view setbacks as temporary barriers to achieving their goals.

- **Willingness to accept calculated risks.** Successful entrepreneurs have the ability to identify risks and weigh their relative dangers. They prefer to take calculated risks that are high but realistic.

- **The ability to delegate.** Although the business owner must be in overall control of the business, it is impossible for one person to perform every task. The ability to delegate some tasks is very important.
- **Able to handle stress, ambiguity and uncertainty.** An entrepreneur must be able to live with the uncertainty of job security and without the guarantee of a regular paycheque. This is the complete opposite of the corporate world. Stress and ambiguity are woven into the very tapestry of a new business: new employees whose jobs may not be totally defined, new customers and unpredictable revenues. Successful entrepreneurs accept uncertainty as an integral part of being in business and take it in stride. You will have to be able to handle temporary failures without panic.
- **Strong goal orientation.** Entrepreneurs set clear goals that are challenging but attainable. They have the ability to focus their energies on achieving their goals and not get sidetracked. In order to be successful, you will need to continually evaluate and adjust your goals to ensure they remain consistent with your business objectives. Rather than being content at attaining new goals, successful entrepreneurs enjoy the challenge that setting new goals brings.
- **Seeking and using feedback.** In order to know how well they are doing, and how they might improve their performance, successful entrepreneurs constantly seek out and use feedback from employees, their management team and professional advisors or mentors. Not only does this provide instant feedback, it also stimulates the people whose advice is solicited.
- **Self-determination.** Successful entrepreneurs have a strong belief in themselves. They believe that they are personally responsible for controlling their own success or failure, and that success or failure is not decided by luck, circumstance or external events.
- **Versatility and resourcefulness.** Entrepreneurs are capable of dealing effectively with many subjects or tasks simultaneously. The ability to multi-task effectively is particularly important for new business owners, as there may be fewer employees available to handle all the tasks.
- **Team building and human relations.** Entrepreneurs have strong leadership qualities. They have the ability to lead by example and can interact well with people of varying personalities and values. This is especially important when dealing with employees, bankers, investors, partners, suppliers or customers and is reflected in characteristics such as sociability, consideration, empathy, cooperation, tact and a sense of humour.

Corporate Refugees

Economic shifts have contributed to the demise of a large number of companies, resulting in massive layoffs, particularly in the field of technology. These shifts have affected mostly white-collar employees including executives and middle management. These people are often referred to as "corporate refugees." Corporate refugees usually have three choices regarding their future: find another job, go into business for themselves, or retire. For many of these workers, the chances of finding a comparable, or acceptable job are minimal. Most corporate refugees are too active to consider retirement. Many have a substantial net worth comprised of savings, equity in their homes and RRSPs, and are financially capable of investing in a business. Many are also well qualified to go into business for themselves because of their relevant management experience.

However, as many corporate refugees are in their 40s and 50s, they are fairly risk-aversive as they do not have a lot of time to recover financially should the business fail. Security can be a motivator or a demotivator depending on whether it is perceived as gained or lost. For example, security becomes a demotivator when you have to give up some of your assets that have taken years to amass, and pledge them as collateral, to get into business.

Some corporate refugees are not suited to running their own business for several reasons:

1. They are accustomed to having a support staff to carry out menial tasks and as a result may find it difficult to fulfill all the roles from janitor to bookkeeper.
2. They are accustomed to working 9 to 5 and taking several weeks' vacation each year.
3. They do not have a bottom-line mentality. Their corporate responsibility may have only related to operating within the guidelines of a departmental budget without influencing, or realizing the implications of their budget on, the net profit of the company as a whole.
4. They are not used to dealing with the stress of totally running the show, particularly if their previous responsibilities or decision-making were limited to a narrow sphere of influence.
5. They lack the drive, commitment and focus that are necessary to achieve success on their own. The corporate structure provided them with a certain security and insulated them from the peaks and valleys associated with the hands-on operation of a small business, particularly in the early stages.

Qualifying as a Business Immigrant

Canada welcomes business immigrants who have the ability and resources to invest in or establish businesses in Canada. During 1998, business immigrants invested more than $437 million in Canada. The Business Immigration Program allows immigrants to enter Canada provided they meet the program's criteria and strictly follow the Ministry or government guidelines. As regulations change from time to time, and vary from province to province, anyone interested in this program should check with the appropriate authorities to ensure that they have the most current information.

All business immigrants must apply for immigration from outside of Canada. Business immigrants must apply at one of nine business immigration centres that are located in Beijing, Berlin, Buffalo, Damascus, Hong Kong, London, Paris, Seoul and Singapore.

Obtaining entry into Canada can take anywhere from a year to 18 months or longer, depending on how complete the submitted application is. The process includes submitting the application, attending a personal interview at a Canadian embassy and medical and security checks. As the application requires the preparation of a business plan or proposal, it is advisable that a prospective immigrant consults a lawyer and a professional accountant for assistance. You can visit the Government of Canada site on immigration information for more information at www.canadainternational.gc.ca. Business immigrants can apply to enter Canada in one of three ways: as an entrepreneur, as an investor or as a self-employed person.

How to Assess Your Financial Comfort Level

The Rule of Two-Thirds

Before you commence your search for a business, it is helpful to have an idea of what you can afford. This prevents you from wasting your time pursuing businesses that are beyond your means. The majority of businesses do not sell for cash, in fact, it is common to finance about two-thirds of the selling price. That means you are looking at making a down payment of around one-third of the selling price. The logic behind the "rule of two-thirds" is that the cash flow from the business must be able to service a debt of two-thirds of the selling price. In other words, after paying all the expenses involved in running the business, there must be enough money left over to cover the payments due on the debt incurred to buy the business. If there is a shortfall, it cannot be considered a high-profit business. If you still decide to buy the business, you will have to either increase the amount of down payment or increase the number of years over which the loan is amortized in order to reduce the amount of monthly or annual debt service.

Based on the rule of two-thirds, if you multiply the amount of cash you have to invest in a business by three, you will have a rough dollar estimate of the size of business you can afford. Some purchasers will ask for a copy of your net worth statement to assess if you are a qualified buyer. The following questions will help in determining your financial investment comfort level so that you know how much cash you have available for a business.

- What is the maximum amount of investment you are willing to undertake, including possible assistance from someone else?
- Are you willing to sign a personal guarantee for a business loan or financial assistance?
- If you do not have enough collateral, are you willing to give up a share of the business to a partner or investor?
- What is the type and amount of collateral that you have available to back up a loan request?
- What is the maximum investment that you can handle without assistance?

Assessing Your Potential Investment Level

The financial factors that are most important in assessing your potential investment level can be divided into two areas:

1. **Your net worth** that relates to your investment potential. In other words, do you have enough money on hand, or enough security or collateral, that you can go to a lender to acquire the capital needed to start the business?

2. **Your own cash-flow requirements.** Are you able to survive during the initial start-up period of the business? Are your own resources adequate or will you use an alternative source, such as your spouse's income?

How to Calculate Your Net Worth

The first step is to calculate your net worth and unencumbered capital. See the "Personal Net Worth Checklist" at Appendix 1.1. Different people may have the same total net worth, but assets can be distributed differently among liquid assets and equity, thereby making it easier for one person to finance a business than another.

Essentially, your personal financial statement appears very much in the same format as that of a company. You have assets on the one hand and liabilities on the other. Your assets are all of the things that you own. Assets include money in the bank, your life insurance surrender value, the value of your home and RRSPs — even small items such as golf clubs.

On the other hand, your liabilities are monies you owe to other entities including banks, mortgage companies, credit cards companies and the government. Your net worth is monies that you consider you owe to yourself. So, in other words, if you take all the things that you own (your assets) and subtract all the money you owe to other entities (your liabilities), you are left with your net worth. For example, if your sole possession is your home, valued at $400,000, and you have a mortgage of $200,000, your net worth would be $200,000. That is the money you would owe to yourself when you sell your home and pay off your liabilities.

From the point of view of calculating your net worth for the purposes of obtaining bank, trust company or credit union financing, it must be understood that a bank is not interested in smaller items that you own, such as golf clubs, nor does the bank necessarily want you to cash in your RRSPs. Banks look at large assets, those items that can be sold realistically in the event of a need to pay off the loan. The most important of these is your home. If you were to own shares in a publicly traded company, which is recognized by the bank as a stable venture, then these shares may also form some additional security or collateral for a loan.

Your investment in a business will come from two sources: loans against assets, and unencumbered capital or liquid assets from which you can obtain cash in order to invest in a business.

Some of your assets may be mortgaged or have other monies owing against them such as your home or vehicle. In a stable housing market, the bank will normally be very interested in using your home as security. The bank must consider, however, that if there is a mortgage against the home, it can effectively reduce the realization value upon resale. The following example may assist in clarifying this situation.

If your home is worth $400,000 and has a mortgage of $300,000 against it, the bank will be unable to use it as collateral for advancing further funds. A bank requires a 25% safety margin on your home to provide for the eventuality of a decrease in real estate values. If your home is worth $400,000 and you have a mortgage of $200,000, then a bank may advance you 75% of the $400,000, minus the $200,000 that is already owed against the home, or $100,000.

"Unencumbered capital" is a term used to describe your liquid assets, or assets that can be readily liquidated or sold for investment purposes. These are assets such as cash in the bank, loans that you have made to others that are easily collectible, stocks and bonds that you can readily sell on the stock market, and RRSPs. These are quite different from assets such as real estate that would not normally be sold, but that can be used for collateral.

Although a bank may be prepared to lend you sufficient monies against your home — given that there is sufficient equity, and you are able to liquidate some of your other assets to raise cash for your investment — you should also pay close attention to the extent of your liabilities. By borrowing additional funds and by liquidating your assets and investing them in a business, you may be placing yourself at undue risk, given that you may already have excessive liabilities for other reasons. To put it simply, if you already owe too much money and have limited cash reserves to use with further borrowings against your home to start a business, you can quickly get yourself into financial difficulties, even if the business is otherwise a good opportunity.

There is a lot to think about when considering whether or not to buy a business. The checklists included at Appendix 1.2 ("Personal Cost-of-Living Budget") and Appendix 1.3 ("Financial Needs for First Three Months") will help in the decision-making. Ultimately, the choice is yours, but your choice should be based on facts. Do your homework, take the time to complete a personal inventory, talk with your spouse and take the pulse of your financial affairs. It could just be the start of something big.

Appendix 1.1
Personal Net Worth Checklist

	You	Your Spouse
Liquid Assets		
(Can be relatively quickly converted into cash)		
Term deposits/GICs	$ _____	$ _____
Chequing accounts	_____	_____
Savings accounts	_____	_____
Stocks	_____	_____
Bonds	_____	_____
Term deposits (savings)	_____	_____
Pensions (government / employer)	_____	_____
Annuities	_____	_____
RRSPs / RRIFs	_____	_____
Life insurance cash surrender value	_____	_____
Demand loans		
— family	_____	_____
— other	_____	_____
Automobile	_____	_____
Tax instalments made / withheld	_____	_____
Other (specify)	_____	_____
Subtotal	$ _____	$ _____
Non-Liquid Assets		
(Takes longer to convert into cash or		
accrue total financial benefit)		
Business interests	$ _____	$ _____
Long-term receivables, loans	_____	_____
Deferred income plans	_____	_____
Interest in trusts	_____	_____
Tax shelters	_____	_____
Principal residence	_____	_____
Other real estate (e.g. second home, revenue		
or investment property)	_____	_____
U.S. / foreign assets	_____	_____
Personal property	_____	_____
Valuable assets (e.g., art, antiques, jewellery, etc.)	_____	_____
Other (specify)	_____	_____
Subtotal	$ _____	$ _____
TOTAL ASSETS (A)	$ _____	$ _____

	You	Your Spouse
Current Liabilities		
(Currently due within a year or on demand)		
Bank loans	$ _____	$ _____
(currently due or on line of credit demand or within 1 year)	_____	_____
Credit cards	_____	_____
Income tax owing	_____	_____
Alimony	_____	_____
Child support	_____	_____
Monthly rent	_____	_____
Other	_____	_____
Subtotal	$ _____	$ _____
Long-Term Liabilities		
(Generally not due for over 1 year)		
Term loans	$ _____	$ _____
Mortgages		
— principal residence	_____	_____
— other (investment revenue recreational or commercial)	_____	_____
— reverse mortgage	_____	_____
Other	_____	_____
Subtotal	$ _____	$ _____
TOTAL LIABILITIES (B)	$ _____	$ _____
Net worth — before tax (A–B)	$ _____	$ _____
Tax cost if assets liquidated (if any)	_____	_____
Net worth — after tax	_____	_____

Appendix 1.2
Personal Cost-of-Living Budget Checklist

	You	Your spouse
I. Income		
(Average monthly income, actual or estimated)		
Salary, bonuses, and commissions	$ _____	$ _____
Dividends	_____	_____
Interest income	_____	_____
Pension income	_____	_____
Other	_____	_____
TOTAL MONTHLY INCOME	$ _____ (A)	$ _____ (X)
II. Expenses		
Regular monthly payments:		
Rent or mortgage payments	$ _____	$ _____
Automobile(s)	_____	_____
Appliances / TV	_____	_____
Home improvement loan	_____	_____
Credit card payments (not covered elsewhere)	_____	_____
Personal loan	_____	_____
Medical plan	_____	_____
Instalment and other loans	_____	_____
Life insurance premiums	_____	_____
House insurance	_____	_____
Other insurance premiums		
(auto, extended medical, etc.)	_____	_____
RRSP deductions	_____	_____
Pension fund (employer)	_____	_____
Investment plan(s)	_____	_____
Miscellaneous	_____	_____
Other	_____	_____
Total Regular Monthly Payments	$ _____	$ _____
Household operating expenses:	$ _____	$ _____
Telephone Gas and electricity	_____	_____
Heat	_____	_____
Water and garbage	_____	_____
Other household expenses (repairs, maintenance, etc.)	_____	_____
Other	_____	_____
Total Household Expenses	$ _____	$ _____

	You	Your spouse
Food expenses:		
At home	$ _____	$ _____
Away from home	_____	_____
Total Food Expenses	$ _____	$ _____
Personal expenses:		
Clothing, cleaning, laundry	$ _____	$ _____
Drugs	_____	_____
Transportation (other than auto)	_____	_____
Medical/dental	_____	_____
Day care	_____	_____
Education (self)	_____	_____
Education (children)	_____	_____
Dues	_____	_____
Gifts, donations and dues	_____	_____
Travel	_____	_____
Recreation	_____	_____
Newspapers, magazines, books	_____	_____
Automobile maintenance, gas and parking	_____	_____
Spending money, allowances	_____	_____
Other	_____	_____
Total Personal Expenses	$ _____	$ _____
Tax expenses:		
Federal and provincial income taxes	$ _____	$ _____
Home property taxes	_____	_____
Other	_____	_____
Total Tax Expenses	$ _____	$ _____

III. Summary of Expenses

	You	Your spouse
Regular monthly payments	$ _____	$ _____
Household operating expenses	$ _____	$ _____
Food expenses	$ _____	$ _____
Personal expenses	$ _____	$ _____
Tax expenses	$ _____	$ _____
TOTAL MONTHLY EXPENSES	$ _____ (B)	$ _____ (Y)

TOTAL MONTHLY DISPOSABLE INCOME AVAILABLE

$ _____ (A–B) $ _____ (X–Y)

(subtract total monthly expenses from total
monthly income)

TOTAL ANNUAL DISPOSAL INCOME AVAILABLE

(multiply x 12) $ _____ $ _____

Appendix 1.3
Projected Financial Needs for the First Three Months
(Business) Checklist

This worksheet will help you to estimate the amount of money you will need for the first three months of business operation.

Cash Available

Owner's cash on hand $ _____

Loan from relative or friend   _____

Other: _____   _____

Total Cash on Hand $ _____

Start-up Costs

Repairs, renovations and decorating $ _____

Equipment (including installation costs)   _____

Furniture   _____

Insurance (homeowners' rider, personal
   and product liability)   _____

Inventory   _____

Product materials and office supplies   _____

Advertising and promotion (Yellow Pages,
   business cards, stationery, flyers,
   newspaper ads, etc.)   _____

Other: _____   _____

Total Start-up Costs $ _____

Operating Costs

Wages of owner   3 x $_____   = $ _____

Utilities   3 x $_____   =   _____

Supplies and inventory 3 x $_____   =   _____

Advertising   3 x $_____   =   _____

Auto and travel   3 x $_____   =   _____

Contingency   3 x $_____   =   _____

Total Operating Costs $ _____

Total Start-up and Three-Month Operating Costs $ _____

**TOTAL MONEY NEEDED FOR FIRST THREE
MONTHS OF BUSINESS** $ ════════════════

2

SELECTING PROFESSIONAL ADVISORS

Introduction

When buying a business, the purchaser must eventually use the services of professional advisors. In particular, it is critical that the purchaser obtain legal and accounting advice sooner rather than later. Consulting with lawyers and accountants early in the negotiation process can usually save both the purchaser and the vendor time and money. Because of the costs associated with hiring a lawyer, accountant or other professional, some people are inclined to try the do-it-yourself approach. This can be a short-sighted decision and can prove to be very costly. For instance, people who process their own personal income tax returns rather than hiring an accountant may miss out on small business tax exemptions that could save far more than the cost of an accountant's time. A person who signs a long-term lease or contract without having it reviewed beforehand by a lawyer may regret it for many years to come. If you are in a partnership or are a shareholder in an incorporated business, you may not find out until it is too late that your partner or partners have the ability to buy you out for less than the value of your share of the business and without you being able to prevent it.

> Because of the costs associated with hiring a lawyer, accountant or other professional, some people are inclined to try the do-it-yourself approach. This can be a short-sighted decision and can prove to be very costly.

You may already have an established relationship with some advisors but they may not have the specific experience that you will require. For example, a lawyer may have a background in family law but little or no expertise in the area of business law. You would not go to a paediatrician if you needed brain surgery. You need to find the person with a successful track record in the specific area you require. The key professionals that you may need are:

- accountant;
- lawyer;
- business broker; and
- insurance agent.

All these professionals serve different functions. You must be selective in your screening process and in the advice you accept from each advisor. Each advisor has a specific area of expertise and the advice that you receive from that advisor should be confined to that specific area: a lawyer should give you legal advice not business advice. Consider the following factors when selecting a professional advisor:

- professional qualifications;
- competency;
- experience in the specific area you are interested in, and
- fee for service.

Competency includes timeliness. If the professional is unable to provide you with what you need within the time-frame required, it may be that you lose your opportunity. It is helpful to prepare a list of questions that allows you to qualify each advisor in the above areas, plus other questions relating to your specific needs. Some people may feel uncomfortable discussing fees and qualifications with a professional, but it is important to establish these matters before you make a decision to use that person's services. Ask professionals if they require a retainer and whether you will be charged at an hourly or a flat rate. If you decide to hire the individual, it is also a good business practice to follow-up on the initial meeting with a letter confirming the fees agreed on and other terms discussed, or request the professional advisor to do so. This is not meant to suggest that you should consider selecting someone strictly on price. Cost is a function of value. It is an integral part of the decision but makes up only one component.

> Remember that these people are advisors. They are not responsible for making the decisions. That is your responsibility. It is your money, your risk and your life.

Remember that these people are advisors. They are not responsible for making the decisions. That is your responsibility. It is your money, your risk and your life. The advisors can only give you the options and the possible consequences.

Locating Professional Advisors

The best method to find professional advisors is to ask friends, relatives, colleagues and business contacts if they can recommend anyone who would be appropriate for your particular needs. However, it is still necessary to carry out due diligence. Check out whether the expert to whom you have been referred has the area of specialization that you need. For example, have you been referred to a lawyer who practises family law and has no experience in business law? You can also look in the Yellow Pages telephone directory under the appropriate heading but you should expect to carry out a more thorough due diligence than you would for a personal referral. A growing number of professionals have their own Web sites, which provide information such as areas of specialty, so you may wish to search the Internet using a keyword search.

Selecting an Accountant

You are looking for an accountant who does more than file tax returns. As in any profession, there are those who are competent and those who are not. It may surprise you to know that many accountants do not have a clue about how to buy a business effectively and have had no training or experience in this area. It is advisable to select an accountant who will remain as your permanent accountant after you have purchased the business. Ideally, you should be looking for an accountant who is heavily experienced in the type of business you are considering. An accountant who is familiar with the type of business you are contemplating purchasing will be conversant with its operating ratios. The accountant should be able to advise you about:

- how much the business is worth;
- what kind of condition it is in;
- how much money you will need to meet the financial requirements of the business;
- how you will meet both the operating costs and the debt service;
- depending on your growth plans, what level of profit you could make and how soon;
- how to minimize your taxes; and
- if you qualify for, and how to obtain, government grants.

Selecting a Lawyer

The lawyer's role in the process may not come until later, as a lawyer's primary responsibility is to make sure that you are protected from any legal land mines. This should not prevent you from retaining legal counsel early. There are a number of areas in which you will need the services of a lawyer including, but not limited to:

- drafting or reviewing the letter of intent (offer to buy the business);
- drafting or reviewing the asset purchase agreement or share purchase agreement;
- determining the proper legal structure;
- drawing up a partnership agreement or shareholders' agreement;
- advising on or drawing up management or employee contracts;
- checking patents, copyrights and trademarks;
- checking title;
- transferring ownership of real estate;
- reviewing lease, franchise, licence, dealership or distributorship agreements;
- suggesting options and strategies for putting the deal together.

The mechanics of reviewing or drafting the documents, checking title and other routine matters can be handled by most lawyers. Keep in mind that a creative lawyer with a wealth of experience in buying and selling businesses may be able to provide you with valuable assistance in the negotiation and structure of the deal.

Select the right lawyer and avoid problems and hassles

Craig was keen about buying a retail sports store. He had been an athlete most of his life, and liked the idea of dealing with customers who shared the same love of sports. However, Craig had heard horror stories from friends who had had bad business experiences. He wanted to avoid as many problems as possible by getting good legal advice from an experienced business lawyer. To make sure that he had a benchmark for comparison, Craig wanted to interview at least three lawyers. If any advice was inconsistent, he would want to know why.

Craig contacted the local lawyer referral service in his phone book. He had heard that all provinces have this service available, offered by the provincial law society or bar association. This service offers initial consultations for free or for a nominal fee, from lawyers in various specialty areas. In order to be organized and to make the meeting productive, Craig listed all the questions he wanted to ask so that he would not forget them, and prioritized them in case he ran out of time.

Craig wanted to make sure that the lawyer he selected would be a good fit for his needs and expectations. He wanted someone who had a positive attitude and warm personality, who exuded confidence and chemistry; and who was candid, forthright and street-smart. In addition, he wanted someone who had a good communication style and who was proactive in pre-empting problems by anticipating and avoiding them. He also wanted experience and expertise dealing with small business. All these attributes and traits were more important to Craig than the hourly fee.

Craig had lots of questions he wanted to ask, including:

- If I bring in a partner, how do I protect myself if there is a falling out? What is a shareholder's agreement?
- If I want to minimize personal liability, what are the benefits of incorporating and what would it cost to incorporate?
- If I want to bring in some private investors, what sort of documentation should I have them sign to show the money is for equity rather than a shareholder's loan?
- If I borrow money from my parents for my business, how can I protect their loan from creditors in case the business goes under? Can I secure their loan with security documentation from my business and a second mortgage on my home?
- I do not want my spouse to have any legal or financial responsibility for my business. If I do not have my spouse as a director or officer of the company and she never signs any personal guarantees, will she be free from any legal exposure?
- I do not want to have any of my personal assets or matrimonial home as security for any business loan from the bank. How do I negotiate out of personal guarantees to the bank, landlord or trade suppliers?

After meeting with the three lawyers, Craig selected a lawyer named Ann. Ann had been specializing in small business for 15 years, and clearly liked dealing with entrepreneurial clients. As she was in her own small business, she could also relate to the ups and downs of being self-employed. Ann was also a marathon runner, skier and overall fitness buff, so she could relate to his love of sports. Ann's fees were $150 an hour, which Craig felt were very reasonable, considering the benefits she would bring to his business.

Selecting a Business Broker

The topic of using a business broker is covered in Chapter 5, "Selecting the Right Business." You can look for a business broker by looking in the Yellow Pages under "Business Brokers" or by typing in these key words as an Internet search. You may also try contacting local real estate offices as some realtors specialize in the sale of businesses.

Selecting an Insurance Agent

An insurance broker is not committed to any particular insurance company, and can compare and contrast the different policies, coverage and premiums from a wide range of companies that provide the type of insurance coverage for which you are looking. Insurance brokers can obtain a premium quotation and coverage availability from insurance company under-writers if the particular business you have is unique or difficult to cover by other existing policies. Insurance brokers generally have a wide range of business insurance available. It is important to have confidence in the broker in terms of expertise, qualifications and objectivity. Ensure that the broker is affiliated with a reputable firm. If you are unable to obtain a referral, you can look for an insurance broker by looking in the Yellow Pages under "Insurance Brokers" or typing in these key words as an Internet search.

When selecting your professional advisors, it is important to make a list of questions beforehand so that you do not forget them. Sort the questions in order of priority in case you run out of time. This will give you a real sense of organization. You will be able to control the agenda and have a productive meeting.

Make note of the key qualities and attributes that are important to you, so that you can make a good selection in your advisor fit. These may include, for example, good communication skills, good chemistry, reliability, trustworthiness, and expertise and experience relevant to your needs. Finally, remember to comparison shop by interviewing various advisors. That way, you will have a basis for making your final selection.

3

CHOOSING THE RIGHT LEGAL STRUCTURE

Types of Legal Structure

One of your first considerations when starting a business is the form of legal structure with which to operate the business. This will be necessary before you set up a company bank account, apply for a business licence, register for coverage under the workplace safety and insurance board or apply for your Revenue Canada business number.

The type of legal structure you decide on for your business depends on several factors including your potential risk and liability, your financing options, the degree of your participation in management, and tax implications. If your potential risk and liability is high, the incorporation process will provide protection from possible disasters. On the other hand, a person starting a business with little or no risk should consider the advantages of having a sole proprietorship. Once you become familiar with the differences between each form of legal structure, you should consult a lawyer and tax accountant. Your decision in this area is an important one. Your main options will include: corporations, sole proprietorships and partnerships. A description of each of these follows, along with advantages and disadvantages of each.

> A corporation is a business that is a legal entity separate from the owner or owners of the business.

Corporations (Limited Company)

The corporation is the most common form of business organization and, despite common belief, it is not restricted to large organizations. Corporations come in all sizes. A corporation is a business that is a legal entity separate from the owner or owners of the business. Shareholders and management have separate legal personalities from the corporation and are therefore subject only to limited liability.

A corporation is a formal business structure that, after being incorporated with the provincial or federal registry, must file annual reports, submit regular tax returns, and pay tax on the profits of the business. The shareholders elect directors who are responsible for managing the business affairs of the corporation. Directors are usually shareholders. The profits of the corporation may be retained for re-investment or, at the discretion of the directors, distributed to the shareholders in the form of dividends. A corporation can carry on business, own property and is subject to all legal and contractual obligations in the same manner as any individual.

Corporations can be incorporated under federal or provincial law. A company that incorporates federally does so under the *Canada Business Corporations Act* ("CBCA") and a corporation that incorporates provincially does so pursuant to the *Company Act* of that particular province. Under the CBCA, a federal corporation has the right to carry on business under its corporate name in any province of Canada, but a provincially incorporated company does not have that same privilege. Although this may seem to be a strong argument to incorporate federally, the CBCA also requires corporations with over $10 million of gross revenues or over $5 million of assets to file financial statements, whereas the *Company Act* only requires public corporations to file financial statements.

Although it is possible to incorporate a company without the benefit of legal advice, it is advisable to obtain legal and tax advice to assist with the preparation of the incorporation documents and shareholders agreements.

Advantages

- **Limited liability.** The shareholders are not personally responsible for any of the debts or obligations of the corporation, unless a shareholder has signed a personal guarantee.
- **Raising capital.** Raising of capital is easier because of financing flexibility. A corporation can attract investors and provide better security to lenders in the form of debentures, common shares, convertible shares and other structures. The corporation may also be eligible for government financing incentive programs that may be unavailable to unincorporated businesses.
- **Perpetual existence.** The corporation's existence has the potential to be perpetual because the departure or death of any or all of its shareholders or managers will not affect it.
- **Possible tax advantages.**
- **Transferable ownership.**

Disadvantages

- Corporations are closely regulated by a legislative scheme.
- Costs of incorporating are higher, but this monetary outlay should be kept in perspective. It is simply another cost of doing business if the reasons for incorporating a business for tax or liability benefits are appropriate.
- Onerous requirements of shareholder and regulatory financial reporting.

- The operating losses and tax credits remain within the corporate entity; they are not available to individual shareholders if the corporation is unable to utilize them.

Sole Proprietorship

The sole proprietorship is the simplest form of business organization because there is only one owner. Ultimate control lies in the hands of the owner, whether the business is operated in the owner's name or through a trade name. All of the assets, responsibilities, rights and obligations belong to that individual owner. This personal responsibility means that the sole proprietor's personal assets may be seized to meet the claims of the business's creditors. The assets of a sole proprietorship are the assets of the owner, meaning that the business has no separate legal personality from its owner, as is the case with a corporation.

While there is no commercial legislation strictly regulating sole proprietorships, a sole proprietor will, depending on the nature of the business, have to comply with federal, provincial and municipal regulations affecting trade and commerce, registration and licensing. In some cases the sole proprietor may be required to register under another regulatory scheme, once again depending on the nature of the business.

> The assets of a sole proprietorship are the assets of the owner, meaning that the business has no separate legal personality from its owner, as is the case with a corporation.

The business income and the owner's personal income are considered the same for tax purposes. Therefore business profits are reported on the owner's personal income tax return, based on federal and provincial income tax schedules. Business expenses and losses are deductible. It is advisable, though, to keep personal and business bank accounts separate. For instance, you should pay yourself a salary from your business account and deposit it into your personal account for your personal needs (food, clothing, lodging, personal savings). A proprietor is personally responsible for all debts or liabilities of the business.

Advantages

- Minimal start-up costs and compliance procedures.
- The owner is in direct control of the decision-making and does not have to report to shareholders or directors.
- Relative freedom from regulation.
- All the profits are for the benefit of the owner.
- The personal tax rate is lower than the rate for corporations in certain situations. Therefore, during the early phases of the business, it may be more advantageous to remain a sole proprietorship or partnership. Once the business is earning substantial sums, the company could be rolled over into a corporation.
- Sole proprietorships are relatively easy to roll over into an incorporated company at some point in the future.
- Non-capital start-up losses can be offset against the owner's income from other sources.

Disadvantages

- The owner is personally liable for all debts and obligations of the business.
- It is difficult to raise capital apart from conventional loans.
- The business can only be transferred by selling the assets.
- Some government loan, subsidy or guarantee programs are available only to limited companies (corporations).
- If the business fails, the owners are not eligible to collect employment insurance benefits.

Partnerships

A partnership is essentially a proprietorship with two or more owners. Taxation considerations are the main reason for organizing a business as a partnership rather than a corporation. Each partner may offset his or her share of the partnership tax losses against income from other sources because income and losses of a partnership are taxed in the hands of the partners. Appendix 3.1 provides a "Partnership Agreement Checklist."

> Partners may contribute money, property or services and unless otherwise stated in the partnership agreement, all contributions are considered equal.

Partners may contribute money, property or services and unless otherwise stated in the partnership agreement, all contributions are considered equal. In a partnership, each partner is personally liable for the full amount of the debts and liabilities of the business. Each partner shares equally in the profits and must contribute equally to sustain the losses. Every partner is generally considered an agent of the partnership and of the other individual partners and every partner is jointly liable with the other partners for all obligations of the business incurred while a partner.

> It is sound business advice not to enter any partnership arrangement without a written agreement between the partners regarding responsibilities for financing the business, sharing the profits and losses, working in the business, specific duties and other important considerations.

Each of the individuals is authorized to act on behalf of the company and can bind the partnership legally, unless stated otherwise in a partnership agreement. It is sound business advice not to enter any partnership arrangement without a written agreement between the partners regarding responsibilities for financing the business, sharing the profits and losses, working in the business, specific duties and other important considerations. Although generally partners are people, corporations or other partnerships may enter into the partnership relationship.

Advantages

- easy to establish;
- minimal start-up costs;
- limited regulation;

- the partners provide additional sources of investment capital; and
- the partners may have diversified management skills.

Disadvantages

- possibility of conflict between the partners;
- difficulty in raising external capital;
- unlimited liability of the partners; and
- partners are bound by the actions of other partners as all partners are considered to be agents of the business.

REAL LIFE

The Right Match can Spell Success

Gayatri had been a very successful corporate salesperson for Downtown Corporate Travel when she learned that the owner was considering selling the company. Gayatri had to make some decisions. She was apprehensive about working for a new owner but did not want to move to another company. She valued the relationships she had established with her clients. Based on these facts, Gayatri decided that her best course of action was to try and purchase the business.

Gayatri had some savings and equity in a condominium but she did not have all of the required capital or enough personal net worth to qualify for bank financing, so she decided to look for an individual investor who could contribute the balance of the required capital. Gayatri had discussions with several potential investors and was close to entering into an agreement with a passive investor when Helena approached Gayatri and suggested they form a partnership to buy the business. Helena was employed as the office manager in Downtown Corporate Travel. Helena explained to Gayatri that she had recently received a small inheritance which, added to her personal savings, would provide the balance of the investment. Helena also thought that their different skill sets would complement each other as Gayatri could go out of the office and do what she did best — service the existing clients and bring in new clients — and Helena could stay in the office to make sure that everything ran smoothly. They discussed how each partner would react in various situations that might occur in the running of the business and concluded that they had the potential to form a good working relationship.

Gayatri and Helena made an offer to the owner of Downtown Corporate Travel, which the owner accepted and even offered to carry some of the financing for them. After two years, Gayatri and Helena had increased the business by 20% and were still good friends.

The Importance of Agreements

If you are contemplating entering into a partnership or shareholder situation, it is essential to have a well-constructed agreement in writing before you start the business relationship. For help in this, see the "Partnership Agreement Checklist" at Appendix 3.1. The checklist will assist you in drafting an agreement for your own use. The contents of these agreements can be thorough and complex, but the underlying issues covered are important to clarify and resolve before starting your business. If an agreement is not in place when a dispute arises, it may be impossible to resolve the situation or for the conflicting parties to continue in business. Be sure to obtain legal assistance before signing any agreement.

REAL LIFE

Establish the Rules Before you Start Playing the Game

Yasser and Denis met when they played on the same rugby team. They forged a relationship over a few beers after rugby practice. Denis became aware of what he considered to be a good opportunity to purchase a janitorial business. As he did not have the financial resources to purchase the business, he approached Yasser to see if he would be interested in going into some form of partnership to acquire the business. Denis knew that Yasser was an experienced entrepreneur and was aware that he had made a significant amount of money in some of his business ventures.

After looking at the track record of the company, Yasser agreed to come up with half of the funds required to close the deal and half of the working capital that would be required, according to the financial projections that Denis had prepared. They incorporated a company in which they were equal shareholders but they did not enter into a shareholders' agreement. Under their verbal agreement, Denis would work in the business (and draw a salary) but Yasser would not be active in the business as he was fully occupied with his other business interests. After six months, they discovered that Denis had overestimated his initial revenue projections and they needed an additional injection of working capital. Denis had exhausted his finances when they bought the business and had to look to Yasser to provide 100% of the additional working capital.

Denis soon saw a side of Yasser he had not seen before as Yasser proved to be very tough when it came to his business dealings. Yasser made it clear that he had relied on Denis's projections when he had made his initial investment and told Denis that he had lost confidence in his ability to run the business. Yasser refused to invest more money if Denis was his partner but instead offered to buy Denis's shares for $50,000, which was around 30% of what Denis had invested in the company. As Denis was between a rock and a hard spot, he had no alternative but to accept Yasser's offer, leaving Yasser as the sole shareholder. The business proved to be a success and Yasser sold it two years later, making himself quite a nice profit. Needless to say, they no longer share a beer after rugby practice.

The type of legal structure you select for your business will have a profound impact on your legal protections, tax benefits and business image. Make sure you understand the pros and cons of the three main types of legal options. If you think there is any form of business risk whatsoever, make sure you incorporate from the outset. In order to further minimize the risk of business problems in the future, make sure you have written agreements wherever prudent to do so, for example, partnership agreements, shareholders agreements and management contracts.

Appendix 3.1
Partnership Agreement Checklist

☐   1. Date of agreement

☐   2. Description of partners

☐   3. Firm name:
      (a) name search to ensure no conflict with existing trade, corporation or partnership name
      (b) registration of name as required by law
      (c) continued use of name after death or withdrawal of any partner or after reorganization
      (d) restriction on use of name in any other activity

☐   4. Term of partnership:
      (a) commencement
      (b) termination at specified time or on specified events

☐   5. Place of business:
      (a) specify geographical limits if desired

☐   6. Business purpose of partnership:
      (a) description of authorized business activities
      (b) limitations on business activities
      (c) provisions for future changes in business activities

☐   7. Capital contributions:
      (a) percentage contribution of each partner
      (b) form of contribution (cash, assets, etc.)
      (c) when contribution to be made
      (d) valuation of non-cash contributions
      (e) interest on contributions
      (f) adjustments to contributions
      (g) contributions by new partners
      (h) loans to partnership
      (i) future capital contributions:
         (i) circumstances when required
         (ii) amount and form
         (iii) apportionment of contribution among partners
      (j) withdrawal of capital

☐   8. Division of profits and losses:
      (a) proportion of division among partners
      (b) salaries and benefits as elements in profits for distribution
      (c) guarantee of minimum profits to certain partners
      (d) reserve fund for partnership expenses paid into prior to distribution

      (e) alteration for work in progress

      (f) limitation on partners' share in profits or losses

      (g) distribution to partnership based on: equal shares, point system, billable hours, seniority of client acquisition or management responsibilities

      (h) timing of distribution

☐ 9. Records of business:

      (a) nature of records

      (b) partners' access

      (c) statements to be given to partners

☐ 10. Appointment of accountant/auditor

☐ 11. Fiscal year

☐ 12. Accounting and valuation principles:

      (a) generally accepted accounting principles (specify if desired)

      (b) valuation principles (book value, multiple of earnings, etc.)

☐ 13. Banking arrangements:

      (a) bank and branch

      (b) kinds of accounts

      (c) signing authority

      (d) maximum loan amount without approval of all partners

☐ 14. Financial restrictions on partners:

      (a) prohibition against partner giving bonds or guarantees, charging partnership interest for personal separate debts or otherwise impairing personal financial position to the detriment of the partnership

      (b) prohibition against any one partner borrowing for partnership or releasing debt of partnership

      (c) indemnity by partner breaching these provisions

☐ 15. Attention to business:

      (a) partners to devote full-time attention to business

      (b) partners not to engage in competing business or any other business

      (c) liability of partners to account for outside income (e.g., director's fees)

      (d) salary for full-time partners

      (e) specify responsibilities

☐ 16. Entitlements and benefits:

      (a) vacations, special vacations, sabbaticals and leaves for sickness or disability

      (b) volunteer at professional and community activities

      (c) attendance at conventions and conferences

      (d) professional development and education

      (e) business or promotion expense

☐   17. Control of policy:

    (a) majority rule or unanimity

    (b) voting:

        (i) one partner — one vote

        (ii) votes proportional to interest

☐   18. Management:

    (a) designation of responsible partners

    (b) division of functions (e.g., administration, sales)

    (c) provision for business meetings

    (d) records of decisions

    (e) establishment of policies

    (f) simple or special majority or unanimous approval

    (g) authority to enter contracts, negotiate loans, pledge credit, hire and fire employees

    (h) provision for review of decisions by all partners

☐   19. Drawing arrangements and benefits:

    (a) frequency

    (b) maximum amount or percentage

    (c) vacations

    (d) other benefits

☐   20. Powers of partners and limitations:

    (a) engaging in non-partnership business

    (b) defining scope of partners' authority, collectively and individually

    (c) delegation of powers to management committee

    (d) acting outside scope of partnership committee

    (e) patents and trade secrets

☐   21. Restrictive covenants (to prevent competition in the event of departure):

    (a) reasonable time, scope and geographic area

☐   22. Retirement or death:

    (a) provide for continuance notwithstanding retirement or death

    (b) purchase of retiring partner's interest — valuation criteria and method of payment

    (c) purchase of deceased partner's interest or provision for estate to act as partner

☐   23. Sale of partnership interest:

    (a) prohibit

    (b) allow, with right of first refusal to remaining partners, compulsory buy-sell, etc.

    (c) restriction on who may purchase

    (d) terms of sale

    (e) right to sell or to compel purchase by partnership on reorganization, or on being out-voted on major decision

24. Expulsion of partner:

    (a) majority vote or unanimity of remaining partners

    (b) specify grounds:

        (i) insolvency

        (ii) fraud

        (iii) bankruptcy

        (iv) incapacity

        (v) age

25. Dissolution:

    (a) specify grounds

    (b) specify events that are not to result in dissolution (e.g., death, insolvency)

    (c) dissolution on vote in case of major split among partners

    (d) tax effects

26. Admission of new partners:

    (a) special majority or unanimity on vote of partners

    (b) acceptance qualifications

    (c) new partner's capital contribution

    (d) allocation of new partner's interest from others

    (e) method of payment

27. Purchase of partner's interest:

    (a) obligation to purchase on death, retirement or expulsion, insolvency

    (b) option-to-purchase terms

    (c) right of first refusal

    (d) compulsory buy-sell

28. Partnership property:

    (a) identification of assets

    (b) valuation of assets, including goodwill

    (c) title to assets

    (d) control of assets

    (e) maintenance, repair and replacement

    (f) restrictions on personal use

    (g) distribution on termination

29. Insurance:

    (a) kinds, limits and deductibles

    (b) fire, theft, automobile, tenant's liability, personal injury, products liability, errors and omissions

    (c) life insurance on other partners sufficient to fund purchase of other partner's share, and agreement of partners to facilitate obtaining such insurance (provision if a partner is uninsurable)

☐ 30. Partners' liability:
   (a) to one another
   (b) to third parties
   (c) partnership liability

☐ 31. Arbitration:
   (a) named individual (auditor for financial matters)
   (b) Arbitration Act

☐ 32. Registrations:
   (a) grant irrevocable power of attorney to other partners for purpose of effecting all necessary registrations

☐ 33. Amendments:
   (a) written
   (b) majority rule or unanimity

☐ 34. Applicable provincial law

☐ 35. No assignment of agreement

☐ 36. Addresses of partners

☐ 37. Partners' signatures on agreement

4

DETERMINING THE BEST BUSINESS FIT FOR YOU

Introduction

Many people have an idealized picture of the rewards of running their own business. Obviously there are benefits, but there are also risks and frustrations. It is important to look objectively at both sides in order to make realistic decisions.

Advantages of Going into Business

You have the opportunity of making more money working for yourself than by being an employee. You have no ceiling on your potential income as it is only limited by your energy, management skill and good judgment. However, studies show that making money is not one of the main motivating factors of business owners. The following are some advantages of owning your own business.

- You have the opportunity to satisfy your creative drive.
- You cannot be laid off. In that sense, you have job security as long as your business is successful.
- You have definite tax advantages over people who are not self-employed.
- You set your own priorities as the decision-maker.
- You have control over your own destiny as you are the only person responsible for the success of your company.
- Your workday will not be routine. There are constant and varied challenges.
- You have the opportunity to see things through to completion.
- You have flexible working hours that can accommodate your personal and lifestyle needs.
- You can determine your own style of work environment.
- You will receive prestige, status and recognition if your business is successful.

Disadvantages of Going into Business

- Your income may be irregular depending on the nature and maturity of the business, economy, competition and other variables.
- Your involvement with the business is generally very time-consuming, especially during the start-up years. This can lead to reduced time with friends or family, and reduced recreation time.
- You will be under pressure to succeed from family, friends, investors and creditors.
- In most cases, you must commit considerable financial resources towards the operation of your business. This could vary of course, depending on partnership or investor involvement or the level of bank financing.
- You are faced with the risk of losing all your money in the business venture due to circumstances beyond your control. Health, family, marital, partnership and competition factors may not always be controllable, avoidable or predictable.
- You must be conversant and able to deal simultaneously with various management areas in order to maintain proper control over the business, especially in the early stages.
- Considerable paperwork and reporting may be required by various levels of government, which is non-revenue generating and time-consuming.

Why Buy a Business Instead of Starting One?

The term "entrepreneur" was initially used to describe an individual who created a business venture. More recently, the term has been applied to any business owner. There is often a significant difference in the abilities between someone who builds a business and someone who manages a business. Put simply, there are builders and custodians and if you understand which group you fit into, this will determine in large part whether you should start or run a business. To help you out in making a decision, try out the "Buying a Business Checklist," at Appendix 4.1.

People who have management skills tend to buy businesses rather than start them as their skill set is in managing people, money, processes and systems. Entrepreneurs like the thrill of being first in the marketplace, the prospect of a big financial upside and the recognition that comes with it. On the other hand, buying a business is usually faster, cheaper, safer and easier to finance as you take over a customer base, cash flow, profit and proven systems (assuming the company is profitable).

Keep in mind that it could take you a year to buy a business from the time you carry out a self-assessment, define your criteria for a business, locate a business, negotiate the purchase, arrange financing, structure the deal and close the sale. Compare that to how long it takes most start-up businesses to generate cash flows and become profitable. A rule of thumb is

People who have management skills tend to buy businesses rather than start them as their skill set is in managing people, money, processes and systems. Entrepreneurs like the thrill of being first in the marketplace, the prospect of a big financial upside and the recognition that comes with it.

business buyers will usually invest the equivalent of two years' salary in purchasing a business. Any remaining balance will be borrowed, either from family and friends, the bank or through seller financing.

The potential and financial upside of a start-up can be enormous. Of course, the risk is also very high.

Starting a business from scratch requires investment in leasehold improvements, equipment, inventory and working capital. However, to compare "apples with apples," the true cost of a start-up business must also include forgone wages. Owners who leave their jobs to start a business and work "free" for an extended time period have a true cost higher than just the cash outflow.

Apart from the ability factor, the other main motivation to start a new venture, rather than buy a business, is the potential. The potential and financial upside of a start-up can be enormous. Of course, the risk is also very high. It is extremely difficult for an acquisition to match the growth potential of a start-up that is on the cutting edge of the market. The good news is that there are plenty of companies that can provide you with an excellent income, secure lifestyle and increase your net worth. These businesses have manageable risks, which although they may have a smaller upside, also have a smaller downside.

Advantages of Buying a Business

- As an operating business will have a track record, you will be able to evaluate its revenues and profit picture. Based on this information, you will be able to reasonably forecast what the business will do for you. With a start-up you have to rely on general industry information to project revenues and profits.
- Unless the business is having difficulties, it should be at or close to operating at the break-even point or be generating some level of profitability. Any start-up business is going to take some time to reach break-even or profitability and substantial losses may be incurred in the process.
- Lenders are more likely to approve financing for an established business than a start-up, as they will have greater confidence in a business with a track record. In addition, the seller may be willing to provide you with all or part of the financing.
- If the business has been operating for some time it should be relatively free of the types of problems that are associated with a start-up. You will benefit from its learning curve, which should save you money and reduce your stress level.
- The cost of buying a business may be less than it would cost to acquire the same tangible assets for a new business.

Advantages of Starting a Business

- You will not have to pay a seller for "goodwill" associated with the business.
- Within certain limits, you will be able to create the type of business that matches your criteria.
- A start-up commences with a clean sheet and does not have any reputation problems that may be inherent with an established business.

What Type of Business Should You be Looking to Acquire?

Go into your business search with an open mind as to what type of business you are looking for as there is a good chance that you will end up buying a type of business that does something you never imagined when you started the process. The criterion of what to search for involves more than the type of business. Many buyers make the fundamental mistake of buying the business that is easiest to get into or one where they think they can make the most money instead of asking themselves which type of business they are best suited for. Most buyers have a reasonably accurate idea of the business they are looking for. Before you start your search you should define the following criteria:

- location;
- size of business;
- cash flow;
- opportunity for continued growth and profits; and
- cash available for a down payment, acquisition costs and working capital.

This should give you some idea of the type of business you are looking for, although you may have expanded or narrowed your search and possibly changed the type of business you initially had in mind: check out the buying a business checklist at Appendix 4.1. Since it is unrealistic to expect to find a business that exactly matches your profile; prepare to be flexible. You will have to seriously consider what, if any, compromises or concessions you are willing to make. For example, would you still proceed if the earnings potential were less than you wanted or needed? What if you were looking for an Italian restaurant and found a business that met all your criteria except that it served French cuisine? What if the business was located in a different area than the one you had in mind? Obviously, it will be easier to be flexible in some areas than in others but if you are too rigid in your requirements prepare to be in for a long search.

> Many buyers make the fundamental mistake of buying the business that is easiest to get into or one where they think they can make the most money instead of asking themselves which type of business they are best suited for.

On the other hand, if you cannot find a business that matches your criteria, it is possible that you are working with unrealistic criteria. You will have to redefine some of your requirements.

Location

Selecting a location involves two separate yet integrated considerations: whether the location is convenient for you and whether it is a good location for the business. You may only be interested in a business that is within an easy commute of your present residence. Alternatively, you may be willing to relocate to certain areas for the right opportunity or may be looking to relocate to a specific area and are wishing to purchase a business in that area. Moving to a new area to buy a business has inherent risks and demands serious consideration for a number of reasons.

1. **Buying and taking ownership of a business is time-consuming.** The additional burden of moving, possibly including selling your home, purchasing a new home, putting your children into a new school, organizing the move, and familiarizing yourself with a new area can be very stressful.

2. **Moving can be an emotional experience for a family.** You have to deal with the double challenge of settling your family into a new community at the same time as taking over a business. The emotional stress associated with a move can place a real strain on a family relationship; add that to the stress associated with getting the business up and going.

3. **Moving can be expensive.** At a time when you are using a lot of your financial resources to make an investment in a business, you do not need the extra financial burden.

Obviously, there are a number of factors to take into consideration and they should all be seriously reviewed and discussed with your family before making a decision.

REAL LIFE

Murphy's Law: "Whatever Can Go Wrong Will Go Wrong"

Réjean had been sales manager for a small pharmaceutical company in Winnipeg for 15 years when a much larger corporation acquired the business. Réjean's position was eliminated as the new corporation already had an established sales force with a sales manager in place. Réjean decided that the time was right to get into business for himself and be in a position to control his own destiny. His severance package had given him enough money for a down payment on a medium-sized business.

Réjean and his wife Natalie had two children, Nicole, who was 13, and Pierre, who was 11 years old. Natalie worked in the personnel department of the local hospital. Every second year for the past 10 years they had enjoyed family vacations at Parksville on Vancouver Island and they had both fantasized about living in the coastal town. They thought that this might be an ideal opportunity to realize their dream by moving out of Winnipeg and buying a business in Parksville.

Réjean found a printing business for sale in Parksville and, after carrying out his due diligence, decided to purchase the company from the current owner. As the owner wanted to move to Ontario to take care of his ailing father, Réjean agreed to an early closing date.

Réjean and Natalie needed to sell their house in Winnipeg in order to purchase a home in Parksville. As Réjean had to take over control of the business immediately, he moved to Parksville and rented a room in a small motel, while Natalie stayed in Winnipeg to sell the family home. After the home had been on the market for three weeks they received an offer, which they accepted after some negotiation. The offer was subject to financing but the purchasers assured them that this would not be a problem. Secure in the fact that their home was sold, Natalie arranged for the movers to transport the contents of their home to Parksville at the end of the month and headed for Parksville in a minivan with Nicole and Pierre and the family dog.

In the meantime, Réjean had signed an offer and paid a deposit to purchase a home in Parksville. Natalie arrived safely in Parksville with the children and the dog and as the closing date on their new home was still three weeks away, they all moved into the motel room with Réjean.

Having received little training from the previous owner, Réjean was experiencing some difficulties with the printing business. First, he grossly underestimated a large print job for a local company, secondly the only employee who understood the business left to take another job and then his main printer broke down and the faulty part had a delivery time of two weeks. In the middle of all this, they learned that the sale had collapsed on their Winnipeg home, which meant that they were unable to proceed with the purchase of a home in Parksville. Réjean and Natalie tried to find a home to lease but nothing was available and they had now been living out of the motel room for three weeks. On top of this, the children were having a hard time adjusting to their new school and making new friends.

It took five months for their Winnipeg home to sell, which put a tremendous drain on their cash resources, as they still had to make their monthly mortgage payments. Natalie was unable to find a job and had to seek medical treatment for depression. After eight months, everything started to fall into place. They were able to purchase a home, the children settled in to their new surroundings, Natalie got a job at a medical clinic and Réjean became more proficient with the printing business. However, they had all been placed under tremendous strain.

If Réjean had it to do over again, he would still relocate but he would do it on his own time-frame and would not be rushed into making decisions.

The Size of Business

Either revenues or the number of employees will define the size of business. A major factor in deciding the size of the business will be your investment level. Another consideration is the size of business you feel confident about and capable of managing.

> You should focus your search on a business that will generate sufficient cash flow to cover your current needs but with the ability to grow in the future.

Cash Flow

It is not enough to define what type of business you are interested in without determining whether the potential earnings will meet your requirements. The first step is to calculate how much money you need. Will the business provide you with that level of income? The common mistake among buyers is to overestimate their earning potential, particularly in the first few years. This is important, as this is the period when you will be repaying any business loans. Excessively optimistic projections often result from buyers being convinced that they can increase profitability by rapidly increasing sales revenues. Of course, such an increase is possible, but in most cases it does not happen and there is a shortfall in income. You should focus your search on a business that will generate sufficient cash flow to cover your current needs but with the ability to grow in the future.

Opportunity for Continued Growth and Profits

If you have sufficient cash reserves, you may be satisfied with a business that is currently losing money if it has a big financial upside. Regardless, most people are looking for a business that has opportunity for growth and increased profits. In addition to providing larger annual cash flows, it increases the value of the business thereby increasing your equity in the business.

Cash Available for a Down Payment, Acquisition Costs and Working Capital

The topic of how much cash you have available or are willing to invest in a down payment is covered under "How to Assess Your Financial Comfort Level," in Chapter 1. You must also consider funds for acquisition costs and sufficient working capital for your business.

The amount of acquisition costs will vary depending on how long it takes you to find your business, since you have to live during this period and fund the cost of travel and long-distance telephone calls. It also depends on how many businesses you investigate and how deeply you investigate them. If you only carry out a preliminary investigation of a business before you eliminate it, you will probably only incur minimal expenses but if your investigation of a business involves due diligence, which requires you to consult with professionals such as lawyers, accountants or appraisers, your expenses will be significantly higher.

There are many factors to consider when deciding what type of business is right for you. You need to understand the pros and cons of business ownership, as well as starting or buying a business. It is also important to do a candid list of your personal and business needs and wants, as well as strengths and weaknesses. You need to determine and assess the type of business that you think would work for you and why. That will help you in deciding on a business that is the right fit for you. Finally, remember to check out a lot of businesses to increase your level of awareness. Shortlist those businesses you are interested in, then do a detailed list of the pros and cons of the shortlist. This type of methodical approach will help you make objective, rather than emotional, decisions. Refer to Appendix 4.1, "Buying a Business Checklist, for some guidelines of key issues to consider.

Keeping your eye on the prize at all times will help you navigate your way through the early stages of identifying and researching potential businesses and business ideas. There is a lot of work to be done in the cause of finding that ideal fit. Prepare and position yourself, then watch for the signs.

Appendix 4.1
Buying a Business Checklist

Check when
answered to your
satisfaction

Preliminary

1. What are your reasons for considering buying a business rather than starting from scratch or buying into a franchise? ☐

2. Have you made a list of what you like and do not like about buying an existing business? ☐

3. Have you compared the costs of buying a business with the costs of starting a new business? ☐

4. Have you talked with other business owners in the area to see what they think of the firm? ☐

5. Have you fully explored the alternative types of businesses that you might be interested in? ☐

6. Have you selected the type of industry that would most interest you? ☐

7. Have you expertise and experience in the type of business you are considering? Is it compatible with your personal goals, personality and financial resources? ☐

8. Have you established the criteria that you require in an existing business for your needs? ☐

9. Are you comparing identical types of businesses for sale so that you can make a comparative value judgment? ☐

10. Do you know the real reasons the business is for sale? How do you know they are accurate? ☐

11. Have you checked out the firm's reputation with the Better Business Bureau, Credit Bureau, Dun & Bradstreet, suppliers, creditors and competitors? ☐

Costs

12. Is inventory accurately shown at true current value for calculating actual cost of goods sold? ☐

13. Did the seller prepay some expenses? Must you reimburse the seller for your share? ☐

14. Are expenses all-inclusive? Will new ownership change them? ☐

15. Is another business involved in the accumulation or payment of expenses? ☐

16. Will some annual expenses be due soon? ☐

17. Have some expenses been delayed (e.g., equipment maintenance)? ☐

18. What new or increased expenses should you anticipate? ☐

19. Was interest paid for money lent to the business? ☐

20. Are wages as well as an attractive profit margin provided for working owners? ☐

21. Must staff salaries be adjusted soon? ☐

22. Does equipment value reflect reasonable annual depreciation? ☐
23. Has your solicitor checked out the lease? ☐
24. What expenses do similar businesses have? ☐
25. How will sales fluctuations affect cost? ☐
26. What costs are allocated to which product? How would a change in product mix affect costs? ☐

Sales

27. What's the future of your product or service? Is it expanding? Becoming oversold? Obsolete? ☐
28. Can sales increase with current resources? ☐
29. Have you checked with the suppliers in terms of the history of the business for sale? ☐
30. Is the location good, or is a poor location the reason for the sale? ☐
31. Are bad debts deducted from records or are they still shown as receivables? ☐
32. Have all sales been reliably recorded? Are the total sales broken down by product line, if applicable? ☐
33. Are some goods on consignment and able to be returned for full credit? ☐
34. Are some goods on warranty? If so, will financial allowance be made for possible warranty commitments? ☐
35. What is the monthly and annual sales pattern? Is it consistent? Seasonal? Related to other cycles? ☐
36. Are sales fluctuations due to one-shot promotions? ☐
37. Is the seller's personal role critical to success? ☐
38. Is there a salesperson who contributes significantly to success? Can you keep this salesperson? ☐
39. Will existing suppliers be available to you? ☐
40. Is reported stock turnover in line with industry practice ratios? Does existing stock include items from another business? ☐
41. Are sales figures solely from this business? ☐
42. Are prices competitive? Who are the competitors? Are the competitors' price strategies gaining them a larger market share? ☐

Profits

43. Do you know minimum and maximum likely sales? ☐
44. How will sales fluctuations affect profits? ☐
45. What are the book values, market values and replacement values of the fixed assets? ☐
46. If inventory and/or work in progress are included, has a value been agreed on at time of offer? Have you agreed on how it will be adjusted at time of closing and within what limits? ☐
47. Is there inventory sold but not shipped? ☐
48. How will inflation affect sales and costs? ☐

49. Are profits enough to take the risk? ☐

50. Based on the history, have you projected future cash flow and profitability? Have you determined your break-even point? ☐

51. Have accurate records been kept? ☐

52. Have you and a qualified accountant analyzed the records thoroughly? Balance sheets? Profit-and-loss statements? Tax returns? Purchases and sales records? Bank statements? How far back have you gone? ☐

53. Must you build up your own accounts receivable? How will this affect cash flow? ☐

54. Is some equipment leased? At what cost? ☐

55. Is equipment in good repair? Efficient? Up-to-date? Easy to service? Saleable? ☐

56. Have you checked with comparable industry profit ratios and are they consistent with the business you are examining? ☐

Liabilities

57. Is the seller cooperative in supplying financial information? ☐

58. Are there any contingencies such as warranties or guaranteed debts or accounts? ☐

59. Are your assets free and clear of debts and liens? Do you have in writing the terms of the debts you are assuming? ☐

60. Will cash flow cover debts? ☐

61. Are you assuming any risk of liability for the seller's actions (e.g., if you are buying shares of a limited company)? Will customers expect you to make refunds or honour warranties or risk losing goodwill, even though you are not legally obliged to do so? ☐

62. How is the business's credit rating with suppliers? ☐

63. Are there advances or prepayments that should be turned over to you? ☐

64. Are there goods that have been prepaid to the business but not delivered by the business? Should these advance payments be given to you? ☐

65. If buying part of a company or entering a partnership, what limitations are there and what authority will you have in the management of the firm? ☐

Purchase Agreement

66. Is the business a limited company? Are you buying assets or shares? Have you consulted with your lawyer and accountant on the pros and cons of this issue? ☐

67. Does the contract of sale cover assets to be purchased and liabilities to be assumed when the business is to be taken over? ☐

68. Are you prepared to negotiate, remembering a business is only worth what someone will pay and what a seller will accept? Do you have the skills to negotiate directly yourself? ☐

69. Did you include escape clauses in the proposed offer to purchase contract covering obtaining finance, inspection of records, receiving licenses, rights and other transfers, and satisfactory review by your lawyer and accountant? ☐

70. Have you discussed the proposed business with someone who understands this type of business? □

71. Will the seller agree not to set up in competition with you for an agreed time and within a specified geographic area? □

72. Will the seller train and assist you after the purchase? □

73. Have you selected a lawyer who is skilled in commercial law, including buying a business? Are you going to discuss the purchase terms with your lawyer before removing the escape clauses or better still, before formally submitting an offer? □

74. Have you selected an accountant who is skilled in the financial evaluation and assessment aspects of buying a business? Are you going to discuss the purchase terms with your accountant before removing the escape clauses or better still, before formally submitting an offer? □

5

SELECTING THE
RIGHT BUSINESS

The Buying Process

Be patient. Buying a business can take as long as one or even two years, assuming you are searching full-time. It is estimated that less than 25% of people seriously searching for a business ever achieve their objective. The process can be extremely time-consuming, frustrating and expensive. Many buyers lose their patience after a couple of months. It is important that you understand that the entire buying process takes time. Be active, be aggressive and be focused. There are a lot of good businesses out there; it is not easy to find the one that is right for you. Your search will require hard work and perseverance. The good news is that your skill and knowledge will increase in direct proportion to the amount of time you search for a business. Therefore, the probability of making the *right* decision should increase proportionately with the length of your search. You may also change your mind about the type of business you are looking for as your knowledge increases.

> It is important that you understand that the entire buying process takes time. Be active, be aggressive and be focused.

Unfortunately, most people choose a business in the worst possible way: by hearing about a business that is available and buying it. Of course, this does not make sense. How many people buy the first house they look at? Even if the business looks attractive, you should not buy the first business offered to you, regardless of how appealing it might be, without looking at other businesses. It is possible that you could miss the business that is right for you, but the alternative is far worse. Take a moment to consider the following questions:

- What happens to you financially if you still have not bought a business after several months?
- Can you get a job quickly?

• Do you have alternative financial resources?

The first thing to understand is that it is difficult to find a good, profitable company with a motivated seller. At any particular point in time only around 5% of businesses are: for sale, profitable and appealing. Some businesses may meet the first two criteria, but fail on the third.

It is important not to rush the decision and to carry out full due diligence. This is especially important for individuals who have been laid off by their firms, or whose positions have been terminated, as there can be a tendency in these cases to hurry the process and base the buying decision on emotion rather than logic. People often do this to counteract the effects of lost self-esteem that can accompany job loss. They may be anxious to prove their worth to family, friends and colleagues. Consider the opinions of your professional advisors. The decision has to have logic at its base. It is important to feel excited about the business, as this will develop into the passion necessary to make the business a success. However, emotion alone is not enough.

One of the biggest mistakes first-time buyers make is to stop investigating other opportunities once they have become interested in a particular company. As they say, "It's not over until the fat lady sings." Only 50% of transactions reaching the letter of intent stage actually close. You should continue to actively pursue other possible acquisitions at the same time as you are negotiating your primary business interest; if the first deal collapses you do not have to start all over again.

> It is important to feel excited about the business, as this will develop into the passion necessary to make the business a success. However, emotion alone is not enough.

> You should continue to actively pursue other possible acquisitions at the same time as you are negotiating your primary business interest; if the first deal collapses you do not have to start all over again.

Timing

Buying a business when the economy is strong may mean that you have to pay more for the business and that interest rates and lease rates will be higher. Generally, when the economy is in a downturn, you will pay less for a business, and interest rates and lease rates will be lower. At the same time, an inordinate number of buyers looking for businesses at the same time means more competition, which could translate into a seller's market and result in higher selling prices for businesses. Other factors also have to be considered when the economy is in a downturn, for example, lower business revenues.

Where to Look for a Business

The reason that most people experience such difficulty locating a profitable and appealing business is that they are located in what is referred to as the "hidden business market." This is the market where businesses are not publicly advertised for sale. In fact, the majority of businesses that are for sale are not advertised publicly. One need only look in the Business

Opportunities section of a metropolitan newspaper to see that this is the case. Typically, you will see a number of ads for businesses such as dry cleaners, restaurants, video outlets, flower stores, fast food franchises, travel agencies, gas stations and convenience stores. The classifieds tend to attract smaller businesses; those that cannot afford to pay a broker's commission or others who are avoiding paying the broker's commission.

There are a number of reasons why some of the most desirable businesses are the most difficult to locate. One of the reasons the business is desirable is because it has established a good reputation in the community and has built solid relationships with its customers and suppliers. In addition, the business probably has excellent long-term employees who have played a large part in the business's success. Consequently, the last thing a business owner wants to do is to create uncertainty about the future of the business. Customers who have been loyal to the business owner may decide to move their business to a competitor as they are unsure what level of service they will receive from the new owner. Suppliers might consider revising their pricing structure before a new owner takes over. Nothing creates anxiety among employees faster than uncertainty about their jobs or working for a new employer, so they may start testing out the job market. It is fairly evident why the seller of a viable company is reluctant to go public with an intention to sell the business. The business owner advertising a business for sale in the classifieds is not usually concerned about confidentiality; the employees may not be such an integral part of the business, their relationship with the customer may not be as important and supplier concerns may be a non-issue.

> The most effective way of reaching the hidden market is by going directly to the source and contacting business owners directly.

Contacting Business Owners Directly

The most effective way of reaching the hidden market is by going directly to the source and contacting business owners directly. This method allows you to target businesses that meet your criteria and circumvent the intermediaries and the competition. However, to be successful, this is a process that requires both professionalism and organization. Understand that owners of successful businesses may be approached frequently by prospective purchasers. Unfortunately, a number of prospective purchasers may be poorly prepared or unqualified tire kickers, which can make the business owner very cynical of interested buyers. Consequently, you need to be well-prepared and capable of convincing the business owner that you are a prospect and not a suspect — that you are credible and capable of buying the owner's business. You must first understand that it can take time to build a relationship of trust, so approach business owners in a series of contacts.

Start by sending a short letter to the business owner, expressing your interest and suggesting that you would like to follow-up within the next few days to discuss your interest. Explain why you are interested in the

> ... you need to be well-prepared and capable of convincing the business owner that you are a prospect and not a suspect — that you are credible and capable of buying the owner's business.

owner's particular business — for example, you have researched the industry and find it appealing; you have a specific interest or passion for that type of business; or you have patronized the business for several years and are impressed by the way it is operated — and you are interested to know if the owner has considered selling it.

Follow-up your letter with a call to the business owner and ask for the opportunity to have a meeting. Try to make the call on a day of the week, or at a time of day, when the business typically would not be busy. If the owner agrees to a meeting, try to keep it as short as possible. Your primary goal is to establish rapport and gain a basic understanding of the business owner's intentions regarding the business. Do not force the owner into giving you a decision about whether or not the owner wishes to sell the business at this time. If you do force the owner into a decision, the answer almost certainly is going to be no. Neither is it appropriate to ask about a selling price. In fact, it is not good negotiating strategy to ask for the owner's selling price at any time as in most cases it will be excessively high. If the owner's response is "everything is for sale, at a price," the probability is that you will never do a deal with that person, certainly not one that is favourable.

> Maintain regular contact even if the owner is uninterested at this time, as you never know when the owner might reconsider selling.

After the meeting, regardless of the outcome, it is appropriate to send a follow-up letter thanking the owner for the time and confirming your interest (assuming, of course, that you are still interested). If there is interest on the part of the owner, you can arrange to meet again to initiate further discussion. Maintain regular contact even if the owner is uninterested at this time, as you never know when the owner might reconsider selling. If this happens, you will want to be the first to know. The key is to appear interested but not over-anxious as this could affect the ultimate selling price.

Using Business Brokers

There are advantages and disadvantages to using business brokers. The first thing to keep in mind is that business brokers are primarily salespeople and they are usually paid on a commission basis if successful in selling the business. As sellers pay their commission, brokers are motivated to sell the business for the highest price and the best terms possible for their client. Consequently, do not expect a broker to volunteer negative information about the business. On the other hand, you know that you have a motivated seller if the business is listed for sale with a broker.

The key is to search out the successful business brokers and ignore the rest. Some brokers specialize in certain types and sizes of businesses, so you should seek out a broker familiar with the type of business you are interested in acquiring. Investigate a broker's reputation in the marketplace before contact. The successful brokers know that the secret to success is to focus on solid profitable businesses, whereas the unsuccessful brokers are not so selective in the businesses they represent. The top brokers know that although it might take greater effort initially to obtain good business listings, it takes less effort to sell them. Consequently, a good broker may have several potential buyers who might be interested in a new listing, so you need to get your name on the broker's priority buyer list. Even then, your chances of finding a business through a business broker are probably less than 50%. Although approximately 90% of homes are sold through realtors, less than 20% of businesses are sold through business brokers. Experienced brokers can also be helpful and creative in structuring a deal. They may be in a position to help you with some financing alternatives if they have established credibility with lenders based on past dealings.

Some business brokers will work on a fixed-fee or hourly basis on behalf of the purchaser. This can work well as you only pay for the specific services you require. It is not advisable, however, to enter into an exclusive arrangement as this limits your ability to search for a business on your own or to work with other agents. The other benefit is that a broker can represent you anonymously, which could be very important if you are still working and do not want your employer to know that you are seeking a business, particularly if it is in the same line of business.

REAL LIFE

Know Yourself, Know your Broker

Travis was interested in buying a restaurant when he saw a couple of restaurants advertised for sale in the newspaper together with a number of other businesses in a display advertisement that had been placed by Reg, a local business broker. Travis called Reg to obtain some preliminary information about the restaurants, but during the phone conversation, Travis sensed that Reg was deliberately moving the focus away from the restaurants, and towards another unrelated business, Exclusive Business Machines. Reg kept saying, "You really should take a look at this business. The owner is quite motivated to sell and it has a lot of potential."

Travis thought it was worthwhile to meet with Reg at his office to obtain more in-depth information about the restaurants; however, once again Reg kept trying to divert Travis's attention to Exclusive Business Machines. Travis explained to Reg that the asking price was $100,000 over Travis's investment range and he was not interested in that type of business in any case. Reg said, "I know how you feel Travis, but believe me you will be glad that you checked this one out. Anyway, I know that the owner will carry a large part of the financing at very attractive terms." Reg really tried to push Travis into making an appointment to look at the business the following morning. Travis began to feel pressured and told Reg that he would think about it and give him a call later in the day if he decided to look at it the next day. As Travis was feeling very uncomfortable, he made an excuse about having another meeting and left Reg's office without even getting information about the restaurants.

Later that day, Travis met his friend Julien for lunch. Travis told Julien how uncomfortable he had felt at Reg's office and how he could not understand why Reg was so forceful about showing him the Exclusive Business Machines business. Julien had known

Reg for quite some time and was able to shed some light on the situation. He explained to Travis that Reg's wife, Carmine, was a partner in Exclusive Business Machines and she urgently needed to liquidate her investment in the company as she needed the funds for another business that she owned. This second business was in financial difficulty. Now it all made sense to Travis, who was quite upset that Reg had not declared his wife's interest in the business. Travis understood that as the seller compensated the business broker, the broker would be acting in the seller's best interest but he was surprised that Reg would blatantly promote a business that did not match Travis's criteria in any way. Travis decided that he would not confront Reg about the situation but he would certainly not do business with him.

Realtors

Some businesses are listed for sale through realtors on the multiple listing service. In rural areas that cannot support a full-time business broker, most businesses go through realtors. Search out realtors who specialize in commercial real estate and not the realtor who does it as a sideline.

Networking

One of the rules of marketing is, "Stand in traffic and you might get hit." The more people who know you are looking for a business, the greater your chances of finding the business that is right for you. Your first circle of influence is friends, family, neighbours and colleagues. Other networking opportunities include joining the Chamber of Commerce, service clubs and trade organizations.

> The more people who know you are looking for a business, the greater your chances of finding the business that is right for you.

Newspaper Ads

There are some publications that specialize in the sale of commercial real estate, franchises and business opportunities. One such publication is *Western Investor*, which covers British Columbia, Alberta, Saskatchewan and Manitoba. Ads frequently appear in the business section and the business opportunities section of the classifieds in newspapers. Check the classified sections of your local and regional newspapers regularly.

Advertising

You could also consider advertising for business opportunities in newspapers, magazines and trade publications. Advertising is not always effective, although there is the chance that it may produce a good lead, and that could be all that you need. Be prepared to be bombarded with calls from business brokers and people offering you all types of business opportunities.

There are many different methods of searching out businesses for sale. It is helpful to try all of them to expand your potential buying opportunities. Remember to have a written system for doing your comparisons and analysis. That way, you can compare and contrast the opportunities, using the same criteria.

6

BUYING A FRANCHISE

Introduction

Buying a franchise can be a good option, especially for someone going into business for the first time. There are essentially two ways of acquiring a franchise: you can acquire a new franchise or you can purchase an established franchise unit from the current franchisee (a resale). In fact, franchisors have existing units for sale from time to time and, depending on the circumstances, these units can be a good investment. If you have the opportunity to purchase a franchised unit that is not operating to its full potential and that is part of a reputable franchise system, it may be a good investment depending on the price and the reason for its underperformance. For example, if the location is good and what is required to raise the performance is related to inferior customer service, poor budgeting, lack of cost controls or inefficient inventory management, it may be a good investment, as these things typically do not require major investment.

> If you have the opportunity to purchase a franchised unit that is not operating to its full potential and that is part of a reputable franchise system, it may be a good investment depending on the price and the reason for its underperformance.

Everything is relative, so when you evaluate the business opportunity, you have to take the price into consideration. If the seller is asking full value and is not discounting the price to reflect the situation, it may not be such a good investment. You will need the franchisor's approval to take over the franchise and in most cases you will be required to attend and pass the franchisor's training program.

What is Franchising?

In basic terms, franchising is a form of distribution or marketing. It is a method of doing business by which the *franchisee* is granted the right to offer, sell or distribute goods or services under a marketing plan or system prescribed in substantial part by the franchisor. It is a strategy for successfully penetrating, developing, dominating and achieving a disproportionately large market share.

The *franchisor* is the company that owns and controls the franchise system and grants the licence to operate the franchise according to a certain method and with the products and/or services that have been developed by the franchisor.

The *franchisee* is the company or person that pays the franchisor for the franchise and the right to use the system.

The *franchise* is the right to use the trademarks and systems, and to promote the products and/or services.

Franchise Legislation

Until 1997, Canada had been relatively free of franchise legislation, with Alberta being the only province in Canada to have legislation directed specifically at franchising. However, the increasing number of lawsuits between franchisors and franchisees has prompted other provinces to reassess the need to introduce some form of franchise legislation. On May 17, 2000 the *Arthur Wishart Act (Franchise Disclosure), 2000* ("the Ontario Act") was passed by the Ontario Legislature and came into force on January 31, 2001. In substance, the Ontario Act is very similar to the Alberta Act. Prince Edward Island is considering adopting franchise legislation using the Alberta and Ontario legislation as the basis for any new legislation.

> Franchising is a method of doing business by which the franchisee is granted the right to offer, sell or distribute goods or services under a marketing plan or system prescribed in substantial part by the franchisor.

Disclosure Requirements

If the franchisor is operating in a province with disclosure requirements and if you are a resident of, or have a permanent residence in one of these provinces, the franchisor is required to provide you with a copy of its disclosure document at least 14 days before the signing of any agreement relating to the franchise, or the payment of any consideration relating to the franchise, whichever is earlier. If you are investigating a franchise in a province that does not have disclosure requirements, and the franchisor is operating in a province with disclosure requirements, you can request a copy of the franchisor's disclosure document that the franchisor is required to provide. The disclosure document must contain copies of all proposed franchise agreements, the franchisor's financial statements, reports and other documents in accordance with the regulations. A certificate stating that the disclosure document contains no untrue statement of a material fact and does not omit to state a material fact must be signed by at least two of the franchisor's officers or directors. The information contained in the disclosure provides a good basis for assessing the merits of a franchise operation but do not assume that the franchisor's compliance with disclosure or registration requirements implies that the regulatory authority has approved or recommends the franchise in any way. It is essential that you verify the information disclosed by the franchisor by speaking with existing franchisees, your lawyer, your accountant or a franchise consultant.

Earnings Claims

The Alberta and Ontario Acts requires the franchisor to provide details of any earnings claims information used by the franchisor, including material assumptions underlying its preparation and presentation, whether it is based on actual results of existing outlets, and the percentage of outlets that meet or exceed each range of results. The earnings claims information must have a reasonable basis at the time it is prepared. The disclosure documents must also state where substantiating information is available for inspection by franchisees. If the information is given in respect of a franchisor-operated outlet, the franchisor must state that the information may differ in respect of a franchisee outlet. Earnings claims consist of information from which a specific level or range of actual or potential sales, costs, income or profit from franchisee or franchisor outlets can be ascertained.

> Unfortunately, a large number of people view franchising as some sort of magic wand or guarantee of success, and fail to carry out proper due diligence. Franchising is not a guarantee of success or the accumulation of great riches.

Franchisee's Right of Rescission

If a franchisee suffers a loss because of a misrepresentation contained in a disclosure document, the franchisee has a right of action for damages against the franchisor and every person who signed the disclosure document. If the franchisor fails to provide the disclosure document within the time requirements, the prospective franchisee may rescind the agreement by giving notice of cancellation no later than 60 days after receiving the disclosure documents, or no later than two years after the granting of the franchise. A franchisor must, within 30 days of receiving a notice of cancellation, compensate the franchisee for any net losses the franchisee has incurred in acquiring, setting up or operating the franchised business.

Fair Dealing between Franchisee and Franchisor

Both the Ontario and Alberta statutes provide that every franchise agreement imposes on each party a duty of fair dealing in its performance and enforcement.

Investigate before You Invest

Unfortunately, a large number of people view franchising as some sort of magic wand or guarantee of success, and fail to carry out proper due diligence. Franchising is not a guarantee of success or the accumulation of great riches. Certainly, some franchisees enjoy a good return on investment in addition to paying themselves a good management salary, but others work harder than they ever imagined with little or no franchisor support, no profits and no chance of selling their business. Franchising is usually a safer investment than opening a similar independent business, if the franchise is part of a solid franchise system. A "Franchise Assessment Checklist" is provided in Appendix 6.1.

When considering a franchise it is essential that you carry out greater due diligence than if you were buying an independent business. If you are interested in acquiring a resale franchise, you need to carry out due diligence on both the franchise and the business itself. Success in franchising is based on mutual dependence, so it naturally follows that the search for a franchise is a mutual investigation process. It is important to evaluate both the franchisor and the franchise. In addition to any legal disclosure requirements, the Canadian Franchise Association has mandatory disclosure requirements for its franchisor members.

REAL LIFE

Check out the Reasons for Poor Performance

Sophia was interested in buying a franchise to operate a small restaurant when she saw an advertisement in her local newspaper to purchase an existing Ms. Monika's Restaurant. The asking price for the business was about 60% of the cost of setting up a new Ms Monika' restaurant.

Sophia met with the franchisee, William, who explained that because of his recent divorce he was unable to focus on the business and wanted to move to another city. William's operating financial statements for the business showed that the restaurant was performing at about 50% of the average of other Ms. Monika's Restaurant franchises. Sophia asked if she could spend a day working in the restaurant to see what it would take to improve the performance.

Sophia concluded that a combination of factors — poor customer service, low staff morale, high staff turnover, inconsistent food quality and excessive food wastage — contributed to the restaurant's poor performance. These were mainly attitudinal things that required time and effort rather than large investments of capital, although Sophia thought it would be worth spending some money on interior painting and a new exterior sign.

Sophia purchased the business and after just three months she was able to achieve her initial target of the average sales of the other restaurants in the chain. She went on to surpass her goal by 25% at the end of the first year.

Reputable franchisors go to great lengths to select a franchisee. If a franchisor fails to investigate you as thoroughly as you investigate them, be cautious. If a franchise is awarded to a franchisee who is unable to operate it successfully, the franchisor will suffer almost as much as the franchisee who fails. Not only does the franchise unit fail to produce an ongoing revenue stream for the franchisor, but it can also take up a tremendous amount of the franchisor's time and effort to either salvage or resell the franchise.

A franchisor is obviously not gambling an entire reputation on you, however, you are probably betting a good deal of your future on the franchisor, so do not hesitate to ask a lot of questions. A franchisor who is offering a legitimate opportunity and who has nothing to hide should have no hesitation in providing the necessary information to a qualified franchise prospect and should respect the fact that you are investigating the franchise in much the same manner as you are being investigated.

Balance Your Decision-Making

To be a successful franchisee you must:

- have a passion for the business;
- understand the business; and
- be capable of financing the business.

Obviously, you should not consider a franchise that is beyond your financial means. Emotion and logic should be equally balanced when making the final decision about purchasing the franchise. You should feel good about the people involved in the franchise and excited about the opportunity. Make sure you thoroughly investigate consumer acceptance, risk analysis, availability of product and demographics. Ask yourself, "Does this all make sense?" Your emotional commitment is only one of the essential elements, and if any of these elements is missing, the franchise is probably not right for you.

The Critical Factors

There are four critical factors that combine to make a good franchise system. Ask yourself the following questions with regard to the four factors.

The Organization

- Does the franchise organization have the ability to develop and maintain a franchise network? It is one thing to build and successfully operate a couple of retail outlets, but it requires a completely different set of skills to build a network of several hundred stores.
- Is there a strong management team that understands the particular industry and possesses the skills necessary to build the franchise organization?
- How long has the franchise company been in business? What are the depth and quality of the franchisor's management team and field-support people?
- What business is the company really in? Is it more interested in selling franchises than in operating a solid franchise system? How does the company make its money — from up-front fees or from continuing royalties? Does the franchisor have adequate financial backing or is it relying on the sale of franchises to develop the system? How long has the franchise concept been tested? Reputable franchisors are interested in the continuing success of their franchisees; money should come from successful franchises and products, not reselling unprofitable franchises.

The Product or Service

- Does the product or service have widespread consumer demand? Selling a new concept to the general public can be expensive and risky. Ideally, consumer demand for the product or service should have already been established. Some potential franchisees, thinking that the market is saturated, shy away from franchise opportunities that are already well represented by other companies. If there is an established consumer demand for a product or service, it then becomes a matter of gaining market share rather than gaining market acceptance.

- Is the product or service marketable in your area?
- Will there only be a seasonal demand?
- Is this a trend or a fad?
- Can the concept be taught or is it a skill unique to the franchisor?
- Is it recession-proof?
- Is the franchisor the only source of supply for the product? What alternatives are there if the franchisor should fail and the supply of product is terminated?

The Competitive Edge

- Does the franchise offer a better way of providing that product or service to the consumer?
- What makes the product or service unique and does it satisfy a particular need in your market?
- Can the product or service be easily copied by a competitor?
- Will you have many competitors?
- Is the product or service protected by a trademark or copyright?
- Is the price competitive?
- Is there a fully developed business format (system) for you to follow?
- What assurance do you have that the franchisor will be able to continue getting you the product at a fair price?

The Entrepreneurial Opportunity

Ask yourself whether the level of investment, the nature of the industry and the appeal of the franchise itself will attract enough other people to become franchisees. If the answer is "yes" to these questions, chances are the system will grow and the franchise can be re-sold in the future.

> In most cases a franchised business should sell faster and for a higher price than an independent business by virtue of its exclusivity, name recognition and other franchise advantages.

Most people do not enter a business with the thought of selling it in the future, but it is a sensible approach to develop a business with the intention of future resale. You must have a way of liquidating your assets and unless you are planning to list your company on a public exchange the only way of realizing the increase in your equity is through the eventual resale of your business. In most cases a franchised business should sell faster and for a higher price than an independent business by virtue of its exclusivity, name recognition and other franchise advantages.

On average, franchises change hands every five years. The reasons for the change of ownership are as varied as the people running them: a fresh challenge; the transfer of a spouse to a new city; an inability to run the business profitably; illness, retirement or personal problems; or simply a franchisee's desire to capitalize on his or her efforts and make a profit.

A franchisee must look at the franchise opportunity through the eyes of other would-be franchisees, taking into consideration all of the factors that will influence the growth of the total franchise system. Unless the system grows, many of the benefits of franchising — such as advertising clout and purchasing power — will be lost.

Pros of Franchising

Reduced Risk
Franchising does not guarantee success, but a good franchise should help reduce the chances of failure.

A Proven System
With a tried and tested operating system, the franchisee loses the obstacles and gains the opportunities. A franchisee should receive a completely proven system that includes initial training, opening assistance, accounting systems, established suppliers, manuals and use of the trademarks. The franchisee avoids repeating previous mistakes and is provided with information on inventory levels, store design, competition, pricing structure and operational data drawn from the entire system.

> ... the purchasing power of the franchisor can reduce the franchisee's initial outlay for equipment and supplies.

Easier Access to Financing and Reduced Cash Requirements
Financial institutions prefer to lend to established franchised systems because of their higher success rate. The consumer awareness created by national or regional name recognition can reduce the costs of grand-opening promotional activity and advertising start-up. As well, the purchasing power of the franchisor can reduce the franchisee's initial outlay for equipment and supplies.

Purchasing Power
Collective purchasing power on products, supplies, extended health and insurance benefits, equipment, and advertising can easily offset any ongoing royalties paid by the franchisee.

Site Selection Assistance
Franchisors can provide expert site selection assistance based on their operating experience and demographic knowledge. Landlords and developers prefer to deal with someone who has an established track record. This enables franchisees to obtain locations in major malls and other developments that might not be available to independent operators.

Advertising Clout
Most independent businesses cannot afford the services of advertising and promotional experts. Consequently, their advertising is often poorly conceived and inconsistent. They also cannot afford to invest in the level of advertising required to maintain a commanding presence in the marketplace. In a franchise system, the advertising cost is spread over many units enabling the franchisor to achieve economies of scale. This also allows the franchisee to create well-conceived promotional campaigns and place the advertising in the most effective medium.

Building Equity
Because of national or regional name recognition and territorial exclusivity, a franchised business should sell faster and for a higher value than an independent business. A buyer is often motivated to buy the franchised business for the same reasons as the original franchisee and may perceive a higher value associated with a recognized name and system.

Stress Reduction
The ability to operate more effectively and efficiently can relieve many business pressures. Systems that control job scheduling, cash flow and inventory levels allow franchisees to run the business instead of the business running them.

Cons of Franchising

Loss of Independence
Loss of independence can be viewed negatively by some franchisees. Although most franchisees invest in a franchise because they want the franchisor's guidance, the moment they enter the franchise system they want to make changes. Unless you are capable of working within a system and can accept a certain amount of regimentation, you should think long and hard before entering into a franchise relationship. One of the greatest strengths of franchising is consistency among units, and with consistency comes compliance.

> Unless you are capable of working within a system and can accept a certain amount of regimentation, you should think long and hard before entering into a franchise relationship.

Franchisor's Failure to Perform
Some franchisors do not deliver what they promise for a couple of reasons. A common reason for failure is the franchisor's shortage of available capital, which can be caused by:

- the franchisor's unrealistic franchise sales projections;
- the franchisor underestimating the expenses associated with the development of the franchise system;
- the franchisor's failure to meet franchise sales projections; or

• high franchisee attrition.

Alternatively, it could be that the franchisor is just not capable of providing the support and assistance, or does not possess the ability to operate a franchise organization.

Misunderstanding the Franchise Agreement

Confusion over the interpretation of certain aspects of the franchise agreement can result in a problem with either the franchisor or the franchisee. A potential franchisee has probably never encountered a document similar to a franchise agreement. A franchise agreement requires careful explanation and scrutiny; failure to do so will inevitably result in a conflict that may end up in the courts.

Misrepresentation by the Franchisor

Misrepresentation by the franchisor can be intentional or unintentional. Projections of income and expense can be provided to the franchisee in good faith, but may turn out to be inappropriate for the location because of the franchisor's inexperience or unfamiliarity with the area's demographics. Conversely, the figures may be total fabrications designed to get the franchisee to sign on the dotted line and hand over the initial franchise fee.

> Consumers are often their own worst enemy, choosing to ignore cautionary advice and warning signals, and basing their investment decisions on emotion without balancing it with logic.

Caveat emptor — let the buyer beware — applies to franchising as it does to any consumer purchase or investment. Consumers are often their own worst enemy, choosing to ignore cautionary advice and warning signals, and basing their investment decisions on emotion without balancing it with logic.

Payment of Fees

The franchisee typically pays an initial fee for being granted the franchise, using the system and receiving initial training. Typically, single-unit franchise fees are in the range of $25,000 to $35,000. The initial fee is paid only once during the term of the agreement, however, franchisors may charge a nominal renewal fee at the commencement of each new term of the agreement. The typical term for a franchise agreement is five or 10 years but may vary to coincide with the terms of a lease. Franchisors sometimes charge a site selection fee of $5,000 or more, in addition to the initial fee, which offsets their costs of site selection and lease negotiation.

In addition to the initial fee, some form of ongoing royalty is paid by the franchisee to the franchisor. In most instances, the royalty is based on a percentage of the franchisee's gross sales, which vary from 1% to10%, or even higher, with a median range of 3% to 6%. Units with high sales volumes often pay 1% or 2% less.

Franchisees are also required to contribute to a national or regional advertising fund, which is in addition to any requirement that the franchisee invest a minimum amount on local advertising.

The Franchise Agreement

A franchise agreement is a contract entered into between the franchisor and the franchisee. It sets out the relationship between the franchisor and franchisee. The franchise agreement will usually appear biased towards the franchisor, which is necessary for the franchisor to maintain control over the franchise system. A franchisor is risking its name and reputation on the franchisee's performance, so it is only fair and reasonable that it has the right to place certain obligations on the franchisee. Consistency among franchise units is a cornerstone of successful franchising.

Despite common beliefs, there is no such thing as a standard franchise agreement; no two franchise agreements are alike. This is understandable because franchises cover many types of businesses in many different industries and have different characteristics. A franchise agreement will be just one of the documents that a franchisee will be required to sign. These may include a non-disclosure/confidentiality agreement, offer to purchase agreement, lease (or sublease) agreement, and a security agreement. We have included a franchise agreement terms checklist at Appendix 6.2.

What is Considered Negotiable?

There are differing opinions regarding just how negotiable a franchisee agreement can be. Franchise agreements can generally be considered non-negotiable, except for items such as location, exclusive territory and opening date. A franchisor may negotiate a point that is specific to a particular franchisee, but will be unwilling to make any changes that will weaken or violate the franchise system. There may be more flexibility or opportunity for negotiation with a new franchisor whose agreement is still evolving and has not yet stood the test of time.

What's Included?

A typical franchise agreement will include:
- the parties to the agreement (the name, address and other details of the franchisor and the franchisee, and any other parties to the agreement)
- the business structure or format being licensed to the franchisee, which is usually referred to as the "system." The system typically includes: trade names, trademarks (for example, logos and slogans), trade secrets, patents, copyright, designs, procedures, techniques, manuals, and the products and/or services that are the subject of the franchise
- the term of the agreement and any renewals or options to renew the franchise at the end of the term;
- the fee or fees payable by the franchisee to the franchisor, some of which may be one-time fees (for example, the initial franchise fee), and some of which may be ongoing fees (for example, a royalty payment, which is generally a percentage of the franchisee's gross sales)
- any territorial limitations on the franchise
- any training and/or re-training requirements

- obligations on the franchisee to abide by the franchisor's system (and the consequences of failing to do so)
- any obligations on the franchisee to modify the system at the request of the franchisor
- any obligations on the franchisee to introduce the franchisor's new products and services, and any obligations to cease selling particular products and services
- any obligations on the franchisee to purchase products or services from the franchisor or from approved suppliers
- any obligations on the franchisee relating to the hours and days of operation of the franchise
- any obligations on the franchisee to advertise or promote the franchise locally or regionally, or to contribute to the franchisor's advertising or promotional program
- any obligations on the franchisee to participate in special promotions (for example, to redeem promotional coupons)
- any obligations on the franchisee regarding the maintenance of financial records, and any obligations to make these records available to the franchisor
- any obligations on the franchisee relating to insurance policies
- any restrictions on the sale of the franchise by the franchisee
- the method or methods by which a franchise may be terminated by the franchisor, and any continuing obligations on a franchisee after termination or expiration of the franchise agreement
- alternative methods for resolving a dispute, for example, mediation and arbitration

Buying a franchise may be one of the options that is right for you. However, it is important that you appreciate the pros and cons of franchising. Operating a franchise is not for everyone. It is also important to thoroughly investigate the franchise that you are considering. There are a variety of critical benchmark factors that will make it easier to weed out unsuitable franchise companies. If you decide on buying a franchise, it is important to make sure that you have a franchise lawyer review all the documents, and help you negotiate the best deal. You want to go through this prudent process before you put any money down or sign any paperwork. The "Franchise Assessment Checklist" at Appendix 6.1, gives you a thorough basis for analyzing a prospective franchise. The "Franchise Agreement Terms Checklist" at Appendix 6.2, covers the types of content that you could expect to see in a franchise agreement. Ask the hard questions outlined in order to make a sound comparative judgment.

Appendix 6.1
Franchise Assessment Checklist

Check when
answered to your
satisfaction

1. How long has the franchise been in business? ☐
2. Is it a well-established company? ☐
3. How long has it been offering franchises? ☐
4. Does it have proven experience of operating a franchise chain? ☐
5. If a new firm, how long has the concept been tested? ☐
6. What are the results of the concept testing? ☐
7. Is it the subsidiary of another company? If so, what is the parent company? Has that company ever franchised other products or services? What was its track record? ☐
8. What business is the company really in? Is it more interested in selling franchises than in marketing a viable product or service? ☐
9. How does the company make its money? From upfront fees or from continuing royalties? ☐
10. How many franchised outlets are currently in operation? How many outlets are company-owned? ☐
11. Have any outlets failed in the past? If so, why? What is the ratio of successful franchises to those that have failed? ☐
12. Have you received the franchisor's recently audited financial statements? Is the company financially stable? Has your accountant analyzed the statements? ☐
13. Who are the franchisor's directors and officers, and what is their business experience? ☐
14. Are these management people employed full-time by the franchise company? ☐
15. How long has the present management been with the company? ☐
16. What is the depth and quality of the franchisor's management team and supervisory personnel? ☐
17. Does the franchisor have a reputation for dealing honestly with its franchisees? With its customers? ☐
18. What is the franchisor's standing with the Chamber of Commerce? The Better Business Bureau? Dun & Bradsheet? Its bank? Your bank? The Canadian Association of Franchisors? ☐
19. Have you discussed the franchisor's plans for future development and expansion or diversification? ☐
20. What effect will development and expansion have on your dealings with the franchisor? ☐

21. What innovations has the franchisor introduced since first starting? ☐
22. Are there immediate plans for further expansion in your area? Will that affect your sales? ☐
23. Where will new franchises be located? ☐
24. Has the company shown a pattern of solid growth? ☐
25. How selective is the franchisor when choosing its franchisees? Have your qualifications and financial standing been reviewed? ☐
26. If the franchise is being offered in Alberta or Ontario, have you been provided with the Franchisor's disclosure document? ☐
27. Is the franchisor connected in any way with any other franchise company handling similar merchandise or services? ☐
28. If the answer to the last question is yes, what is your protection against this second organization? ☐
29. Are there any lawsuits pending against the franchisor or its key people? What is the nature of the claim? Has there been a history of dissatisfied franchisees litigating against the franchisor? ☐

The Product or Service

30. How is the firm's image in the community? How is the product regarded? ☐
31. Are you prepared to spend the rest of your business life with this product or service? ☐
32. Will this product or service sell year-round or will you be out of business for some months each year? Would you be prepared for such a slack period? ☐
33. Might this product or service just be a fad? Will demand increase? Is it a luxury? ☐
34. Is it well-packaged to promote sales? ☐
35. Where is the product or service now sold? ☐
36. What assurance do you have that the franchisor will be able to continue getting the product for you at a fair price? ☐
37. How many people in the area are potential customers? ☐
38. Is the product or service protected by a trademark or copyright? Is it patented? ☐
39. What makes the product or service unique? Does it satisfy a particular need in your market? ☐
40. Can the product or service be easily duplicated by your competitor? ☐
41. How much of this product or service is presently sold? Have sales been increasing or decreasing? ☐
42. Would you buy the product or service on its own merits? ☐
43. How long has it been on the market in its present form? ☐
44. Is the product or service marketable in your territory? ☐
45. Is the price competitive with similar products or services on the market? ☐
46. Have you reviewed the federal and provincial standards and regulations governing the product or service? ☐

47. Are there product warranties or guarantees? Are they your responsibility or the franchisor's? ☐

48. Are you allowed by the franchisor to carry other product lines? ☐

The Location and Territory

49. How well defined is the exclusive territory? Is it outlined on a map? In the franchise agreement? ☐

50. Are there proposed changes in traffic patterns or redevelopment that could affect the business in the proposed location? (Check municipal offices about local bylaws.) ☐

51. How expensive are taxes and insurance in the area? ☐

52. Are your franchised rights exclusive for the area? What guarantee do you have? Can the company open its own outlets? ☐

53. What competition is in the area? ☐

54. Can you select your own location? ☐

55. Do you lease or own the premises? What are the terms? ☐

56. Will you receive assistance in selecting a location? Is there a fee for this? ☐

57. Will the population in the territory increase, remain static or decrease over the next five years? Does the franchisor have information on these matters? ☐

58. Will the product or service you are considering be in greater demand, about the same demand, or in less demand five years from now? ☐

59. Can you, or the franchisor, change the size of your territory in the future? ☐

60. Do you have a profile of the people in your area, including age, income and occupation? ☐

The Experience of Current Franchisees

61. Was the profit projection by the franchisor accurate? ☐

62. What reports to the company are necessary? Are they reasonable? ☐

63. Is there a minimum quota of sales? Is it difficult to achieve? ☐

64. Are the products and equipment supplied by the franchisor satisfactory and delivered promptly? ☐

65. How reliable is delivery from the franchisor? ☐

66. What problems have been encountered with the franchisor? ☐

67. How did the franchisor's income projections compare with the results experienced by existing franchisees? ☐

68. What was the total investment required by the franchisor? ☐

69. Were there any hidden or unexpected costs? ☐

70. Has the franchise been as profitable as expected? ☐

71. How long was it before the operating expenses were covered? ☐

72. How long was the franchise in operation before the business became profitable? ☐

73. How long was it before the franchise was able to pay a reasonable management salary? ☐

74. Does the franchisor respond promptly and helpfully to questions asked? ☐

75. Has there ever been a serious disagreement with the franchisor? What about? Was it settled amicably? ☐

76. What kind of management and staff training was provided? Did it meet expectations? Where was it held? ☐

77. Is the marketing, promotional and advertising assistance received from the franchisor satisfactory? ☐

78. What steps have been taken to make the franchise location successful? ☐

79. Do franchisees advise anyone else to start a franchise with this particular franchisor? ☐

80. If the contract could be changed, what would be changed? ☐

Note: Further franchise checklists can be obtained from the Canadian Franchise Association, the provincial government, accounting firms and banks.

Appendix 6.2
Franchise Agreement Terms Checklist

As franchise agreements vary from franchise to franchise, it would be impossible to identify every term and issue that should be considered in every situation. However, this checklist should be a valuable tool if you are interested in buying a franchise.

Check when
answered to your
satisfaction

Fees, Royalties and Other Costs

How much is the initial franchise fee? ☐

Is any part or the entire initial franchise fee refundable under any
circumstances? ☐

What is the total initial investment? ☐

What are the terms of payment? ☐

Does the franchisor offer any financing, or provide assistance in finding
financing? ☐

How much are the ongoing royalties and how are they determined? ☐

How and when are sales and royalties reported, and how are they paid? ☐

Is the franchisee required to contribute to an advertising fund administered by
the franchisor? If so, how much? ☐

How is the advertising fund administered? Is it national, regional or local? ☐

What are the franchisor's responsibilities regarding accounting of the
advertising fund? ☐

Franchisor's Obligations to the Franchisee

Are accounting and bookkeeping services included or available? ☐

What degree of control does the franchisor have over franchise operations,
particularly in maintaining franchise identity and product quality? ☐

Does the franchisor provide an initial training program? If so, where and when
is it presented, what is the duration and is the franchisee responsible for any
costs such as travel, accommodation and living expenses. ☐

What ongoing management support, assistance and training programs are
provided by the franchisor? Are there any additional costs involved? ☐

Does the franchisor provide promotional aids, point-of-purchase materials,
mail programs and the like? What is the cost? ☐

Franchisee's Obligations

Is the franchisee required to maintain a specific amount of working capital? ☐

Is the franchisee required to commit full-time and best efforts to the operation
of the franchised business? ☐

Is the franchisee required to purchase equipment or supplies from the franchisor or from a supplier approved by the franchisor? ☐

Is the franchisee required to purchase a minimum product quota? ☐

Is the franchisee required to meet specific performance requirements? If so, what are the penalties for not meeting them? ☐

What controls does the franchisor have concerning facility appearance, equipment, fixture and furnishings, and maintenance or replacement of the same? ☐

Is the franchisee required to purchase all, or some of their products from the franchisor? ☐

Is the franchisee required to obtain insurance coverage as specified by the franchisor? ☐

Is the franchisee required to name the franchisor as an "additional named insured" on the franchisee liability coverage? ☐

Is the franchisee required to expend a minimum amount with respect to local advertising? ☐

Are operating hours and days set out in the franchise agreement? ☐

Are there restrictions on what the franchisee can sell? ☐

Premises, Locations and Territory

Are premises required? ☐

Is the franchisee required to lease or sublease premises from the franchisor? ☐

If there is a lease, does it coincide with the term of the franchise agreement? ☐

Who is responsible for site selection and lease negotiation? ☐

Does the franchisor determine the plans and specifications for the premises? ☐

Is the franchisor or the franchisee responsible for the development of the premises? ☐

Is the franchisor responsible for supervision of development of the premises? ☐

Who is responsible for selecting the contractor? ☐

How is the development of the premises financed? ☐

Are there any restrictions on remodelling or redecorating? ☐

Does the franchisee receive an exclusive territory? ☐

Is the size of the exclusive territory subject to reduction or modification under certain conditions? ☐

Does the franchisee have a first refusal option as to any additional franchises in the original territory if it is not exclusive? ☐

Termination and Renewal

Under what circumstances can the franchisor terminate the franchise agreement? ☐

Does the franchise agreement spell out the terms under which the franchisor may repurchase the business? ☐

Does the franchisor have an option or duty to buy any or all of the franchisee's equipment, furnishings, inventory or other assets in the event the franchise is terminated for good cause, by either party? If so, how is the value determined and what are the payment terms? ☐

What provisions are there in the event of the death or permanent incapacity of the franchisee? Is the franchise assignable to heirs, or may it be sold by the franchisee's estate on death or disability? ☐

Is the franchisee restricted from engaging in a similar business after termination or expiration of the franchise agreement? If so, for how many years and in what area? ☐

Term, Renewal and Assignment

Can the franchisee sell the franchised business and assign the franchise agreement to the buyer? If so, what are the conditions of assignment? ☐

Is the franchisee required to pay an assignment fee? ☐

Does the franchisor have the first right of refusal in the event of an assignment? ☐

What is the initial term of the agreement? ☐

What are the terms of renewal? ☐

Is the franchisee required to pay a renewal fee? ☐

Other Points to Consider

Are all trademarks, trade names, or other marks registered to the franchisor? ☐

Has the franchisor met all provincial legal requirements regarding full disclosure? ☐

7

UNDERSTANDING FINANCIAL STATEMENTS

Introduction

There is a perception that financial statements are complex and can only be interpreted by professional accountants. On the contrary, once you become familiar with the overall concepts and the terminology used, you will have an appreciation for the valuable information they contain and will understand how to apply your knowledge to evaluate the business.

What are Financial Statements?

Financial statements consist primarily of the balance sheet and an income statement.

Balance Sheet

The statement of financial position, or balance sheet, reports a company's financial status at a set date noted on the statement. The statement is like a snapshot because it shows what the company is worth at that set date. The statement shows:

- what the company owns;
- what the company owes; and
- what belongs to the owners.

The statement of financial position is also referred to as the balance sheet because of the way one part — assets — is in balance with the sum of the other two parts — liabilities and stockholders' equity. In other words, the amount of money invested in the business, plus the amount that has been borrowed by the business, must equal the assets.

When the owner of the business is an individual, net worth is usually referred to as owner's equity, however, when dealing with a corporation there can be several shareholders so net worth is referred to as shareholders' equity. Annual financial statements normally include information for at least the last two years to allow comparison of changes between years.

The balance sheet shows three main categories of information for each year:
- assets;
- liabilities; and
- shareholder's equity.

Assets

The things that a company owns are called assets. These things might be physical assets such as buildings, trucks, inventory, equipment, and cash, or they might be intangible assets such as goodwill, trademarks and patents.

Assets are either current or non-current (fixed assets). Current assets include cash, government securities, marketable securities, accounts receivable, notes receivable (other than from officers or employees), inventories, prepaid expenses and any other item that could be converted into cash within one year in the normal course of business.

> Annual financial statements normally include information for at least the last two years to allow comparison of changes between years.

Fixed assets are those assets acquired for long-term use in a business such as land, plant, equipment, machinery, leasehold improvements, furniture, fixtures and any other items with an expected useful business life measured in years (as opposed to items that will wear out or be used up in less than one year and are usually expensed when they are purchased). Fixed assets are typically not for resale and are recorded on the balance sheet at their net cost less accumulated depreciation.

Other assets include intangible assets, such as patents, royalty arrangements, copyrights, exclusive use contracts, and notes receivable from officers and employees.

The amounts of fixed assets vary by company and industry. For example, manufacturing companies generally have a large investment in fixed assets because making things requires property, plant and equipment. Service companies usually have fewer fixed assets.

Liabilities

On the balance sheet, debts are called liabilities. All companies have liabilities. Examples of liabilities include:
- money owed to banks and other lenders;
- money owed to suppliers of goods and services (accounts payable);
- taxes owed to government authorities; and
- rents owed to owners of land and buildings.

Liabilities are either current (short-term) or long-term. Current liabilities are due within one year. Long-term liabilities are due after one year.

Shareholders' Equity

Shareholders' equity is the amount owners invested in new stock plus the earnings the company retained since it started (retained earnings is the amount of profit kept after dividends are paid). On the balance sheet the amount of shareholders' equity always equals the value of all the assets minus all the liabilities, for example, if a company's assets are valued at $100,000 and liabilities total $60,000, the equity is $40,000.

The sample balance sheet in Appendix 7.1 is a typical format for a limited company. The shareholders' equity section is made up of share capital and retained earnings. For a proprietorship or partnership, this section is referred to as owner's equity and partner's equity respectively. Owner's equity consists of paid in capital and retained earnings. Paid in capital reflects the total amount of money paid by shareholders to purchase company stock (shares).

Income Statement

Unlike the balance sheet, which is a snapshot of the company's financial position at a particular point in time, the income statement (or profit and loss statement) provides a picture of what has happened over a period of time, for example, a month, a quarter or a year. The sample income statement shown in Appendix 7.2 shows a typical income statement format. It contains specific revenue and expense categories regardless of the nature of the business as described below:

Gross Revenues (revenues from the sale of products and services)   −   Cost of Goods Sold (cost of inventories)

Gross Margin (gross profit on sales before operating expenses)

Gross Margin   −   Operating Expenses (salaries, wages, payroll taxes and benefits, rent, utilities, maintenance, supplies, postage, etc.)

Operating Profit (profit before other non-operating income or expense)

Operating Profit   +   Other Income (income from discounts, investments, customer charge accounts)   −   Other Expenses (interest expense)

Net Profit (or Loss) before Tax (the figure on which your tax is calculated)

Net Profit (or Loss) before Tax   −   Income Taxes (if any are due)

Net Profit (or Loss) after Tax

How to Evaluate the Financials

When evaluating a company, you need to examine the financials for a number of different reasons.

1. The current balance sheet and income statement will provide a snapshot of the company's performance

2. Reviewing a minimum of three years' statements (preferably five years) will give you an indication of management efficiency.

3. The recent financials will indicate the extent to which you can leverage the balance sheet to finance the acquisition of the business.

There are three factors that ultimately determine the financial viability of a small- or medium-sized business:

- the owner's salary level;
- sufficient cash flow to cover debt service; and
- a return on investment commensurate with the level of risk.

In arriving at a valuation for the business, assessing management's ability is different than analyzing the financials (see Chapter 9, "Establishing a Value"). Although you may think that the procedure is the same in both instances, that is not the case. For example, consider a family-owned and operated company that has manufactured a very successful product for many years with a strong balance sheet and an income statement with high gross margins but that is producing minimal profits. The possibility is that the company has not been managed well and has good profit potential. The key is to identify what changes should be made to increase profitability, whether those changes can be made and what the associated costs will be.

Gross Revenues

Is the business gaining or losing market share? You need to determine if annual sales have increased in excess of any price increases that have been implemented. If not, it means the business is either losing customers or its customers are buying less from the business. Are the revenues seasonal? For example, some businesses generate the majority of their revenues during a few months of the year. If you take over such a business at the beginning of its low revenue period, you may need to substantially increase your amount of working capital.

> ... some businesses generate the majority of their revenues during a few months of the year. If you take over such a business at the beginning of its low revenue period, you may need to substantially increase your amount of working capital.

Calculating the Cost of Goods Sold

Calculation of the cost of goods sold varies depending on whether the business is retail, wholesale or manufacturing. In retailing and wholesaling, computing the cost of goods sold during the accounting period involves beginning and ending inventories. This, of course, includes purchases made during the accounting period. In manufacturing it involves not only finished-goods inventories, but also raw materials inventories, goods-in-process inventories, direct labour, and direct factory overhead costs. Regardless of how the cost of goods sold is calculated, it is deducted from sales revenue to get gross margin (or gross profit). From gross profit, general or indirect overhead, such as selling expenses, office expenses and interest expenses are deducted to calculate net profit. This is the final profit after all costs and expenses for the accounting period have been deducted.

Operating Expenses

The operating expenses explain what is happening to most of the cash the business is generating. The majority of fixed expenses should generally be the same amount from year to year. Big variances in fixed expenses may require further investigation.

These numbers will tell you where there may be opportunity for increasing the bottom line by decreasing some of the operational costs. You need to understand the major costs involved with doing business. Does the rent seem high for this type of business? Does the payroll seem excessively high? One of your primary concerns should be cost control. Have costs been increasing each year? Keep in mind that small business owners do everything possible to reduce taxable income. This is where you need to read between the lines, as some of the operating expenses may not be exactly what they seem. Are travel and entertainment expenses legitimate business expenses? Is the owner paying his spouse a monthly salary even though she only comes into the office once a week and performs minor tasks? Is a lease payment for the owner's luxury vehicle included under the travel or automobile categories? Are there other fringe benefits that are not immediately obvious?

> Keep in mind that small business owners do everything possible to reduce taxable income, as a result some of the operating expenses may not be exactly what they seem.

Net Profit

Net profit is what is left over after the total of other costs of goods and the operating expenses are deducted from the revenue. Net profit as a percentage of net sales is called the profit margin. For example, if a business has $1 million in net sales and $100,000 in net income after tax, the net profit margin is 10%. The acceptable range for this margin varies from industry to industry, however 5% is considered acceptable.

Notes to Financial Statements

Financial statements may or may not contain accompanying notes. If there are notes they should be read and interpreted carefully as they may contain important information about the business, such as contingent liabilities or contractual obligations.

The Importance of Ratios

The true meaning of figures from the financial statements emerges only when they are compared to other figures. Various ratios can be established from key figures on the financial statements. Analysing these ratios enables you to spot trends in a business and to compare its performance and condition with the average performance of similar businesses in the same industry. Your accountant should be a good source of information on how your business compares to similar businesses. When you compare changes in the business's ratios from period to period, you can pinpoint improvements in performance or developing problem areas.

Balance Sheet Ratio Analysis

Important balance sheet ratios measure liquidity and solvency (the ability of a business to pay its bills as they come due) and leverage (the extent to which the business is dependent on creditors' funding). Balance sheet ratios include the following ratios:

Liquidity Ratios

These ratios indicate the ease of turning assets into cash. They include the current ratio, quick ratio, working capital and leverage ratio. Generally, the higher these ratios are, the better.

Current Ratios

The current ratio is one indicator of a company's liquidity. This ratio addresses whether the business has enough current assets to meet the payment schedule of its current debts with a margin of safety for possible losses in current assets, such as inventory shrinkage or collectable accounts. It is calculated as shown below:

$$\text{Current Ratio} = \frac{\text{Total Current Assets}}{\text{Total Current Liabilities}}$$

> When you compare changes in the business's ratios from period to period, you can pinpoint improvements in performance or developing problem areas.

The higher the ratio, the better, but a drop in the ratio may indicate trouble, such as using a demand line of credit to finance the purchase of new capital equipment or other long-term assets. Another reason for deterioration in the current ratio may be recent decreases in operating cash flow to pay suppliers and other current debts. A generally acceptable current ratio is 2 to 1. Whether or not a specific ratio is satisfactory depends on the nature of the business and the characteristics of its current assets and liabilities. The minimum acceptable current ratio is obviously 1 to 1, but that relationship is usually playing it too close for comfort.

Quick Ratios

The quick ratio, sometimes referred to as the "acid-test" ratio, is another good indicator of liquidity. It is calculated as shown below:

$$\text{Quick Ratio} = \frac{\text{Cash} + \text{Government Securities} + \text{Receivables}}{\text{Total Current Liabilities}}$$

The quick ratio is a much more exacting measure than the current ratio. By excluding inventories, it concentrates on the really liquid assets, with value that is fairly certain. It helps answer the question: "If all sales revenues should disappear, could the business meet its current obligations with funds on hand or from items that could quickly be converted into cash?" A ratio of 1 to 1 is considered satisfactory unless the majority of the quick assets are in accounts receivable, and the pattern of accounts receivable collection lags behind the schedule for paying current liabilities.

Working Capital

Working capital is more a measure of cash flow than a ratio. The result of this calculation must be a positive number. It is calculated as shown below:

Working Capital = Total Current Assets − Total Current Liabilities

Cash flow is one of the most crucial financial statements in business. It is possible for a business to show a profit on the income statement, but have no money available to pay bills. A successful business will always have sufficient cash (working capital) available to cover operating expenses such as raw materials, inventory and labour costs.

Leverage Ratio

The debt/worth or leverage ratio indicates the extent to which the business is reliant on debt financing (creditor money versus owner's equity). Generally, the higher this ratio, the more risky a creditor will perceive its exposure to the business, making it correspondingly harder to obtain credit. This ratio is calculated as follows:

$$\text{Debt/Worth Ratio} = \frac{\text{Total Liabilities}}{\text{Net Worth}}$$

Income Statement Ratio Analysis

The two following statement of income ratios measure profitability.

Gross Margin Ratio

The gross profit (or gross margin) represents the excess of sales over cost of sales. It measures the percentage of sales income (after obtaining or manufacturing the goods sold) available to pay the overhead expenses of the company. Comparison of the business ratios to those of similar businesses will reveal the relative strengths or weaknesses in the business. A change in the gross profit ratio may be caused by a number of factors. It could mean that the business has been able to maintain its margins, or that it has reduced them due to competitive forces. A change may also mean that suppliers have increased or cut their prices. If the business is a manufacturer, it may also mean the business is using various production elements more or less efficiently. If you are able to analyze the sales and cost of sales figures by major categories, you may be able to spot a trend for a type of product, rather than for the company as a whole. The gross margin ratio is calculated as follows:

$$\text{Gross Margin Ratio} = \frac{\text{Gross Profit}}{\text{Net Sales}}$$

(Gross Profit = Net Sales − Cost of Goods Sold)

Net Profit Margin Ratio

The net profit margin ratio is the percentage of sales dollars left after subtracting the cost of goods sold and all expenses, except income taxes. It provides a good opportunity to compare the company's return on sales with the performance of other companies in the same industry. It is calculated before income tax because tax rates and tax liabilities vary from company to company for a wide variety of reasons, making comparisons after taxes much more difficult. The net profit margin ratio is calculated as follows:

$$\text{Net Profit Margin Ratio} = \frac{\text{Net Profit Before Tax}}{\text{Net Sales}}$$

Management Ratios

Other important ratios, often referred to as management ratios, are also derived from information contained in the balance sheet and income statement.

Inventory Turnover Ratio

This ratio reveals how well inventory is being managed. It is important because the more times inventory can be turned over in a given operating cycle, the greater the profit. The higher the ratio, the better. A drop in the turnover ratio, however, may reveal an overstock situation that has yet to be corrected. The acceptable ratio of the inventory turnover ratio varies from industry to industry but there should be consistency among businesses in the same industry. The inventory turnover ratio is calculated as follows:

$$\text{Inventory Turnover Ratio} = \frac{\text{Net Sales}}{\text{Average Inventory at Cost}}$$

Accounts Receivable Turnover Ratio

To analyze accounts receivable, you should use the accounts receivable turnover ratio. This ratio indicates how well accounts receivable are being collected. When this ratio drops, it means that it is taking longer to collect receivables, which might be a widespread problem in the customer base, or which might be concentrated with just a few of the major customers. Although both situations require corrective action, the latter is especially dangerous as the business may get hit with a big loss because of an unhappy customer or because of the customer's own financial difficulties. If receivables are not collected reasonably in accordance with their terms, the collection policy may need to be changed. If receivables are excessively slow in being converted to cash, liquidity could be severely impaired. The accounts receivable turnover ratio is calculated as follows:

$$\frac{\text{Net Credit Sales/Year}}{\text{365 Days/Year}} = \text{Daily Credit Sales}$$

$$\text{Accounts Receivable Turnover (in days)} \; = \; \frac{\text{Accounts Receivable}}{\text{Daily Credit Sales}}$$

Return on Assets Ratio

The return on assets ratio measures how efficiently profits are being generated from the assets employed in the business when compared with the ratios of firms in a similar business. A low ratio in comparison with industry averages indicates an inefficient use of business assets. The return on assets ratio is calculated as follows:

$$\text{Return on Assets} \; = \; \frac{\text{Net Profit Before Tax}}{\text{Total Assets}}$$

Return on Investment (ROI) Ratio

The return on investment ratio is perhaps the most important ratio of all. It shows a shareholder's yield on the shareholder's investment in the business. In short, this ratio tells the owner whether or not all the effort put into the business has been worthwhile. An unusually low ratio may mean that the company's profitability is not what it should be when compared to prior years or to industry standards. The return on investment ratio is calculated as follows:

$$\text{Return on Investment} \; = \; \frac{\text{Net Profit before Tax}}{\text{Net Worth}}$$

How Reliable are the Financials?

Audited or Unaudited

Obtaining accurate financial information can be one of the most difficult tasks facing a potential purchaser. Many financial statements prepared by small businesses are not prepared in accordance with generally accepted accounting principles. Often, it can be difficult to differentiate between the operations of the business and the owner's personal business affairs such as travel and automotive expenses. The balance sheet may even include the owner's personal residence as an asset. Subsequently, the financial statements are only as valuable as the quality of information and the degree of care that went into them.

> The financial statements are only as valuable as the quality of information and the degree of care that went into them.

Financial statements are either audited or unaudited depending on the amount of due diligence performed by the company's accounting firm. Although there will be differences in the accuracy of unaudited financial statements, the biggest difference will be between financial statements that are audited and those that are not. If you are interested in purchasing a "closely held" business (that is, a business that does not have shares traded on a stock exchange), you will probably receive unaudited statements, as most closely held businesses are not required to have their books audited and consequently have no reason to incur what is a significant expense. If you receive unaudited statements, an employee of the business or an independent accountant may have prepared them. Obviously, you will have a greater level of comfort if an independent accountant prepared them and that level of comfort will increase if the accountant has a professional designation such as a CGA, CA or CMA. If the statements were prepared by an independent accountant, they will be accompanied by a report letter outlining whether they are audited or unaudited. If the statements are unaudited, it means that the accountant has relied on the information supplied by the business owner in preparing the financial statements.

There is probably little chance that you can persuade the business owner to have an audit conducted on the books before you buy, however, you may agree to have up-to-date financial statements prepared by an independent accountant as a condition of closing.

How Current are the Statements?

The statements you are provided with should be no older than 90 days. If they are too stale-dated, the information may not be relevant. A business should have financial statements prepared at the end of each calendar year, with interim reports (monthly or quarterly) during the year.

Cash-Basis or Accrual Accounting

Statements can be prepared using cash-basis or accrual accounting. It is important to determine which method has been used and understand the difference between the two systems. If financial statements are prepared strictly on a cash basis, all cash *actually received* by the business would be recognized as revenue and all cash *actually paid out* would be recognized as expense. Even assets such as fixed plant and equipment would be recorded as expense items at the time they were paid for, rather than writing them off over the life of the assets through depreciation charges.

If the accrual accounting method is used, all items of income are included in gross revenue *when earned* even though payment is not received at that time. Expenses are deducted *as soon as they are incurred,* whether or not they are paid for at that time.

> ... it is important to examine the financials carefully as accrual accounting can actually make a bad company appear better.

Normally, the accrual method of accounting is the only one that gives an accurate picture of past operations, however, it is important to examine the financials carefully as accrual accounting can actually make a bad company appear better. For example, if the business shows a large revenue number and no accounts receivable, it presents a good picture. However, if the business's account receivables are high and represent a large percentage of its total revenues, the picture is not so attractive. It could mean that one of its major customers is experiencing financial difficulties and has been unable to make its payments and the business has not yet written off the receivable as uncollectible.

Most businesses use the accrual method for their daily operation as they offer credit to their customers and receive credit terms from their suppliers. If the seller's financial statements have been prepared on a cash basis, you should make the necessary adjustments to convert the statements to an accrual basis.

When deciding on a particular business, you need to understand the financial statements. They need to make sense to you. You also need to have a professional accountant analyze and evaluate them, and give you candid feedback. Financial statements can be misleading, as they do not give you the total picture of the business. Tough questions need to be asked and additional information obtained. You should also look at the past financial history of the business over — at a minimum — a five-year period and the projections for the immediate future. It is also important to consider different types of ratios, which mean comparative industry standards. With the right professional advice, you should be able to get the objective feedback you need to assist your decision-making.

Appendix 7.1
Sample Balance Sheet

As of (Current Date/Year)

	20____ (Current Year)	20____ (Previous Year)
Assets		
Current Assets		
Accounts receivable (attach aged list)	$ _____	$ _____
Less: Allowance for bad debts (net)	_____	_____
Cash and balance in bank accounts	_____	_____
Prepaid expenses (e.g., insurance, rent, etc.)	_____	_____
Inventory at market value	_____	_____
Other current assets	_____	_____
Total Current Assets	$ _____	$ _____
Fixed Assets (net book value after depreciation)		
Land and buildings	$ _____	$ _____
Furniture, equipment and fixtures	_____	_____
Other fixed assets	_____	_____
Total Fixed Assets	_____	_____
Other Assets (nonfixed, *e.g.*, automobiles)	$ _____	$ _____
TOTAL ASSETS	$ _____	$ _____
Liabilities		
Current (due within 12 months)		
Accounts payable	$ _____	$ _____
Bank loans	_____	_____
Loans — other	_____	_____
Employee deductions and sales taxes payable	_____	_____
Income taxes payable	_____	_____
Current portion of long-term debt	_____	_____
Other current liabilities	_____	_____
Total Current Liabilities	$ _____	$ _____

	20____ (Current Year)	20____ (Previous Year)
Long Term (over one year)		
Mortgages payable	$ _____	$ _____
Less: Current portion noted above	_____	_____
Loans from shareholders and partners	_____	_____
Other loans of long-term nature	_____	_____
Total Long-Term Liabilities	$ _____	$ _____
TOTAL LIABILITIES	$ _____	$ _____
NET WORTH (Total Assets – Total Liabilities)	$ _____	$ _____

Shareholders' Equity

	20____ (Current Year)	20____ (Previous Year)
Share capital	$ _____	$ _____
Retained earnings	_____	_____
TOTAL SHAREHOLDERS' EQUITY	$ _____	$ _____
TOTAL LIABILITIES AND SHAREHOLDERS' EQUITY	$ _____	$ _____

Appendix 7.2
Sample Income Statement

ABC COMPANY LTD.

Income Statement

For the Year Ended _____

Gross Revenue

Gross sales	$ _____	_____ %
Less cost of goods sold	$ _____	_____ %

GROSS MARGIN	$ _____	_____ %

Operating Expenses

Advertising and promotion	$ _____
Automotive	$ _____
Bad debts	$ _____
Bank service charges	$ _____
Credit card fees	$ _____
Insurance	$ _____
Miscellaneous	$ _____
Office supplies	$ _____
Owner's salary	$ _____
Permits and licences	$ _____
Rent	$ _____
Repairs and maintenance	$ _____
Telephone	$ _____
Travel	$ _____
Utilities	$ _____
Wages	$ _____

TOTAL OPERATING EXPENSES	$ _____	_____ %

OPERATING PROFIT	$ _____	_____ %

Plus Other Income

Gain (loss) on sale of assets	$ _____
Interest income	$ _____

TOTAL OTHER INCOME	$ _____	_____ %

Less Other Expenses

Amortization $ _____

Depreciation $ _____

Interest $ _____

             TOTAL OTHER EXPENSES $ _____   _____%

Net Income (Loss) $ _____

Less income tax $ _____

             NET PROFIT (LOSS) $ _____   _____%

8

METHODS OF BUYING
A BUSINESS

Introduction

During the negotiation process, you will be faced with the question of how the deal will be structured. The first thing to understand is that as a general rule sellers prefer to sell shares and buyers would rather buy assets. If the seller operates the business as a sole proprietorship or partnership, you have no option but to purchase the seller's assets. If the seller conducts business as a corporation, and provided that the corporation owns the assets of the business, there are two possible ways to buy the business. You can buy the assets from the business (asset purchase), or you can acquire the assets by buying the business itself from the company's shareholders (share purchase). Regardless of whether you are the buyer or the seller, you should be fully aware of your tax obligations before the deal is structured. The method of buying the business should be determined prior to entering into a letter of intent as it affects the type of legal due diligence process to be performed by the buyer's lawyer.

> The method of buying the business should be determined prior to entering into a letter of intent as it affects the type of legal due diligence process to be performed by the buyer's lawyer.

The Issue of Taxes

How the deal is structured is primarily a tax issue. Many people would think that taxes would only affect the seller, as the seller is the one who receives the money. This may be true in many situations, but not in this particular case, as there are implications for the buyer that need to be given serious consideration and can also make a difference to the purchase price. Canada has a number of different levels of taxation. On the purchase or sale of a business, the federal government primarily imposes tax in two areas: income tax and goods and services tax

(GST). All the provinces, with the exception of Quebec, impose a provincial sales tax (PST) on the sale of assets. Any assets purchased from the seller may be subject to provincial sales tax.

The Maritimes combine GST and provincial sales taxes into one sales tax, referred to as the harmonized sales tax (HST). The normal procedure is for the seller to collect all sales taxes and remit them to the appropriate government department. In addition, there are a number of other taxes, for example, Quebec, Ontario, Manitoba and British Columbia charge a land transfer tax (or property purchase tax), which is imposed on the purchase of real estate.

The buyer's preference is to structure the deal as an asset purchase in order to increase the value of the hard assets such as equipment and inventory while the seller would rather sell shares to alleviate capital gains tax and avoid the recapture tax. In addition, the seller is concerned about tax implications for the year in which the business is sold while the buyer is more concerned about tax implications in the ensuing years.

> The buyer's preference is to structure the deal as an asset purchase ... while the seller would rather sell shares.

The question of which method to use may be one of the most difficult parts of the negotiation process. It may even prove to be a deal breaker, as on occasion a seller will insist on selling shares and a buyer will only consider buying assets. Adjusting the actual purchase price can sometimes break this deadlock. Often sellers will accept a lower price for the shares than they would have accepted for the sale of the business assets. In addition the buyer may save PST on equipment and other chattels. In some instances, buyers will pay more if they are purchasing assets.

Exemption from GST

If both the purchaser and the seller are registered for purposes of GST; the purchased assets comprise all, or substantially all, of the property used in the business; and the business is a commercial activity (as defined in the governing legislation), then both parties can file an election pursuant to section 167(1) of the *Excise Tax Act* (Canada) to exempt the sale of the assets from GST.

Why Sellers Prefer to Sell Shares

Obviously the seller wants to receive the highest amount possible from the sale of the business. The federal government's retention of the $500,000 small business capital gains deduction is a strong incentive for shareholders to sell company shares rather than business assets. This is one of the few tax shelters available to small businesses and could be reduced or eliminated at any time. The basis of the program is that if individuals sell the shares of their businesses, they could be exempt from tax on up to two-thirds of their capital gain on the sale. The maximum amount of exemption would be $500,000, assuming that the seller has not already used up the $100,000 personal tax portion of the $500,000 in the past.

There are two levels of taxation when a company sells assets. In the first instance, the company receives the proceeds and is responsible for the payment of applicable taxes at the time the sale closes. Once the taxes have been paid, the company distributes the funds to its shareholders, which as individuals are subject to normal income tax considerations. On the other hand, if an individual receives money from the sale of shares, there is only one level of taxation.

Why Buyers Prefer to Buy Assets

There are a number of reasons why buyers would rather purchase assets than shares. The first one involves potential liabilities, as buyers inherit all of the target company's liabilities. In addition, the company may have a reduced cost base for depreciating capital assets of the business, whereas if the sale is an asset purchase, the buyer can claim depreciation as an income tax deduction. As previously mentioned, the buyer's focus is on the tax consequences in the years following the sale as the buyer wants to ensure that capital cost allowances or depreciation will continue to be available to them as deductions for tax purposes. On the other hand, if the buyer purchased shares, the buyer is saddled with the seller's undepreciated capital cost of each class of assets. It is fairly easy to see why, from a taxation point of view, buyers would prefer to purchase assets at fair market value, as by claiming higher capital cost allowances the purchase price can be written off over a shorter period of time.

Other advantages to purchasing shares include continuation of the goodwill of the business and the continuation of existing trade credit. Similarly, business licences and some leases may not require a third party's consent to assignment. As an additional administrative benefit, many government-related registrations, such as workplace safety and insurance, income tax and PST and GST, remain in place, as do telephone numbers and other standing accounts.

Allocation of the Purchase Price

If the deal is structured as an asset purchase, once the purchase price has been agreed on, it will be necessary to allocate the purchase price among the various assets of the business (for example, land, buildings, equipment, patents, inventory and goodwill), for tax purposes. As the seller's goal is to minimize tax liability in the year of the sale, the seller will be motivated to allocate the purchase price so that it will result in no taxable income. If the deal involves the transfer of land, the seller will want as much of the purchase price to be allocated to that particular asset as land is not depreciable. Consequently, the sale of land could result in a capital gain, which is subject to more favourable tax treatment. Next on the purchaser's list will probably be buildings, which are depreciable, but at a lower rate than other assets and consequently any recaptured capital cost allowance will be relatively small.

On the other hand, buyers will want a relatively low value allocated to land and buildings and higher values allocated to other depreciable assets allowing them to take advantage of higher capital cost allowances and making it possible for them to write off the purchase price faster.

As there is the possibility of an increased recapture of the capital costs allowance for assets such as machinery and other equipment, sellers prefer to allocate lower values to these assets. If higher values are allocated to these types of assets, the seller can be subject to higher tax liability, since recaptures of capital cost allowance are treated as income. Conversely, buyers like to see higher values assigned to these types of assets.

The seller always wants the lowest amount allocated to assets, such as inventory, since assets are treated as ordinary business income. The sale proceeds from inventory are treated as ordinary income and taxed accordingly. From the buyer's perspective, the cost of inventory is essentially the cost of acquiring goods that will be resold. This means that inventory will be deemed to be an expense at the time it is purchased; the buyer will then be able to deduct it from income in that particular year.

Overall, this is a complex situation because both parties have conflicting needs. It makes good business sense to have experienced and competent professional advisors to advise you on the best way to structure the deal and to guide you through the negotiation process. It is possible to structure the deal so that taxes are minimized, or possibly avoided altogether, however, this requires both the buyer and the seller working in cooperation.

There are different types of methods of buying a business, all of which have financial and tax implications to you. Make sure you have professional accounting advice to assist you in this important process. You can buy the shares of the business or the assets — there are pros and cons to each. Another critical factor is the allocation of the purchase price for goodwill and assets. Your final decision on how to buy the business will make a big difference in the amount of money you save in taxes down the road.

9

ESTABLISHING A VALUE

Sellers' and Buyers' Objectives

Obviously sellers and buyers have different objectives. The seller's objective is to get the *best possible price* for the business; whereas the buyer's objective is to buy the business for the *lowest possible price.* In addition, each party has a distinct rationale, and that rationale may be based on logic or emotion. The buyer may believe that the purchase will create synergy or an economy of scale because of the way the business will be operated under new ownership. The buyer may also see the business as an especially good lifestyle fit. These factors are likely to increase the amount of money a buyer is willing to pay for a business.

On the other hand, the seller may have a greater than normal desire to sell due to a number of factors. The most common reasons are:
- partnership dispute;
- retirement;
- the illness or death of one of the principals;
- the business is losing money;
- divorce; and
- financial difficulties.

Fair Market Value

"Fair market value" has been defined for Canadian tax purposes to mean the highest price expressed as money obtainable in an open and unrestricted market, between knowledgeable, prudent and willing parties dealing at arm's length who are fully informed and not under compulsion to act. This is a situation that rarely happens in the real world, as the majority of sellers are motivated to sell for one reason or another. In other words, fair market value is the price at which a hypothetical sale transaction will occur: as first, the sale transaction is an attempt to simulate a market and, as such, does not involve a real buyer or a real seller, and secondly, the sale transaction assumes and/or implies a number of underlying conditions that may or may not be present in an actual sale. Consequently, the fair market value that may be set by a business appraiser may or may not be the sale price that an actual sale transaction would derive. The fair market value hypothetical sale transaction assumes that:

- the transaction is cash or a cash-equivalent price and the seller is not providing any financing to the buyer;
- there is no compulsion existing upon either party to consummate the transaction;
- a market composed of potential buyers and sellers of similar businesses exists;
- the buyer does not have a specific motive for purchasing the business (for example, a potential synergistic relationship with another business owned by the buyer); and
- there is a reasonable amount of time available to achieve the contemplated sale price.

What this hypothetical sale scenario does not consider are the following real world factors:

- a well-planned strategy for the sale of a business, effectively implemented, will achieve a higher selling price than the hypothetical price;
- sellers with time on their side will achieve a higher price than the hypothetical price;
- effective negotiation by the seller will usually obtain a higher sale price;
- providing vendor financing to the buyer may result in an overall higher sale price; and
- a consulting contract with the seller may add value to the sale price.

Estimating the Value of a Business

Estimating the value of a business is not a simple task. The topic of business evaluation is so complex that it could fill a whole book on its own. It can also be said that it is an art, not a science. The first thing to understand is that there is a difference between value and price. The valuation of a business makes certain assumptions and is established at an historical point in time. The price is a function of the value, the perception of the future, the terms and conditions of the deal, and other factors. The value of a business can vary weekly, depending on several factors such as interest rates, the strength of the economy and the availability of capital. The complexity is further compounded by the fact that business owners' purposes, motives and goals in valuing their businesses can vary greatly. The process has to take into account numerous variables and requires that a number of assumptions be made. Six of the most important factors that determine fair market value are:

- recent profit history;
- general condition of the company (for example, condition of facilities and equipment, completeness and accuracy of books and records, employee morale, and state of inventory);
- market demand for the particular type of business;

> The value of a business can vary weekly, depending on several factors such as interest rates, the strength of the economy and the availability of capital.

- economic conditions — especially cost and availability of capital and any economic factors that directly affect the business;
- ability to transfer goodwill or other intangible values to a new owner; and
- future profit potential.

However, there is really no such thing as fair market value as three other factors often influence the agreed-upon price.

- special circumstances of the particular buyer and seller;
- trade-offs between cash and terms; and
- relative tax consequences for the buyer and seller, which depend on how the transaction is structured.

REAL LIFE

A Case of Apples and Oranges

Sadru had owned and operated Fairview Distributors for almost 15 years. The company imported various product lines from manufacturers in Asia and distributed them to retailers who in turn sold them to the general public. Sadru traveled to Asia twice a year to see what new products were available and to negotiate with suppliers. He did not have any exclusive agreements with his suppliers, as his practice had been to deal with whichever supplier gave him the best deal at the particular time. Recently Sadru had decided to sell the business as over the past few years an increasing number of his large customers were cutting him out of the loop by sending their own buyers to Asia and dealing directly with his suppliers. As a result of these changes, Fairview Distributors had lost money for the first time in its business history during the past two years and Sadru saw the situation as getting worse rather than better.

Sadru was unsure how much to ask for his business but he was aware that Exclusive Importers, who were in the same line of business, had sold six months earlier for $500,000 and he was confident that his company was just as valuable. Sadru advertised the business for sale in the local newspapers at $525,000, which he thought was fair market value (leaving some room for negotiation), based on Exclusive Importer's selling price. The advertisement attracted a few interested parties; they all told Sadru that his asking price was too high. At first Sadru felt insulted, but after hearing the same comment a number of times, he thought he should reconsider his asking price. He decided to seek advice from Ben, an experienced business broker. Ben explained to him that although both companies were essentially in the same line of business, it was like comparing apples and oranges, as there were a number of significant differences that affected the value of the business. Ben explained that unlike Sadru's company, the majority of Exclusive Importers' agreements with its Asian suppliers were exclusive and had at least 10 years remaining before they had to be renewed. Consequently, the retailers they supplied were unable to circumvent them and deal directly with the suppliers. Also, Exclusive Importers had increased its revenues by at least 20% annually in the last two years and had improved its bottom line as compared to Sadru, whose business had declined.

In addition, Exclusive Distributors had not been on the market, but was approached by the eventual purchaser who had a specific motive for purchasing the business. The purchaser imported non-competing products from Europe and sold them to many of Exclusive Import's customers, therefore the purchase of the business created a valuable synergistic relationship for which the purchaser was prepared to pay a premium. In addition, the deal had not been all cash but the vendor had received some cash while shares in the purchaser's company made up the balance of the selling price. When he took all these factors into consideration Sadru realized that he was not comparing apples and apples and decided to have his business appraised to obtain a proper evaluation and have some rationale to support his asking price.

Methods for Valuing a Business

Businesses really have only two things to sell: assets and the ability of those assets to produce earnings. Businesses are valued on either their assets or on their earnings, but not on a combination of the two. There are several different methods than can be used to value a business. The value of a particular method is entirely based on the relative circumstances involved in each individual case. The most common methods for valuing small and medium businesses are:

- rules of thumb;
- comparable sales;
- book value;
- capitalization of earnings; and
- liquidation.

Rules of Thumb

There are some formulas that give businesses in particular industries an easy and quick way to estimate a value. These formulas are generally referred to as rules of thumb. Rules of thumb usually provide a range of values — often a wide range of possible values — but a simple formula cannot establish the fair market value of a business. The problem with rule-of-thumb formulas is that they address few of the factors that affect the value of a business. They rely on a one-size-fits-all approach — but no two businesses are

> Businesses are valued on either their assets or on their earnings, but not on a combination of the two.

identical. These formulas are best used as checks for reasonableness instead of appraisal methods. Ultimately, the value of a business is what a buyer agrees to pay and what a seller is willing to accept.

Comparable Sales

Using comparable sales as a means of valuing a business has the same inherent flaw as rule-of-thumb formulas. Rarely, if ever, are two businesses truly comparable. However, businesses in the same industry do have some characteristics in common, and a careful comparison may allow a conclusion to be drawn about a range of values.

Book Value

This form of valuation is based on the books of a business, where the owner's equity — total assets minus total liabilities — is used to establish a price. It is usually not an accurate measure of the real value of the company as there are a couple of problems with this approach. First, unless statements are audited (or you can carry out an audit), you cannot be certain that the information is correct. Secondly, the value of some assets, such as buildings, equipment and furniture or fixtures, may be overstated on the books, and may not reflect the maintenance or replacement costs for older assets. As a result, some business valuation experts will use an adjusted book value. The book valuation method is usually used in the following situations:

> Ultimately, the value of a business is what a buyer agrees to pay and what a seller is willing to accept.

- when the company has operating losses, since there are no earnings on which to apply multiples; or
- for small distribution companies with sales of under $20 million, since these types of businesses are often successful because of the owner's customer and supplier relationships. These types of businesses typically sell at their book value, plus a modest premium.

When the book value technique is used, there is an important variation that a seller will probably want the buyer to consider. The assets may have a far greater value if the values are recast to reflect fair market value for machinery, equipment, buildings and land. Also, the inventory might be adjusted to reflect current values and to pick up items that have been written off in order to minimize taxes. The buyer must also determine whether all the assets are actually earning money for the business. If they are not, the buyer should request an adjustment in the purchase price to reflect this condition.

Capitalization of Earnings

The concept of income capitalization is simple: determine what amount of income is realistic and proper under the circumstances and then apply a capitalization rate that meets the same criteria. In essence, the capitalization rate is the desired rate of return: the rate of return an investor would be willing to accept for the given level of risk. It places no value on the equipment and other hard assets. It is assumed that the equipment and assets have no value other than the ability to produce income for the business. Service businesses, which are usually not asset-intensive, are often valued using this method.

A high-risk investment would equate to a high capitalization rate, which in turn results in a lower value. The asset or business is then presumed to be worth the result when adjusted earnings are divided by the capitalization rate. The first step is to adjust the company's five-year average after-tax profits. Following is an example of typical adjustments:

- Add back excessive salaries.
- Reduce earnings if salaries are too low.
- Add back compensation for unproductive relatives and excessive fringe benefits, such luxury vehicles and golf club memberships.
- Eliminate non-recurring income or expense items.
- Adjust for excessive depreciation.
- Adjust earnings for major changes in accounting procedures, widely fluctuating or cyclical profits or abnormally inflated (or deflated) earnings.
- If there has been a strong upward or downward earnings trend, weight the average to obtain a more realistic appraisal of the company's prospects.

The next step is to select a capitalization rate based on the return on investment, which a buyer should expect, considering the risk factor. Divide the company's adjusted average annual revenue for the five-year period by the capitalization rate. For example, a business earning annual revenues of $200,000 with an applied capitalization rate of 20% would be valued at $1,000,000 (200,000 ÷ 0.20).

> The buyer must also determine whether all the assets are actually earning money for the business. If they are not, the buyer should request an adjustment in the purchase price to reflect this condition.

Liquidation Value

The liquidation value of a company is the value of its individual assets, valued as if the company was not going to continue to carry on business. This is a variation of the book value method but instead of using current market values in the balance sheet, liquidation values are used. Liquidation value is of little interest to you if you are buying a profitable business. There are actually two levels of liquidation value, depending on the time available for the liquidation process.

Orderly Liquidation Value

This value assumes an orderly sale process where the company has the time available to sell its assets to the highest bidder. This may involve selling each asset in its appropriate season and through channels of sale and distribution that fetch the highest price reasonably available.

Distress Liquidation Value

Distress liquidation value is what is often called a "fire sale" price. It assumes that the company does not have the luxury of time and must sell all its assets at or near the same time, to one or more purchasers. The typical asset purchaser in this situation is a dealer who specializes in the liquidation of the entire assets of a company. Obviously, the distress liquidation value will always be lower than the orderly liquidation value and may be significantly different depending on the nature of the business and the type of assets to be liquidated.

How do you figure out what price to pay for your business? The buyer and the seller, of course, have opposite objectives. The concept of establishing value can be very subjective, with the goodwill factor being the most emotional for the vendor. There are pros and cons to the different methods of evaluating a business. You should try to utilize all of these methods, if possible. Out of the process should come some sense of the price you are prepared to pay, or whether you just want to walk away.

10

THE INVESTIGATION PROCESS

The Importance of Due Diligence

Due diligence is the process of investigation by a purchaser in conjunction with the purchaser's legal and accounting advisors before agreeing to proceed with the purchase of a business. Whether buying shares or assets, you use the due diligence process to verify the information that the seller has provided you about the business and its operations in order that there are no surprises at the time of closing or after you have taken over control of the business. Most sellers genuinely intend to fairly and honestly present their business for sale but it would be naive to assume that everything you are told is the absolute truth. The responsibility of investigating the business belongs to you — the buyer. There is not much point in undertaking in-depth due diligence until and unless you and the seller have reached at least a tentative agreement on price and terms.

> Most sellers genuinely intend to fairly and honestly present their business for sale but it would be naive to assume that everything you are told is the absolute truth.

Although you will have carried out some preliminary due diligence in your initial investigation of the business, the in-depth due diligence investigation process actually begins with the signing of the letter of intent (the drafting and execution of a letter of intent is covered in Chapter 11, "The Negotiating Process"). Negotiations continue during this phase and the end result of the investigation process is, if all goes well, a purchase and sale agreement. A due diligence investigation can be expensive and time-consuming, however, it is critical that it is carried out thoroughly. It will help you to determine if you still wish to proceed with the purchase of the business, or if you should renegotiate the price and terms that are in the letter of intent, based on what you discover during the due diligence process. All the factors identified in this chapter should be carefully examined and weighed. Some factors will have a positive influence on the decision to buy and others will have a negative influence. The important thing is to obtain all the information needed to make a decision. All business records should be made available to the buyer, but certain information may be withheld until a bona fide offer, contingent upon obtaining that information, has been made.

Carrying out due diligence is not exclusive to the buyer. The seller may also conduct due diligence on the buyer in situations where the seller is providing some of the financing or is receiving shares or other securities of the buyer as part of the purchase price. A detailed due diligence checklist is provided in Appendix 10.1.

Two Main Categories of Due Diligence

Generally, due diligence falls into two main categories — business due diligence and legal due diligence — although there is some overlap between these two categories. Lawyers normally carry out the legal due diligence and business people (either the buyer or the advisor) conduct the business due diligence. Business due diligence involves such items as reviewing inventories and work in progress, employee relations and status of payables and receivables, as well as contacting suppliers and key customers, and checking the condition of equipment and premises. Legal due diligence varies, depending on whether the buyer is purchasing assets or shares, but can involve reviewing minute books, checking the company documents, company bylaws and directors' resolutions; reviewing and confirming lease agreements, and undertaking title searches to determine if the vendor owns the shares or assets being sold and if they are free from all encumbrances.

> The seller may also conduct due diligence on the buyer in situations where the seller is providing some of the financing or is receiving shares or other securities of the buyer as part of the purchase price.

Components

Due diligence involves a thorough investigation of the business in which you are interested. The following areas should be researched and assessed within the due diligence process. For a detailed breakdown of areas to investigate, see the due diligence checklist in Appendix 10.1.

Premises

1. Obtain a schedule of real estate owned by the business.
2. Determine the condition and age of improvements.
3. Determine the fair market value of each of the buildings and land.
4. Obtain appraisals if necessary.
5. Determine if any repairs or improvements are required.
6. Check the maintenance costs contained in the financial statements. Determine whether they are reasonable.
7. Determine if the premises are an essential part of the business.
8. Determine how the real estate is financed and whether the mortgages are assumable.

9. Check whether the premises comply with all zoning, occupational safety and health requirements, food and hygiene regulations, and whether any work is required to bring the premises up to standard.

10. Check the remaining term of the lease, whether there are any option periods and how the options are exercised. Is there a percentage-of-sales clause? Are there any additional fees (for example, common area maintenance or merchants' association dues)? Is the tenant or landlord responsible for maintaining the roof and the heating and air-conditioning system? Is a periodic rental increase required to adjust for changes in the consumer price index or for an increase in real estate tax assessment? Is there a demolition clause? Under what terms and conditions will the landlord permit an assumption or extension of the existing lease?

Machinery and Equipment

1. Obtain a schedule of machinery and equipment owned or leased by the business.
2. Determine the condition and age of the machinery and equipment. Is it in good working order? Is it state-of-the-art or is it obsolete and in need of replacement? Will immediate repairs be required?

Accounts Payable

These are monies owed *by* the company.

1. Obtain a schedule of accounts payable and determine if there is a concentration among a few accounts.
2. Determine the age of the amounts due.
3. Identify all amounts in dispute and determine the reason.
4. Review transactions to determine undisclosed and/or contingent liabilities.

Accounts Receivable

These are monies owed *to* the company.

1. Obtain a schedule of accounts receivable and determine if there is a concentration among a few accounts.
2. Determine the age of the amounts due.
3. Identify all amounts in dispute and determine the reason.
4. Review transactions to determine undisclosed and/or contingent liabilities.

Accrued Liabilities

1. Obtain a schedule of accrued liabilities.
2. Determine the accounting treatment of:
   - unpaid wages at the end of each period;
   - accrued vacation pay;
   - accrued sick leave;

- payroll taxes due and payable;
- accrued federal, state and local income taxes;
- other accruals.

3. Search for unrecorded accrued liabilities:
    - obtain a schedule of notes payable and mortgages payable;
    - identify the reason for the indebtedness;
    - determine the terms and payment schedule;
    - investigate whether acquisition will accelerate the note or mortgage;
    - determine whether there is a prepayment penalty;
    - determine if there are any balloon payments to be made and the amounts and dates due;
    - investigate whether the notes or mortgages are assumable.

Marketing

1. Are any of the products proprietary?
2. Determine any potential new products or services.
3. Determine the company's geographic market area.
4. Determine the company's percentage of market share.
5. Assess the company's competitive advantages.
6. Determine the company's annual marketing expenditures.
7. Obtain all sales records, such as sales journals and sales reports, to verify sales information on the income statement and to determine the level of sales concentration among key customers.
8. Determine the business's customers. Will you lose any of their business because of a personal relationship that customers have with the seller? Are there some sales that do not come through the door?
9. Determine the business's suppliers. Are there any special relationships that will end once the business is sold?

Personnel

1. Determine the job responsibilities, rates of pay and benefits of each employee.
2. What is the level of each employee's skill in his or her position?
3. Review all employee agreements.
4. Determine whether key employees will stay after the company is purchased.
5. Determine whether any employees are union members. Is a union-organizing effort a possibility?
6. Determine what employee benefits the company offers.
7. Review any employment handbooks or policy manuals.

Intellectual Property

1. Obtain a list of trade names, trademarks, logos, patents and copyrights, with expiry dates.

Legal Issues

1. Determine whether there are there any lawsuits — currently or soon to commence — against the company.
2. Determine if all federal, provincial and municipal registration requirements and regulations are being met.
3. Determine if all local zoning requirements are being met.
4. Review the articles of incorporation, minute books, bylaws and/or shareholder agreements.
5. Determine the classes of stock issued by the corporation and the restrictions of each, if any. Find out if any stock has been cancelled or repurchased.
7. Review the relevant agreements if the business is a franchise, dealership or distributorship. Are any licences required to operate the business transferable?
8. Determine the company's returned goods policy and the extent of its liability for returned goods.
9. Determine the company's liability for product warranty claims.

REAL LIFE

Look before You Leap

Franco had been laid off from his position as sales and marketing manager by his former employer as part of a corporate downsizing. As there was little chance of finding a comparable job in the immediate area, Franco decided to use the proceeds of his severance package to buy a business. Through a business acquaintance, Franco learned of a business that was about to come on the market. The company had the exclusive distribution rights for a number of automotive products in the surrounding area. Franco thought this would be an ideal business for him because of his sales background and his passion for automobiles.

As the business had not yet been listed with a business broker, Franco approached the owner, Serena, directly. Serena told Franco that she had a number of people interested in purchasing the business, Franco became very excited about the prospect of purchasing the business and decided to move quickly as he did not want to miss the opportunity. Franco ignored the advice of his wife, Isabel, who cautioned him to take his time and get professional help. Franco was concerned about wasting time, as he only just had enough available capital to cover the price of the business and did not want to use up his money on living expenses for several months while he searched for a business.

Franco did some surface due diligence on the business and closed the deal within a few weeks. Serena had decided to return to her native Australia, so she left the area soon after the sale had closed.

Just three weeks after Franco had taken over the business; two of his biggest customers closed their doors. Franco was initially concerned to think he had lost two of his biggest accounts, but he became even more upset when he realized that they had gone into receivership and he would have to write off the majority of the accounts receivable that came with the business. He had reviewed the total amount of accounts receivable as part of his basic due diligence but he had not asked for a detailed summary. If he had done so, he would have discovered that not only were the accounts receivable concentrated on just a few customers, the probability of collecting them was unlikely. In fact, he found out later that Serena was aware that her two major accounts were insolvent and knew that the money was uncollectible.

The loss of these two receivables, totalling over $40,000, was a real problem for Franco as he was depending on collecting this money to buy inventory for the winter season. There was little Franco could do as Serena had left the country and in any case she had not provided any warranty that the accounts receivable were current and collectible in the ordinary course of business. As Franco now needed additional operating capital, he had no alternative but to take a second mortgage on his home. This meant that he and Isabel had to postpone starting a family as they needed Isabel's income to service the debt on the second mortgage.

Obtaining the vendor's warranty that accounts receivable are current and collectible is very important because if a major customer is insolvent, the purchaser is potentially at risk for the amount of the receivable and the value of the business is probably considerably reduced due to the pending failure of a major customer.

Executing a Confidentiality/Non-Disclosure Agreement

Because of the sensitive nature of the information found through due diligence, at some point in the due diligence process, the seller typically requires the buyer to sign a confidentiality/non-disclosure agreement that legally binds the buyer from disclosing any information about the seller's business. A sample confidentiality/nondisclosure agreement is included in Appendix 10.2.

Remember to have your lawyer review any agreement you are asked to sign beforehand. Refer to the due diligence checklist at Appendix 10.1 for specific examples of issues to examine and questions to ask. Also review the sample confidentiality/non-disclosure agreement at Appendix 10.2, for a typical format.

Appendix 10.1
Due Diligence Checklist

Corporate Organization

☐ Articles of incorporation

☐ Bylaws

☐ Recent changes in corporate structure

☐ Shareholder list

   Show number of outstanding shares and
      percent owned

   Stock option or share appreciation
      rights plans

☐ Parent, subsidiaries and affiliates

☐ Shareholder's agreements

☐ Minutes of the board of directors

Business Information

☐ Product offering

☐ Depreciation method

☐ Patents

☐ Management information system

Marketing

☐ Pricing strategy

☐ Patents

☐ Distribution channels

☐ Promotion tactics

☐ Customer base

   Top 10 customers by product line —
      showing volume

   Market share by product line

Business Plan

☐ Most recent five-year business plan

☐ Prior business plan

Financial Statements

☐ Five years of historical audited statements

   Income statement

   Balance sheet

   Statement of cash flows

   Change in equity statement

☐ Year-to-date internally generated monthly
      statements

☐ Most recent five-year projections

☐ Monthly sales projections taking seasonality
      into account

Tax Status

☐ Historical tax rate

☐ Net operating losses

Operating Data

☐ Accounts receivable

   Turnover or days

   Aging

   Control and credit policy

   Seasonality

☐ Inventory

   Turnover or days

   Obsolescence Policy

   Sources of supply

   Valuation method

☐ Backlog

   By product line

   Five-year history

   Current

   Seasonal issues

Contracts

☐ List major contracts by product line

☐ Terms

Capital Expenditures

☐ Last five years

☐ Five year gross projection

☐ Detailed priority list with as much analysis
      as possible

Equipment

☐ List

☐ Age

☐ Appraisal

   Orderly liquidation value

   Replacement value

Debt and Leases

☐ Lender

☐ Terms

☐ Interest rate

☐ Payment schedule

Litigation

☐ Current

    Description

    Potential damages

☐ Potential

    Description

    Potential damages

Property

☐ Description

☐ Recent acquisitions or spin-offs

☐ Expansion plans

Insurance

☐ Property

☐ Liability

☐ Workman's compensation

☐ Other

Competition

☐ By product line

    Name, address and phone number

    Size of overall company

    Size of the business unit that is the

    competitor

    Market share

    Competitive advantages and disadvantages

☐ Trade publications

    Name, address and phone numbers

Management

☐ Organizational chart

☐ Resumes

☐ Ownership interest

☐ Compensation and contracts

☐ Performance evaluation criteria

☐ Profit or gain sharing policies

Employee Relations

☐ Unions

    Name of union

    Name of local president, address and

        phone number

    Copy of contract

Pension Plans

☐ Funding status

☐ Balance sheet treatment

☐ Ten-year projected cash expense

Retiree Medical Benefits Liabilities

☐ Funding status

☐ Balance sheet treatment

☐ Ten year projected cash expense

Environmental Liabilities

☐ Description

☐ Phase one studies

☐ Phase two studies

☐ Five-year projected remediation cost

☐ Five-year projected compliance cost

Last Corporate Transactions

☐ Description of each transaction

☐ Purchase and sale agreement of each transaction

Appendix 10.2
Sample Confidentiality/Non-Disclosure Agreement

THIS NON-DISCLOSURE AGREEMENT made the 20th day of August, 2003.

BETWEEN: ABC Sign Makers Ltd.

           having a place of business at

           200 – 1234 Larch St.,

           Winnipeg, Manitoba

           (the Company)

AND: William Smith

           8996 Jackson Ave.,

           Winnipeg, Manitoba

           (the Applicant)

WHEREAS:

A. The Company has developed and is the owner of ABC Sign Makers located at 200 – 1234 Larch St., Winnipeg, Manitoba;

B. The Company wishes to maintain the development secret and confidential and to protect trade ideas, business concepts and systems so developed;

C. The Applicant is desirous of having the developments disclosed to it and is willing to evaluate the developments in confidence and not to make use thereof except pursuant to mutual agreement between the Company and the Applicant;

D. The Applicant considers the disclosure to be real and valuable consideration.

NOW THEREFORE THE PARTIES AGREE AS FOLLOWS:

1. The Company will disclose the developments to the Applicant. The Applicant shall endorse receipt of any written documents comprising part of this disclosure by signing and dating a copy thereof to be retained by the Company if the Company so elects.

2. The Applicant agrees not to communicate the developments to any person, firm, corporation or business without the Company's prior written consent. The Applicant specifically agrees not to use, for personal gain, any trade ideas, business concepts, or systems introduced by the Company.

3. The Applicant shall not make copies of any information, documents, materials, diskettes, tapes or other information appertaining or relating to the developments without the Company's prior written consent. The Applicant will forthwith upon demand by the Company return to the Company all specifications, documents, materials, diskettes, tapes and any copies thereof or any materials of any kind delivered to

the Applicant or any materials arising out of the foregoing and shall not retain copies thereof for any purpose.

4. If the Applicant contends that any concepts or information disclosed to it by the Company are in the public domain or were in the possession of the Applicant prior to such disclosure, the Applicant shall, within ten (10) days of the receipt by the Applicant of such disclosure, give written notice of such contention to the Company, which written notice shall include a complete identification of the information in question and the derivation thereof, including particulars of any contract in which the Applicant or any other person has made use of such concept or information. If the Applicant has not, within ten (10) days of the receipt of the disclosure as contemplated in this Agreement, given such written notice to the Company, then and in that event it shall be conclusively presumed that all information disclosed by the Company to the Applicant concerning the developments originated with the Company and constituted secret and confidential information and know-how.

5. The Company makes no warranty that any information or concept in any disclosure made pursuant to this Agreement is or may be of value to the Applicant. The Applicant, however, shall be bound by the terms of this Agreement whether or not the applicant elects to enter into any future written agreement with the Company for the exploitation of the developments to the mutual advantage of the parties.

6. It is expressly understood and agreed that the agreement herein shall not be construed as to create any partnership, joint venture, agency or any other business relationship which would authorize either party to act in the name of or on behalf of the other party and it is further understood and agreed that each of the parties are to remain completely independent of one from the other and that neither party has authority of any kind to create any liability or obligation on behalf of the other party.

SIGNED BY THE APPLICANT on the date first above written.

_____

Applicant

(11)

THE NEGOTIATION PROCESS

The Art of Negotiation

The art of negotiation is an important part of the process of buying a business. The purpose of the negotiation process is to agree on the details of the deal that will be incorporated into a written agreement. Some of the details — such as price, amount and terms of vendor financing (if any), allocation of price, form of the transaction (shares or assets), condition of equipment, liabilities, and warranties, are often issues where the interests and motivations of the buyer and seller may be in sharp conflict.

It is important to understand that negotiating is not a contest where there is a loser and a winner. Simply put, you have a desire to buy a business and the seller has a desire to sell his business. You do not have to buy it and the seller does not have to sell it to you (unless it is a desperation sale and you are the only likely purchaser around). In other words, neither of you can force the other to do something the other does not want to do. Therefore, the only realistic solution is to create a situation where both parties can come out as winners. When the negotiation process is approached in this manner, it is possible to find creative solutions to any problem.

> It is important to understand that negotiating is not a contest where there is a loser and a winner.

Differences of opinion are a natural part of the negotiation process, but it is important to keep in mind that it is not personal — it is simply business. In fact, it is critical that both parties assume a non-adversarial posture if they wish to achieve an agreement where both parties are satisfied with the price and terms of the deal. Regardless, there are two immutable laws of negotiating that are worth remembering:

1. Sellers do better when they make high demands.
2. Buyers do better when they make low offers.

Motivation of Both Parties

The buyer's objective is to:

- pay the lowest possible price;
- negotiate the most favourable payment terms;
- obtain a favourable tax basis for purposes of resale and depreciation; and
- receive warranty protection against false statements and representations of the seller, inaccurate financial data, and undisclosed or potential liabilities.

The seller wants to:

- get the best possible price;
- receive all his or her money;
- obtain a favourable tax treatment of gains from the sale; and
- sever past and future liability ties.

Too often the negotiations are focused entirely on price, which although the central bargaining issue, is only one part of the transaction. The value you assigned to the business during the valuation process in Chapter 9, "Establishing a Value," will provide a useful benchmark, but it is unlikely to be the final purchase price. Price is what is actually paid for a business, whereas value relates to what the business is worth.

> ... it is critical that both parties assume a non-adversarial posture if they wish to achieve an agreement where both parties are satisfied with the price and terms of the deal.

Strategy and compromise play a part in price determination, but other non-price factors that bear no relation to the value of the business play an important part in the bargaining process. Intangibles enter the equation and, depending on the factors that motivate each party, the final purchase price could be higher or lower than the value previously established. The price paid often reflects the bargaining position of one of the parties, for example, the seller's desire to sell is stronger than the buyer's desire to buy, or vice versa. If the buyer knows that the seller urgently needs to sell the business, the buyer will be more aggressive in negotiating a lower price. Another important factor affecting bargaining position is timing. The seller is more likely to achieve a higher price for the business when the economy is strong and overall business conditions are good.

Equal to or sometimes more important than price are the terms of the deal, such as the amount and term of repayment of any vendor financing and the allocation of the purchase price for tax purposes. The seller's willingness to finance part of the price — or perhaps all of it — may also depend on the urgency of the seller's need to sell. Sellers will naturally have the upper hand in negotiations since sellers know the business better than buyers, but a buyer can minimize the seller's advantages by learning as much as possible about the business prior to the negotiation process.

Part of the learning process should be devoted to trying to understand the seller's motivation for wanting to sell the business. One of the most important things in negotiations is to be able to see things from the other party's perspective as this eliminates much of the difficulty of reaching an agreement and prevents both parties from wasting time. During the negotiation process, it is important to be empathetic and to sincerely try to understand why the seller has adopted a position on a certain issue. The whole process will be much smoother if both parties know the issues and understand the positions that are important to one another.

Sellers will naturally have the upper hand in negotiations since sellers know the business better than buyers, but a buyer can minimize the seller's advantages by learning as much as possible about the business prior to the negotiation process.

As discussed in Chapter 8, "Methods of Buying a Business," one of your negotiating objectives is to allocate as little as possible to goodwill and as much as possible to tangible assets, which depreciate at a much faster rate. Conversely, the more a seller can allocate to goodwill the better off the seller will be for tax purposes.

Getting to a Win-Win Deal

The following tips will help you to negotiate a win-win deal.

1. Request that the seller not negotiate with other buyers while the offer is being negotiated. Sellers have what could be considered an unfair advantage when they are in a position to negotiate with more than one buyer at a time.

2. Before you start the negotiation process, decide on the highest amount that you are willing to pay for the business.

3. Practice your presentation. Assemble all the documents you may require and establish a sequence for your presentation. Leave the difficult issues to last.

4. Prepare in writing a list of facts that validate your position on an issue.

5. Think through possible weaknesses in your reasoning to help you anticipate and respond to the objections that the seller may raise.

6. Try to stick to your sequence during the meeting. Skilled negotiators may deliberately jump from one item to another in an attempt to confuse you.

7. Take notes during the meeting to reduce the chance of misunderstanding.

8. Avoid confrontational language that may terminate discussion. Remain calm at all times.

9. Be prepared to practice a little give and take. If you are firm on an issue, then look for other areas where you can be flexible. Be prepared with alternatives, for example, terms, collateral and intangibles.

10. Never tell the other party what you will not do, such as saying, "I won't pay a cent more that $350,000." Keep all your options open as long as possible. For example, you may wish to increase the sale price if you are unable to obtain outside financing and the seller is willing to provide you with financing on reasonable terms.

11. Always be prepared to walk away if you cannot negotiate a deal that you can live with.

12. If you plan to use an intermediary to handle the negotiations on your behalf and you both plan to be in attendance during negotiations, your respective roles must be clearly defined in advance.

Using an Intermediary

You may wish to consider using an intermediary such as a business broker, accountant or lawyer to conduct the negotiations on your behalf. The use of an intermediary can be helpful because:

- it can remove any emotional involvement that might impede your ability to negotiate effectively;
- the intermediary may have relevant technical expertise that will assist in the negotiation;
- it can prevent you from being in a situation where you have to react on the spot;
- the intermediary can float a trial balloon, without committing you to anything;

On the other hand, there are a few potential negatives to consider before deciding to use an intermediary:

- intermediaries may have their own agenda and may not act in your best interests; and
- there may be poor communication and feedback.

The Sequence of Events

In some situations it is possible for the buyer and the seller to have a meeting of the minds and reach a tentative agreement on the major terms of the sale, which are then incorporated into a letter of intent. On the other hand, the buyer may prefer to present the offer in writing to use in the buyer's presentation to the seller and to avoid any misunderstanding between the parties about the terms of the proposal.

Letter of Intent

The letter of intent is a pre-contractual written proposal that attempts to set out the basic terms and conditions of the intended transaction in layman's language. A letter of intent is also sometimes referred to as a memorandum of understanding. A sample letter of intent is provided in Appendix 11.1. The letter of intent does not set out binding or enforceable obligations except in the following three areas:

- the obligations of the buyer and seller to negotiate in good faith towards the execution of a binding agreement of purchase and sale;
- the right of the proposed buyer to conduct an investigation on the business affairs of the corporation in the case of a share purchase, or to carry out due diligence of the business carried on with the assets that are the subject-matter of a proposed asset purchase; and
- the obligation of the proposed buyer to maintain confidentiality regarding any information it receives during the due diligence process and to use the information only in connection with the proposed purchase. See Appendix 10.2 for a sample confidentiality and non-disclosure agreement, which should also be signed.

It is also common for a buyer to require a provision in the letter of intent preventing the seller from seeking other offers or conducting negotiations with other prospective buyers for a period long enough to allow completion of the buyer's due diligence and to negotiate and execute a purchase and sale agreement. Entering into a letter of intent should not be taken to mean that a sale would be finalized; approximately 50% of deals that reach the letter of intent stage are not completed for a variety of reasons.

There are essentially two approaches to the drafting of a letter of intent. The first approach is to keep it succinct and cover only the really important elements of the deal. The second approach is to draft a more comprehensive letter of intent that addresses every major point that will ultimately be incorporated into the sales agreement in order to minimize or eliminate any potential stumbling blocks at the time of closing. If the latter approach is adopted, the letter of intent can be very similar to the actual purchase agreement in appearance. The approach you select will depend on a number of circumstances, for example, your level of confidence that any issues that may arise as the deal proceeds can be easily resolved with the seller. If your level of confidence is high in that respect, you may wish to opt for the shorter version. If you are unsure that issues can be easily resolved, it may be prudent to draft a more detailed letter of intent.

Because this document can become legally binding, it should be drafted by your legal counsel and reviewed by your accountant. Lawyers prefer to be involved in the construction of the agreement, as it is difficult to make material changes after the fact if they become necessary.

When the due diligence process has progressed to the point where both parties are confident that a deal can be negotiated, one of the parties' lawyers will commence drafting the definitive purchase and sale agreement. The buyer's lawyer normally carries this out.

Contents

At a minimum, the letter of intent should include the following elements:
- a description of what is being purchased and what is not;
- the basic structure of the deal, for example, shares or assets;
- the seller(s) name(s);
- the date of the offer;
- the date on which the offer expires;
- the proposed closing date;
- the price; and
- the terms (this should include the form of consideration [for example, stock, cash or debt], vendor financing [with details of interest rate, term, amortization, secured or unsecured, contingencies], and exactly what is being purchased);
- the amount of deposit and conditions regarding escrow and treatment of deposit;
- whether the discussions are to be kept confidential;
- an indication of whether the negotiations are to be exclusive for a period of time (for example, the seller must not enter into negotiations with any other party and will take the business off the market for a designated period of time);
- a statement that the agreement is non-binding subject to (a) the buyer being satisfied with his review of the business, and (b) the buyer having secured the financing necessary to close the deal; and

- permission for the buyer or the buyer's lawyer to contact the seller's lawyer, accountant, banker, etc., to carry out due diligence on the business.

Payment of Deposit

Typically, at the time of execution of the letter of intent, the buyer pays a monetary deposit on the purchase price, similar to the earnest money used in a real estate deal. If the deposit is large, the seller may agree to a "no-shop" agreement, which prevents the seller from further marketing the company. However, the letter is usually non-binding in the sense that at any point either party can break off negotiations, and the buyer's deposit will be returned.

> A good faith deposit of $5,000 to $10,000 is fairly typical for a small- to medium-sized business.

The size of the deposit will normally depend on the price being offered for the business, but in any event should be sufficiently large to give the seller a level of comfort that the buyer will not abandon the deal, and adequate compensation if the buyer does. A good faith deposit of $5,000 to $10,000 is fairly typical for a small- to medium-sized business, although it is not unusual for the seller to require a deposit of at least 5% of the purchase price.

Once you have decided on the business you want, knowing how to negotiate or having an experienced third party negotiating for you, is an important next step. It is helpful to understand the art and science of the negotiating process. For example, the power of motivation, the stages of the process itself and the benefits of using a third party intermediary — such as a lawyer or broker. Once you have finalized your wishes, a letter of intent tends to be the next step. Throughout this whole process, you want to have the assistance of an experienced business lawyer.

Appendix 11.1
Sample Letter of Intent

July 22, 2002

MARCONI'S REGIONAL DISTRIBUTORS INC.
123 – 1674 Spruce Dr.
Calgary, Alberta
Canada

Re: Purchase of Marconi's Distributors.

Dear Sir:

I am interested in acquiring the business known as Marconi's Distributors.

1. The transfer shall be through a sale of assets (not shares in the seller corporation). The assets would consist of all inventory, fixtures, furniture, equipment and the name and goodwill of the business.

2. The seller would retain all cash on hand, accounts and notes receivable, prepaid expenses, motor vehicles, tax rebates and any pending claims owed by the corporation.

3. The offered purchase price for the business is $200,000 based on an inventory level of $30,000 based on wholesale cost at the time of transfer. In the event the inventory is less than $30,000, the difference shall be added to or subtracted from the purchase price.

4. We would expect the final documents to reflect that the purchase price shall, for tax purposes, be allocated as follows:

   $ 30,000 for inventory (or as adjusted)
   $120,000 for fixtures and equipment
   $ 50,000 for goodwill
   $200,000 total purchase price

5. The proposed purchase price would be paid in the following manner:

$10,000	cash down payment (tendered as a deposit herein)
$50,000	deposit upon signing formal agreement
$50,000	by assumption of seller's existing liabilities at the time of closing
$90,000	to be financed by seller, payable over five years with 6% interest. The note would be guaranteed by William McAffie Enterprises, and secured by a first mortgage on assets and an assignment of the lease if assented to by the landlord.

   Any adjustment based on any increase or decrease in either inventory or liabilities shall be added to or subtracted from the note balance, and not the down payment.

6. Except for liabilities expressly to be assumed, the assets shall be sold free and clear from all claims, debts, liens or other liabilities with William McAffie Enterprises receiving good and marketable title.

7. We shall expect the seller and Dino Marconi to agree to a non-compete agreement preventing them from engaging in the distribution of automotive parts for two years, within two miles of the present business address.

8. This offer is expressly conditional upon:

   (a) The buyer obtaining a lease on the premises on such terms, rents and conditions as it deems acceptable.

   (b) The buyer's accountant verifying further additional information and his satisfaction of the same.

   In the event these two conditions are not fully satisfied, this offer, or any subsequent formal agreement, may be terminated by the buyer and all deposits shall be promptly refunded.

9. We enclose a certified cheque for $10,000 to be held in escrow pending the closing and transfer.

   If this offer is acceptable, please signify by signing where indicated and return a signed copy to me at the above address within 10 days of the above date. In the event that we do not receive a signed copy by that date, you should consider the offer withdrawn. Upon acceptance, we propose to immediately enter into a formal purchase and sale agreement on these terms.

   We understand that the seller shall pay all brokerage fees and that an acceptable date of closing would be on or about September 31, 2002.

Yours truly

William McAffie
President
William McAffie Enterprises

The foregoing offer is accepted on its terms:

By: _____
                    President

_____
William McAffie as an individual

12

RAISING FINANCING

Deciding between Debt and Equity Financing

Essentially, there are two types of financing: debt and equity. The use of either method — or both — to finance the business is of critical importance to the business. The nature of financing will strongly determine the company's very chances of survival, as well as its rate of growth. An explanation of both methods of financing together with their respective advantages and disadvantages are explained below. Keep in mind, however, that your professional advisors should assist you in making the ultimate decision on the best combination of debt and equity.

Debt Financing

With debt financing, you borrow money and have to pay interest for the privilege. If you take on too much debt, it could become cumbersome and you could find yourself at the mercy of the lender if things do not go according to plan and you are unable to service the debt.

There are numerous methods of debt financing from straightforward loans, lines of credit, accounts receivable financing, business improvement loans, leasing and second mortgages to debentures secured by the company's assets and intellectual property. Debentures are often convertible into equity on various terms and conditions at the option of the lender. Lenders — outside of family and friends — will almost always require security other than the business itself.

The primary advantage of debt financing is that you keep all the ownership of the company in your hands unless the lender has a convertible debenture and elects to convert its debt into equity at some time. The disadvantage is that you may lose all of your security if the business fails.

Bank financing is usually only part of your entire financing package. You will need a substantial number of assets of your own to pledge as collateral before the bank will come up with any money. Banks are lenders, not venture capitalists.

There are various government programs available to small business owners who need capital. Among them are federal or provincial government equity plans, which provide capital directly (through the Business Development Bank of Canada or provincial government development corporations) or indirectly (through incentive programs for the private sector to fund small businesses). These programs can be an alternative when conventional methods of borrowing are unavailable. Dealing with these programs often requires patience and persistence as most involve a lot of paperwork and the approval process can be lengthy.

Equity Financing

Equity is the money that is put into a business in exchange for shares. Equity financing means you sell a share of your ownership, which means a reduction in control.

Sources of Financing

The source of financing depends in part on the size of the business being purchased. The majority of small- and medium-sized businesses are purchased with a significant portion of the purchase price financed by the owner. The chances of obtaining outside financing improve as the size of the business being acquired increases, because the number of potential lenders increases. Banks, insurance companies, commercial finance companies and venture capital companies may be interested in lending money for a relatively large acquisition.

Personal Equity

The primary source of equity financing is usually the owner of the company. Typically, the buyer and the buyer's family provide anywhere from 20% to 50% of the funds needed to purchase a business. This usually comes from personal savings, the sale of real estate, loans against assets such as real estate, or the liquidation of other assets or investments.

> Typically, the buyer and the buyer's family provide anywhere from 20% to 50% of the funds needed to purchase a business.

Family and Friends

A common source of equity financing is what is referred to as other people's money. In many cases, this means family and friends. These people usually believe in you and do not require the same kind of collateral as banks do. Careful consideration should be given before involving family and friends in the financing of your business. Consider how you would feel obligated to them and their financial capability to provide funds before you approach them to invest.

If you do decide to approach family and friends, deal with the situation in a business-like manner and present them with a formal proposal just as you would with any other potential investor. If they agree to invest, structure a formal agreement with agreed terms of repayment and interest. In other words, treat their investment as a business arrangement and not as a gift. If they decline your proposal, do not take it personally.

Partnership

You may consider bringing a partner into the business to provide some of the financing, share the work and some of the risk. If you choose the partnership route, understand that the casualty rate of partnerships is very high. As in any form of business relationship, it is critical to enter into an agreement that sets out the responsibilities and obligations of each party before you commence business.

Seller Financing

As noted above, the majority of small- and medium-sized businesses are purchased with a significant portion of the purchase price financed by the owner. Owners may be motivated to provide vendor financing if they feel it is necessary to get the price desired for the business, have confidence in the buyer or are influenced by their own tax situation.

Typically, a seller will require the buyer to make a down payment and execute a promissory note for the balance. The down payment can vary from 10% to 40% of the selling price. The assets of the business usually secure the note, however, the seller could require the buyer to put up a personal residence as additional collateral or personally guarantee the loan. The interest rate charged on the note normally varies with the prime rate and is usually less than the interest rate charged by banks for business loans.

> In most cases, financing provided by the seller will be for a relatively short term although the loan will be amortized over a much longer payment schedule to keep the payments to a manageable amount.

In some situations, the seller may require the buyer to take out a life insurance policy with the seller as beneficiary, so that the loan will be paid off if the buyer dies. In addition, the purchase and sale agreement may restrict the new owner's sale of assets, acquisitions and expansions until the note is paid off, and provide that the seller be provided with regular financial statements so the seller can keep track of the financial health of the business.

In most cases, financing provided by the seller will be for a relatively short term although the loan will be amortized over a much longer payment schedule to keep the payments to a manageable amount. At the end of the term (for example, five years), there will still be a substantial portion of principal remaining and the seller will require the buyer to obtain outside financing to pay off the balance of the loan. The basic philosophy behind this is that at that point, the business will have a solid track record and it will be easier for the buyer to obtain bank financing.

Earn-outs

An "earn-out" is essentially an agreement in which a minimum purchase price is agreed on, with a provision that the seller will be entitled to more money if the business reaches certain financial goals in the future. Such goals should be stated in terms of percentages of gross sales or revenues, rather than net revenues, because expenses are relatively easy to manipulate, which can result in a distortion of net revenues.

An earn-out can be calculated as a percentage of sales, gross profit, net profit or another figure. It is not uncommon to establish a floor or ceiling for the earn-out.

Earn-outs do not preclude the payment of a portion of the purchase price in cash or instalment notes. Rather, they are normally paid in addition to other forms of payment. Because the payment of money to the seller under the provisions of the earn-out is predicated on the performance of the business, it is important that the seller continue to operate the business through the period of the earn-out.

> You will have a far greater chance of obtaining bank financing if you have a large net worth, liquid assets or a reliable source of income.

An earn-out is often used in situations where there is disagreement between the parties about how much the business is actually worth. An earn-out can also be a good solution if the buyer is uncertain about the future of the business since the performance payments can often be financed internally.

Lending Institutions

The most common sources for business loans are financial institutions such as banks although banks turn down far more loan applications than they approve. Before approving a loan request, a bank must be convinced that the loan's risk of failure is minimal and represents a profitable transaction. Institutional lenders are generally conservative and concentrate primarily on repayment. You will have a far greater chance of obtaining bank financing if you have a large net worth, liquid assets or a reliable source of income. In addition, a borrower must be of good character, have a clear source of repayment and have a good business plan.

Collateral

It is unusual for a loan to be secured only by the assets of the business. An institutional lender is almost certain to require personal collateral for a loan. Collateral is essentially property that secures a loan or other debt, so that the lender may seize the property if the borrower fails to make proper payments on the loan. The most attractive types of personal collateral from the lender's point of view are real estate, marketable securities and cash value of life insurance. In start-up business, the most commonly used source of collateral is the equity value in real estate. The borrower may simply take out a new, or second, mortgage on the borrower's residence.

When lenders demand collateral for a secured loan, they are seeking to minimize the risks of extending credit. In order to ensure that the particular collateral provides appropriate security, the lender will want to match the type of collateral with the loan being made. For example, the useful life of the collateral will typically have to exceed, or at least meet, the term of the loan, otherwise the lender's secured interest would be jeopardized.

Consequently, short-term assets such as receivables and inventory will not be acceptable as security for a long-term loan, but they are appropriate for short-term financing such as a line of credit.

If a bank is willing to provide financing, it will typically finance 50% to 75% of the value of real estate, 75% to 90% of new equipment value, or 50% of inventory. The only intangible assets attractive to banks are accounts receivable, which they will finance from 80% to 90% provided the accounts are current, that is, no older than 30 days.

Although the terms may sound attractive, most business buyers are unwise to look toward conventional lending institutions to finance their acquisition.

The *Small Business Loans Act*

Business improvement loans are administered by the *Small Business Loans Act* and are guaranteed by the federal government. Business improvement loans are designed to help small businesses obtain intermediate-term loans from chartered banks and other designated lenders to help finance specific fixed asset needs. Business improvement loans are made directly by approved lenders to small businesses with a loss-sharing agreement signed between the lender and the federal government. In the event you go out of business, the federal government will reimburse the lender for the debt outstanding up to a certain level (currently 90%).

The maximum value of a loan cannot exceed $250,000. Loan proceeds may be used to finance up to 90% of the cost of the fixed asset, including non-refundable taxes and duties. Lenders are obligated to take security in the assets financed. Under this program, the lender cannot ask for a personal guarantee from you that will exceed 25% of the original amount of the loan.

Loan proceeds may be used to finance:
- the purchase or improvement of real property;
- the renovation, improvement or modernization of premises; or
- the purchase and installation of new or used equipment.

The period during which a loan must be repaid will coincide with the expected economic life of the asset being financed, up to a maximum of 10 years. Instalment payments on the loan principal must be scheduled at least annually, but monthly payments are usually called for depending on arrangements between borrower and lender. Borrowers may choose between:
- floating rate loans, where the interest rate fluctuates with changes in the lender's prime lending rate over the term of the loan, but cannot be more than 3% over the lender's prime lending rate; and
- fixed rate loans, where the interest rate is fixed for the term of the loan, cannot be more than 3% over the lender's residential mortgage rate for the applicable term. This 3% includes an annual administration fee of 1.25% payable by the lender to the government.

A loan can be prepaid or the interest rate can be converted to a fixed or floating rate. The lender may charge a penalty for the prepayment or conversion of the loan.

Lenders are also required to pay a one-time loan registration fee on behalf of the borrower, to the government equal to 2% of the amount loaned. The fee is recoverable from borrowers who may reimburse the lenders when their loans are advanced or have the amount of the fee added to their loan balances, provided that the individual borrower's loan maximum of $250,000 in total is not exceeded.

Developing a Loan Proposal

One of the least understood concepts is how to make an effective loan presentation to a lender. A borrower is often told to create a business plan and to include various required documents. This generic approach may result in the loan request being relegated to a stack on the loan officer's desk and perhaps a rejection. If you wish to have any chance of success, you need to develop a strong external business plan. The internal business plan that you develop as your management and operating guide contains more details than a banker has time to read. An internal business plan is for your use and helps you stay on track for the goals you have established for the business. A winning loan presentation has substantially more sizzle than a business plan designed as a personal planning tool. It may also use a more aggressive interpretation of the *pro forma* operating numbers.

To obtain outside financing it is important to be well-prepared and have the information that a lender needs to make a decision. Approval of your loan request depends on how well you present yourself, your business, and your financial needs to a lender. Lenders want to be assured that your business will repay the proposed loan and that there are sufficient assets (collateral) to pay off the principal in the event the loan goes into default. You must provide the lender with these two assurances in a clear and concise format. Lenders reject loan requests when they cannot understand the risk or the risk is greater than acceptable to them. Keep in mind that an acceptable entrepreneur's risk is often greater than an acceptable lender's risk. See Appendix 12.1 for a sample business plan outline, Appendix 12.2 for a sample loan financing/proposal outline, Appendix 12.3 for a sample bank loan proposal letter, and Appendix 12.4 for a sample business loan application.

> Keep in mind that an acceptable entrepreneur's risk is often greater than an acceptable lender's risk.

Choosing the Right Lender

Do not scatter your loan request to many lenders. Instead, tailor it to the specific lender most likely to grant your request. The first lender to consider is the bank where you currently maintain your bank account, as it is more difficult for a lending institution to reject a customer. However, you need to obtain some preliminary information before preparing and presenting your loan request.

- Do they finance start-up companies?
- Do you determine the size of loan you require?
- What are the lender's minimum collateral requirements?
- Does the lender make equipment or working capital loans?

Do not hesitate to switch to a lender that can better accommodate your borrowing needs. When reviewing a loan request, the lender is primarily concerned about repayment. To help determine this ability, many loan officers will order a copy of your credit report from a credit–reporting agency. Avoid making a formal submission if there is not a good chance of being approved because other lenders may find out that you were turned down when they run a credit report.

Business Plan/Proposal

A well-prepared business plan demonstrates management's ability to focus on long-term achievable goals, provides a guide for effectively imple-menting the articulated goals once the capital has been committed, and constitutes a yardstick by which actual performance can be evaluated. Any potential lender or investor will expect to be presented with a meaningful business plan.

> Positive first impressions of the proposal are very important in order to instil confidence in the viability and management of the business.

Positive first impressions of the proposal are very important in order to instil confidence in the viability and management of the business. If it is necessary to re-submit the proposal because it was incomplete, or poorly prepared, that fact alone could influence the final decision and result in your application being rejected.

The Cover Letter

The cover letter that accompanies your loan request is your first opportunity to sell your loan. Make it great! Lenders have been known to reject loans after reading a poorly constructed cover letter or one that is so impersonal that the presentation looks like it is being sent to every institution in town. Relate the cover letter to specific discussions you previously had with the loan officer and verbal understandings. The cover letter should be no more than one or two pages long. Explain how the loan will be used. Highlight the strongest aspects. Note the weak points and how you plan to overcome them. If your collateral is particularly strong, emphasize it in your cover letter. It should include the name, address and telephone number of the business and the names of all principals. In the description of your business, describe its unique aspects and how or why those aspects will appeal to consumers. Emphasize any special features you feel will appeal to customers and explain how and why these features are appealing.

Always recommend approval of the loan as your final thought rather than meekly asking the loan officer to call if there are any questions. If you cannot recommend your loan to the loan officer, do not expect the loan officer to recommend it to the loan committee.

REAL LIFE

Home Equity Can Help Your Financing

Sylvie had received $110,000 from her employer as a golden handshake when her job was eliminated as a result of company downsizing. Sylvie decided to use the opportunity to get into business for herself so that she would be in a position to control her own destiny. She decided to invest in Sammy's Deli, which required a capital investment of $150,000 plus $30,000 working capital. Sylvie calculated that, based on conservative projections of revenue and provided that she took a wage of no more than $2,000 a month, the business could comfortably service a debt of $40,000. Sylvie had originally purchased her house for $90,000 but in the current market it was worth $275,000, with only $35,000 remaining on the mortgage. The Central Bank of Canada agreed to lend Sylvie the additional $40,000 capital she required, and arranged for a $30,000 line of credit for the working capital using her house as collateral.

Understanding how to raise financing for your business purchase is vital. You need to know the advantages and disadvantages of debt and equity financing, and the various sources of financing. You also need to understand the types of collateral you may be asked to sign, and how to effectively negotiate what security you are prepared to offer in exchange for the money you are receiving. Again, having a skilled business lawyer involved will save you a lot of money and potential financial risk. In order to get a better sense of common documents, refer to the appendices. They can provide direction when looking for money.

Appendix 12.1
Sample Business Plan Outline

Elements of a Business Plan

1. Cover sheet
2. Statement of purpose
3. Table of contents

III. The Business

   A. Description of business

   B. Marketing

   C. Competition

   D. Operating procedures

   E. Personnel

   F. Business insurance

   G. Financial data

II. Financial Data

   A. Loan applications

   B. Capital equipment and supply list

   C. Balance sheet

   D. Breakeven analysis

   E. Pro forma income projections (profit and loss statements)

   Three-year summary

   Detail by month, first year

   Detail by quarters, second and third years

   Assumptions upon which projections were based

   F. Pro forma cash flow

   (Follow guidelines for E, above.)

III. Supporting Documents

   Tax returns of principals for last three years

   Personal financial statement (all banks have these forms)

   In the case of a franchised business, a copy of franchise contract and all supporting documents
       provided by the franchisor

   Copy of proposed lease or purchase agreement for building space

   Copy of licenses and other legal documents

   Copy of resumes of all principals

   Copies of letters of intent from suppliers, etc.

WHAT IT INCLUDES

What goes in a business plan? This is an excellent question. And, it is one that many new and potential small business owners should ask, but oftentimes do not ask. The body of the business plan can be divided into four distinct sections: 1) the description of the business, 2) the marketing plan, 3) the management plan and 4) the financial management plan. Addenda to the business plan should include the executive summary, supporting documents and financial projections.

DESCRIPTION OF THE BUSINESS

In this section, provide a detailed description of your business. An excellent question to ask yourself is: "What business am I in?" In answering this question include your products, market and services as well as a thorough description of what makes your business unique. Remember, however, that as you develop your business plan, you may have to modify or revise your initial questions.

The business description section is divided into three primary sections. Section 1 describes your business, Section 2 describes the product or service you will be offering and Section 3 describes the location of your business and why this location is desirable (if you have a franchise, some franchisors assist in site selection).

1. Business Description

When describing your business, generally you should explain:

- Legalities — business form: proprietorship, partnership, corporation. The licenses or permits you will need.
- Business type: merchandizing, manufacturing or service.
- What is your product or service?
- Is it a new independent business, a takeover, an expansion or a franchise?
- Why your business will be profitable. What are the growth opportunities? Will franchising affect growth opportunities?
- When will your business be open (hours of operation)?
- What you have learned about your kind of business from outside sources (trade suppliers, bankers, other franchise owners, the franchisor or publications).

A cover sheet goes before the description. It includes the name, address and telephone number of the business and the names of all principals. In the description of your business, describe the unique aspects and how or why they will appeal to consumers. Emphasize any special features that you feel will appeal to customers and explain how and why these features are appealing.

The description of your business should clearly identify goals and objectives and it should clarify why you are, or why you want to be, in business.

2. Product/Service

Try to describe the benefits of your goods and services from your customers' perspective. Successful business owners know or at least have an idea of what their customers want or expect from them. This type of anticipation can be helpful in building customer satisfaction and loyalty. It certainly is a good strategy for beating the competition or retaining your competitiveness. Describe:

- What you are selling.
- How your product or service will benefit the customer.
- Which products/services are in demand; will there be a steady flow of cash?
- What is different about the product or service your business is offering.

3. The Location

The location of your business can play a decisive role in its success or failure. Your location should be built around your customers, it should be accessible and it should provide a sense of security. Consider these questions when addressing this section of your business plan:

- What are your location needs?
- What kind of space will you need?
- Is the area desirable? Is the building desirable?
- Is it easily accessible? Is public transportation available? Is street lighting adequate?
- Are market shifts or demographic shifts occurring?
- It may be a good idea to make a checklist of questions you identify when developing your business plan. Categorize your questions and, as you answer each question, remove it from your list.

THE MARKETING PLAN

Marketing plays a vital role in successful business ventures. How well you market your business, along with a few other considerations, will ultimately determine your degree of success or failure. The key element of a successful marketing plan is to know your customers — their likes, dislikes and expectations. By identifying these factors, you can develop a marketing strategy that will allow you to arouse and fulfill their needs.

Identify your customers by their age, sex, income or educational level and residence. At first, target only those customers who are more likely to purchase your product or service. As your customer base expands, you may need to consider modifying the marketing plan to include other customers.

Develop a marketing plan for your business by answering these questions. (Potential franchise owners will have to use the marketing strategy the franchisor has developed.) Your marketing plan should be included in your business plan and contain answers to the questions outlined below.

- Who are your customers? Define your target market(s).
- Are your markets growing? steady? declining?
- Is your market share growing? steady? declining?
- If a franchise, how is your market segmented?
- Are your markets large enough to expand?
- How will you attract, hold and increase your market share? If your business is a franchise, will the franchisor provide assistance in this area? Based on the franchisor's strategy, how will you promote your sales?
- What pricing strategy have you devised?

1. Competition

Competition is a way of life. We compete for jobs, promotions, scholarships to institutes of higher learning, in sports — and in almost every aspect of our lives. Nations compete for the consumer in the global marketplace as do individual business owners. Advances in technology can send the profit margins of a successful business into a tailspin, causing them to plummet overnight or within a few hours. When considering these and other factors, we can conclude that business is a highly competitive, volatile arena. Because of this volatility and competitiveness, it is important to know your competitors.

Questions like these can help you:

- Who are your five nearest direct competitors?
- Who are your indirect competitors?
- How are their businesses: steady? increasing? decreasing?
- What have you learned from their operations? from their advertising?
- What are their strengths and weaknesses?
- How does their product or service differ from yours?

Start a file on each of your competitors. Keep manila envelopes of their advertising and promotional materials and their pricing strategy techniques. Review these files periodically, determining when and how often they advertise, sponsor promotions and offer sales. Study the copy used in the advertising and promotional materials, and their sales strategies. For example, is their copy short? descriptive? catchy? or how much do they reduce prices for sales? Using this technique can help you to understand your competitors better and how they operate their businesses.

2. Pricing and Sales

Your pricing strategy is another marketing technique you can use to improve your overall competitiveness. Get a feel for the pricing strategy your competitors are using so you can determine if your prices are in line with competitors in your market area and if they are in line with industry averages.

Some of the pricing strategies are:

- retail cost and pricing;
- competitive position;
- pricing below competition;
- pricing above competition;
- price lining;
- multiple pricing;
- service costs and pricing (for service businesses only);
- service components;
- material costs;
- labour costs; and
- overhead costs.

The key to success is to have a well-planned strategy, to establish your policies and to constantly monitor prices and operating costs to ensure profits. Even in a franchise where the franchisor provides operational procedures and materials, it is a good policy to keep abreast of the changes in the market-place because these changes can affect your competitiveness and profit margins.

3. Advertising and Public Relations

How you advertise and promote your goods and services may make or break your business. Having a good product or service and not advertising and promoting it is like not having a business at all. Many business owners operate under the mistaken concept that the business will promote itself, and channel money that should be used for advertising and promotions to other areas of the business. Advertising and promotions, however, are the life line of a business and should be treated as such.

Devise a plan that uses advertising and networking as a means to promote your business. Develop short, descriptive copy (text material) that clearly identifies your goods or services, your location and price. Use catchy phrases to arouse the interest of your readers, listeners or viewers.

In the case of a franchise, the franchisor will provide advertising and promotional materials as part of the franchise package, you may need approval to use any materials that you and your staff develop. Whether or not this is the case, as a courtesy, allow the franchisor the opportunity to review, comment on and, if required, approve these materials before using them. Make sure the advertisements you create are consistent with the image the franchisor is trying to project. Remember the more care and attention you devote to your marketing program, the more successful your business will be.

THE MANAGEMENT PLAN

Managing a business requires more than just the desire to be your own boss. It demands dedication, persistence, the ability to make decisions and to manage both employees and finances. Your management plan, along with your marketing and financial management plans, sets the foundation for and facilitates the success of your business.

Like plants and equipment, people are resources — they are the most valuable asset a business has. You will soon discover that employees and staff will play an important role in the total operation of your business. Consequently, it is imperative that you know what skills you possess and those you lack since you will have to hire personnel to supply the skills that you lack. Additionally, it is imperative that you know how to manage and treat your employees. Make them a part of the team. Keep them informed of and get their feedback regarding changes. Employees oftentimes have excellent ideas that can lead to new market areas, innovations to existing products or services or new product lines or services that can improve your overall competitiveness.

Your management plan should answer questions such as:

- How does your background and business experience help you in this business?
- What are your weaknesses and how can you compensate for them?
- Who will be on the management team?

- What are their strengths and weaknesses?
- What are their duties?
- Are these duties clearly defined?
- If a franchise, what type of assistance can you expect from the franchisor?
- Will this assistance be ongoing?
- What are your current personnel needs?
- What are your plans for hiring and training personnel?
- What salaries, benefits, vacations and holidays will you offer? If a franchise, are these issues covered in the management package the franchisor will provide?
- What benefits, if any, can you afford at this point?
- If a franchise, the operating procedures, manuals and materials devised by the franchisor should be included in this section of the business plan. Study these documents carefully when writing your business plan and be sure to incorporate this material. The franchisor should assist you with managing your franchise. Take advantage of the franchisor's expertise and develop a management plan that will ensure the success of your franchise and satisfy the needs and expectations of employees, as well as the franchisor.

THE FINANCIAL MANAGEMENT PLAN

Sound financial management is one of the best ways for your business to remain profitable and solvent. How well you manage the finances of your business is the cornerstone of every successful business venture. Each year, thousands of potentially successful businesses fail because of poor financial management. As a business owner, you will need to identify and implement policies that will lead to and ensure that you will meet your financial obligations.

To effectively manage your finances, plan a sound, realistic budget by determining the actual amount of money needed to open your business (start-up costs) and the amount needed to keep it open (operating costs). The first step to building a sound financial plan is to devise a start-up budget. Your start-up budget will usually include such one-time-only costs as major equipment, utility deposits and down payments.

The start-up budget should allow for these expenses.

1. Start-up Budget

- personnel (costs prior to opening)
- legal and professional fees
- occupancy
- licences and permits
- equipment
- insurance
- supplies
- advertising and promotions
- salaries and wages
- accounting

- income
- utilities
- payroll expenses

An operating budget is prepared when you are actually ready to open for business. The operating budget will reflect your priorities in terms of how you spend your money, the expenses you will incur and how you will meet those expenses (income). Your operating budget also should include money to cover the first three to six months of operation. It should allow for the following expenses.

2. Operating Budget

- personnel
- insurance
- rent
- depreciation
- loan payments
- advertising and promotions
- legal and accounting
- miscellaneous expenses
- supplies
- payroll expenses
- salaries and wages
- utilities
- dues, subscriptions and fees
- taxes
- repairs and maintenance

The financial section of your business plan should include any loan applications you have filed, a capital equipment and supply list, balance sheet, breakeven analysis, pro forma income projections (profit and loss statement) and pro forma cash flow. The income statement and cash flow projections should include a three-year summary, detail by month for the first year, and detail by quarter for the second and third years.

The accounting system and the inventory control system that you will be using are generally addressed in this section of the business plan also. If a franchise, the franchisor may stipulate in the franchise contract the type of accounting and inventory systems you may use. If this is the case, the franchisor should have a system already intact and you will be required to adopt this system. Whether you develop the accounting and inventory systems yourself, have an outside financial advisor develop the systems or the franchisor provides these systems, you will need to acquire a thorough understanding of each segment and how it operates. Your financial advisor can assist you in developing this section of your business plan.

The following questions should help you determine the amount of start-up capital you will need to purchase and open a franchise.

- How much money do you have?
- How much money will you need to purchase the franchise?
- How much money will you need for start-up?
- How much money will you need to stay in business?

Other questions that you will need to consider are:

- What type of accounting system will you use? Is it a single entry or dual entry system?
- What will your sales goals and profit goals be for the coming year? If a franchise, will the franchisor set your sales and profit goals? Or, will the franchisor expect you to reach and retain a certain sales level and profit margin?
- What financial projections will you need to include in your business plan?
- What kind of inventory control system will you use?
- Your plan should include an explanation of all projections. Unless you are thoroughly familiar with financial statements, get help in preparing your cash flow and income statements and your balance sheet. Your aim is not to become a financial wizard, but to understand the financial tools well enough to gain their benefits. Your accountant or financial advisor can help you accomplish this goal.

Appendix 12.2
Sample Loan/Financing Proposal Outline

A. Summary

1. Nature of business

2. Amount and purpose of loan

3. Repayment terms

4. Equity percentage of borrower (debt/equity ratio after loan)

5. Security or collateral (listed with market value estimates and quotes on cost of equipment to be purchased with the loan proceeds, if applicable)

6. If private investor, the amount of equity offered

B. Personal Information

(On all corporate officers, directors and individuals owning any equity in the business)

1. Education, work history and business experience

2. Credit references (if requested)

3. Financial net worth statements

C. Company Information

(Whichever is applicable below: 1 or 2)

1. New business:

   (a) Business plan (attach copy of your business plan)

   (b) Projections (this may have already been covered in your business plan):

   - profit-and-loss projection (monthly, for one year); explanation of projections and assumptions

   - cash flow projection (monthly, for one year); explanation of projections and assumptions

   - projected balance sheet (one year after loan); explanation of projections and assumptions

2. Purchasing a business/Expanding an existing business:

   (a) Information on existing business or business to be acquired:

   - copy of offer to purchase agreement (if applicable)

   - business history (include seller's name, reasons for sale)

   - current profit-and-loss statements (preferably less than 60 days old) and previous three years

   - cash flow statements for last year

   - business income tax returns, as submitted to Revenue Canada (past three to five years)

   - copy of sales agreement with breakdown of inventory, fixtures, equipment, licences, goodwill and other costs

   - description and dates of permits or licences already existing

   - lease agreement

   - other relevant material

   (b) Business plan (attach copy of your business plan)

   (c) Insurance coverage

   (d) Partnership, corporation or franchise papers, if applicable

Appendix 12.3
Sample Bank Loan Proposal Letter — prepared by lender

From: XYZ Bank
To: ABC Limited

Term Sheet

(for discussion purposes only)

Confidential

Borrower	ABC Limited
Lender	XYZ Bank
Amount	$70,000 Demand Operating Facility
	$3,000 Corporate VISA
Availment	Operating facility may be availed of by way of overdraft.
Purpose	To assist with general corporate financing and specifically to finance day-to-day operations and purchase of inventory.
Repayment	Demand facility to fluctuate.
Interest Rates/ Fees, etc.	Demand overdraft facility – bank prime + 1% payable monthly. Operating overdraft will be subject to an administration fee of $25 per month; Service Charge will be at the standard rate plus $10 per month; night deposit service will be at the standard rate of $1.10 per deposit bag.
Security	General assignment of accounts receivable registered in (province). Assignment of inventory under Section 178 of the Bank Act, with fire insurance over inventory, loss payable to the bank firstly.
Covenants	1. Total debt to equity shall not exceed 1:1. Equity shall be defined as the sum of paid-up capital, retained earnings, shareholders' loans and deferred management salaries less advances made to shareholders or associated companies.
	2. Operating overdrafts will not exceed 50% of total assigned inventories and eligible assigned accounts receivable.
	3. There are to be no dividend payments, unusual withdrawals or redemption of shares without the prior written consent of the Bank.
	4. Capital expenditures in any one year shall not exceed $10,000 non-cumulative without the prior written consent of the Bank, such consent not to be unreasonably withheld.

5. Monthly inventory declarations and receivable listings will be provided during those periods where an operating facility is in effect.

6. Annual financial statements prepared consistent with generally acceptable accounting principles by an accredited accounting firm shall be provided within 120 days of the borrower's fiscal year end.

7. Monthly profit-and-loss statement prepared internally shall be provided monthly.

8. The bank may request any other financial information it considers necessary for the ongoing administration of the credit facility.

9. The bank agrees to pay interest on credit balances in excess of $10,000 in your current account #0000 at the rate of the Bank's Prime Lending Rate less 3% per annum to be calculated on the average daily credit balance and payable monthly.

Events of Default The usual events of default shall apply.

Review of Credit The credit is subject to periodic review relative to the financial information to be provided, as well as an annual review by no later than May 30, 20___, in light of the annual statements.

This term sheet is for discussion purposes only, is not an offer and represents no commitment, express or implied, on the Bank's part. During our further analysis, information could come to our attention which would detract from the merits of the application and we reserve the right to discontinue the application at any time.

R.B. Jones
Manager

Appendix 12.4
Sample Business Loan Application

Please check:

☐ Proprietorship   ☐ Corporation   ☐ General Partnership   ☐ Limited Partnership

_____
Business Name
_____
Nature of Business
_____
Business Address (Street, City, Postal Code)
_____

(   )
_____
Business Telephone   Year Business Established
_____
How long under present ownership?   Number of employees?

Amount of loan(s)   1. Please describe below how you plan to use your business loan(s)

$ _____   _____

$ _____   _____

$ _____   _____

2. What will be your primary source?_____

3. What are the usual terms of sale you offer

   of repaying the loan(s)?_____   your customers? _____

4. What are the usual terms of sale offered by your major suppliers? _____

5. Do you wish this loan(s) to be insured?   ☐ YES   ☐ NO

6. Please describe any seasonality or business cycle requirements related to your business.

_____

_____

_____

Principals/Owners

Full Name and Address   *% Ownership*   *Title/Position*

_____   _____   _____

_____   _____   _____

_____   _____   _____

Historical/Projected Summary

- Existing businesses please provide financial information for the last 3 fiscal years.
- New businesses please provide projected financial information.

Financial Statements Prepared by	☐ Self	☐ Self	☐ Self
	☐ Acct't	☐ Acct't	☐ Acct't
	☐ Other	☐ Other	☐ Other
Year Ending (Date)	20____	20____	20____
Sales	$_____	$_____	$_____
Gross Profit	$_____	$_____	$_____
Net Profit After Tax	$_____	$_____	$_____
Depreciation/Amortization	$_____	$_____	$_____
Current Assets	$_____	$_____	$_____
Total Assets	$_____	$_____	$_____
Current Liabilities	$_____	$_____	$_____
Total Liabilities	$_____	$_____	$_____
Business Net Worth	$_____	$_____	$_____

Credit Relationships

- Please provide details of your business credit relationships below.

Name of Creditor and Address	Purpose of Loan/Credit Limit	Original Amount	Current Amount Owing	Repayment Terms	Maturity Date if Any
_____	_____	$_____	$_____	_____	_____
_____	_____	$_____	$_____	_____	_____
_____	_____	$_____	$_____	_____	_____
_____	_____	$_____	$_____	_____	_____

Sundry Obligations

- Please provide details below if you answer YES to any of the following questions.

Is the business providing support for obligations not listed on its financial statements (i.e. co-signer, endorser, guarantor)?   ☐ YES   ☐ NO

If yes, please indicate total contingency liability $_____

Is the business a party to any claim or lawsuit?   ☐ YES   ☐ NO

Has your business ever sought legal protection from its creditors (i.e. bankruptcy, receiver, receiver-manager)?

☐ YES   ☐ NO

Does the business owe any taxes for years prior to the current year (i.e. sales tax, income tax, property tax, municipal business taxes or provincial corporation taxes)?   ☐ YES   ☐ NO

Amount $_____   Owed to _____

Amount $_____   Owed to _____

Amount $_____   Owed to _____

Details of any of the above

_____

_____

_____

Business References

- Trade creditor, personal, etc., in addition to those noted.

Name	Address	Business Phone
Banker		
Accountant		
Other		

Insurance Coverage

- Existing businesses, please provide details of present coverage.
- New businesses, please state planned coverage.

Type of Coverage	Insurance Company	Amount of Coverage	Annual Premiums
_____	_____	$_____	$_____
_____	_____	$_____	$_____
_____	_____	$_____	$_____

The undersigned declare(s) that the statements made herein are for the purpose of obtaining business financing and are to the best of my/our knowledge true and correct. The applicant(s) consent(s) to the Bank making any inquiries it deems necessary to reach a decision on this application from a credit reporting agency or otherwise, and consent(s) to the disclosure at any time of any credit information about me/us to any credit reporting agency or to anyone with whom I/we have financial relations.

Per: Per:

_____   _____
Signature   Signature

_____   _____
Date   Date

_____   _____
Title   Title

Appendix 12.5
Sources of Financing Checklist

	Possible Source	Need Further Info	Further Info Obtained
Conventional Sources of Financing			
1. Banks			
(a) Short-term loans:			
▪ demand loans	☐	☐	☐
▪ secured commercial loans	☐	☐	☐
▪ unsecured commercial loans	☐	☐	☐
▪ operating loans	☐	☐	☐
▪ lines of credit	☐	☐	☐
▪ accounts receivable loans	☐	☐	☐
▪ warehouse receipt loans	☐	☐	☐
▪ bridge financing	☐	☐	☐
(b) Medium- and long-term loans:			
▪ term loans	☐	☐	☐
▪ fixed charge debentures	☐	☐	☐
▪ floating charge debentures	☐	☐	☐
▪ conventional mortgages	☐	☐	☐
▪ collateral mortgages	☐	☐	☐
▪ business improvement loan	☐	☐	☐
▪ chattel mortgages	☐	☐	☐
▪ leasing	☐	☐	☐
(c) Other financing services:			
▪ charge card for business expenses	☐	☐	☐
▪ charge card for personal use	☐	☐	☐
▪ factoring services	☐	☐	☐
▪ leasing services	☐	☐	☐
▪ letters of credit	☐	☐	☐
▪ letters of guarantee	☐	☐	☐
2. Business Development Bank of Canada			
▪ term loans	☐	☐	☐
▪ loan guarantees	☐	☐	☐
▪ bridge financing	☐	☐	☐
▪ equity financing	☐	☐	☐
▪ leasing	☐	☐	☐
▪ financial broker program (packaging loans to external lenders)	☐	☐	☐

- joint ventures ☐ ☐ ☐
- equity participation ☐ ☐ ☐

3. Trust Companies
   - long-term loan ☐ ☐ ☐
   - mortgage financing ☐ ☐ ☐

4. Credit Unions
   - term loans ☐ ☐ ☐
   - working capital loans ☐ ☐ ☐
   - mortgage financing ☐ ☐ ☐
   - equity participation ☐ ☐ ☐

5. Insurance Companies
   - mortgage loans ☐ ☐ ☐
   - loans based on insurance policy (cash surrender value) ☐ ☐ ☐

6. Investment Dealers
   - equity purchase ☐ ☐ ☐
   - private placement ☐ ☐ ☐
   - public issue of stock ☐ ☐ ☐

7. Commercial Finance Companies
   - equipment leasing ☐ ☐ ☐
   - real estate loans ☐ ☐ ☐
   - factoring ☐ ☐ ☐
   - machinery and equipment loans ☐ ☐ ☐
   - inventory financing ☐ ☐ ☐
   - accounts or notes receivable financing ☐ ☐ ☐

8. Government Funding/Incentive/Purchasing Services
   - (a) Federal government:
     - Department of External Affairs (PEMB Program) ☐ ☐ ☐
     - Department of Industry, Science and Technology ☐ ☐ ☐
     - Canadian Commercial Corporation ☐ ☐ ☐
     - Canadian International Development Agency (Crown corporation) ☐ ☐ ☐
     - Export Development Corporation (Crown corporation) ☐ ☐ ☐
     - Supply and Services Canada ☐ ☐ ☐
     - *Small Business Loans Act* ☐ ☐ ☐
     - Small business bond program ☐ ☐ ☐
     - Business development centre (Community futures program) ☐ ☐ ☐
     - Other _____ ☐ ☐ ☐
   - (b) Provincial government:
     - Small business ministries ☐ ☐ ☐
     - Provincial development corporations (Crown corporations) ☐ ☐ ☐

- Provincial purchasing commissions ☐ ☐ ☐
- Other _____ ☐ ☐ ☐

(c) Municipal/regional governments:

- Economic development commissions ☐ ☐ ☐
- Municipal government ☐ ☐ ☐
- Small business incubator start-up program ☐ ☐ ☐
- Other _____ ☐ ☐ ☐

Creative Sources of Financing or Saving Money

1. Modifying Personal Lifestyle

- reducing personal long-distance telephone calls ☐ ☐ ☐
- minimizing entertainment expenses ☐ ☐ ☐
- minimizing transportation costs (*e.g.,* car pool, using more gas-efficient car) ☐ ☐ ☐
- cutting down on tobacco and alcohol ☐ ☐ ☐
- reducing number of restaurant meals by packing your own lunch ☐ ☐ ☐
- combining personal and business travel ☐ ☐ ☐
- taking on a part-time job ☐ ☐ ☐

2. Using Personal Assets

- using credit cards ☐ ☐ ☐
- using personal line of credit ☐ ☐ ☐
- reducing premiums by reassessing insurance policy ☐ ☐ ☐
- using funds in personal bank accounts ☐ ☐ ☐
- renting out part of your home or garage ☐ ☐ ☐
- selling stocks and bonds ☐ ☐ ☐
- cashing in pension plans (e.g., RRSP) ☐ ☐ ☐
- selling unnecessary personal possessions (e.g., second car) ☐ ☐ ☐
- selling personal assets to the business ☐ ☐ ☐
- remortgaging your home ☐ ☐ ☐

3. Using Private Investors Known to You

- previous employers ☐ ☐ ☐
- previous co-workers ☐ ☐ ☐
- friends ☐ ☐ ☐
- neighbours ☐ ☐ ☐
- doctor ☐ ☐ ☐
- lawyer ☐ ☐ ☐
- accountant ☐ ☐ ☐
- dentist ☐ ☐ ☐
- stockbroker ☐ ☐ ☐

4. Using Other Private Investors
   - through word-of-mouth contacts (various network groups) ☐ ☐ ☐
   - answering ads in newspapers and magazines that read "investment capital available" ☐ ☐ ☐
   - placing ads for a private investor in newspapers and magazines ☐ ☐ ☐

5. Family Assistance
   - loans from relatives ☐ ☐ ☐
   - loans from immediate family members ☐ ☐ ☐
   - equity financing from relatives ☐ ☐ ☐
   - equity financing from immediate family ☐ ☐ ☐
   - employing family members ☐ ☐ ☐
   - sharing an office used by family members ☐ ☐ ☐
   - using a family investment company ☐ ☐ ☐

6. Using Customers' Funds
   - having a cash-only policy ☐ ☐ ☐
   - invoicing on an interim basis ☐ ☐ ☐
   - asking for advance payments or deposits ☐ ☐ ☐
   - providing discounts for prompt payments ☐ ☐ ☐
   - charging purchases on customers' credit card accounts ☐ ☐ ☐
   - getting signed purchase orders or contracts (collateral for bank) ☐ ☐ ☐
   - third-party billing long-distance phone calls to customer's account ☐ ☐ ☐

7. Employees as Investors
   - asking staff to co-sign on loan guarantees ☐ ☐ ☐
   - asking staff to invest in the business ☐ ☐ ☐
   - direct loans from staff ☐ ☐ ☐
   - paying partial salary in the form of stock ☐ ☐ ☐

8. Using Suppliers' Funds
   - supplier loans ☐ ☐ ☐
   - establishing credit accounts with suppliers ☐ ☐ ☐
   - buying goods on consignment ☐ ☐ ☐
   - floor planning ☐ ☐ ☐
   - equipment loans from manufacturer ☐ ☐ ☐
   - rack jobbers ☐ ☐ ☐
   - instalment financing ☐ ☐ ☐
   - conditional sales agreement ☐ ☐ ☐
   - leasing equipment ☐ ☐ ☐
   - co-op advertising ☐ ☐ ☐

9. Selling Ownership
   - incorporating and selling shares ☐ ☐ ☐
   - taking on partners or shareholders ☐ ☐ ☐

10. Renting
   - sharing or subletting rental space, staff, and equipment
     costs with another business ☐ ☐ ☐
   - renting a packaged office (office space, telephone
     answering, mailing address, secretarial services,
     equipment, etc.) ☐ ☐ ☐
   - renting office space, furniture and equipment ☐ ☐ ☐

11. Leasing
   - selling your assets and leasing them back through a
     commercial leasing company ☐ ☐ ☐
   - leasing assets rather than purchasing ☐ ☐ ☐

12. Factoring Companies
   - factoring without recourse ☐ ☐ ☐
   - factoring with recourse ☐ ☐ ☐
   - company sets up its own factor ☐ ☐ ☐
   - block discounting ☐ ☐ ☐

13. Volume Discounts
   - buying groups ☐ ☐ ☐
   - agency discounts ☐ ☐ ☐
   - co-op advertising ☐ ☐ ☐
   - group rates on insurance ☐ ☐ ☐

14. Financial Matchmaking Services
    (Lists of interested private investors)
   - federal government — entrepreneur immigrants under
     Immigration Act ☐ ☐ ☐
   - provincial government small business departments ☐ ☐ ☐
   - regional/municipal economic development commissions ☐ ☐ ☐
   - Business Development Bank of Canada ☐ ☐ ☐
   - chartered banks ☐ ☐ ☐

15. Other Creative Financing Techniques
   - advance royalty deals ☐ ☐ ☐
   - licensing your product or service ☐ ☐ ☐
   - franchiser financing ☐ ☐ ☐
   - franchising your business ☐ ☐ ☐
   - joint ventures ☐ ☐ ☐
   - limited partnerships ☐ ☐ ☐
   - business brokers ☐ ☐ ☐
   - mortgage brokers ☐ ☐ ☐

- mortgage discounters   ☐ ☐ ☐
- mutual fund companies   ☐ ☐ ☐
- overseas lenders and investors   ☐ ☐ ☐
- pension fund companies   ☐ ☐ ☐
- small business stock savings plans (provincially regulated)   ☐ ☐ ☐
- small business venture capital corporations (provincially regulated)   ☐ ☐ ☐
- venture capital companies   ☐ ☐ ☐
- local venture capital clubs   ☐ ☐ ☐
- financial consultants   ☐ ☐ ☐
- business consultants   ☐ ☐ ☐
- obtaining services in exchange for equity   ☐ ☐ ☐
- contra bartering (exchanging service/product for service/product)   ☐ ☐ ☐
- RRSP (defer tax)   ☐ ☐ ☐
- assigning exclusive rights to copyright or patent, etc.   ☐ ☐ ☐
- proposal under *Bankruptcy and Insolvency Act*   ☐ ☐ ☐

13

LOCATION AND LEASES

The Importance of Location

The location of your business is as important to your success as having a good product to offer to your customers. For retail businesses in particular, the location can make — or break — the business. It is important that the demographic profiles of people who work or live in the trading area match the target customer profile for income level and age group.

Manufacturing or distribution business may be less dependent on the need to be close to its customers or have drive-by visibility. Instead, it may be more important to have larger premises at a lower rental cost.

Businesses such as motels, doughnut shops, gasoline service stations and small family restaurants may be better located near a highway.

Walk-By Traffic

Consider whether the business requires a high level of walk-by traffic to be successful. If so, does the location provide sufficient pedestrian traffic to provide sufficient growth? If not, you may have to consider relocation at some point in the future.

Drive-By Traffic

Ask yourself whether the business depends on drive-by traffic. Look at parking and consider whether it is accessible. Is the parking free, as in a shopping mall, or will your customers have to pay to park in an underground lot or in a coin-metered space? If you have a business that serves trade customers and delivers products to them (for example, automobile parts), then parking for your customers may not be an important factor. Try to investigate traffic patterns throughout the day. Keep in mind the following questions: is traffic congested, or just at various peak times during the day, evening or weekend? Do any of these traffic problems seriously affect a customer's access to the business?

Shopping Centre

If your acquisition target is located in a shopping centre, you should do your research thoroughly. Evaluate the type of tenants in the mall where the business is located to determine whether other tenants would draw traffic to you or be in competition with you. If the shopping centre has several major or national anchor stores, this should attract a large volume of potential customers. Major tenants might include department stores, large supermarkets and many national chain or franchise retail or service operations.

Take the time to check out other malls within the trading area to see how they compare with the mall in which the business is located. You should also check out if any other shopping centres are in the planning stages and how they might affect consumer traffic in the future.

Shopping centre leases tend to be very complex and have stringent clauses in terms of the landlord's rights and requirements. It is also common for the landlord to request a percentage of the tenant's gross sales in addition to the base rent and this needs to be weighed against the benefit of exposure to a high volume of potential customers.

> Look for such warning signs as too many vacant units in the building, for-lease signs, or going-out-of-business sales.

History of the Location

At first glance a location might appear to have all the necessary ingredients for the business to be a success, but upon further research it may turn out to be a location where many businesses have failed. Look for such warning signs as too many vacant units in the building, for-lease signs, or going-out-of-business sales. Another factor could be adjacent buildings to the location. They could be drawing away traffic because of better promotions, nicer facilities and more attractive leasing rates. Possibly the landlord is difficult to get along with, and that is why many tenants are not renewing their leases. Maybe there has been a turnover of landlords or property management companies, which has caused instability in the operation of the building.

Changing Patterns of Neighbourhood

Take a look at the surrounding area. Is there building or housing growth indicating an increase in a potential market? On the other hand, if there is a declining pattern, it could negatively affect the business in the future. Contact the municipal office and make inquiries regarding the development in your geographic market area over the next few years.

Competition

Thoroughly research the competition that is in the market area. There may be very little competition, or the kind of competition that could be threatening to you. For example, a large national chain or franchise operation could spend a lot of money on advertising and promotion. Also look at the proximity of the competition and determine its strengths and weaknesses. Would you have a competitive edge?

Hours of Operation

If hours of operation are important to the success of the business, check to see if the landlord has stipulations in the lease that the building is open for operation only within specified hours. If the business is located in a shopping mall, you may be required to be open for business at all times that the mall is open and restricted from opening outside of those hours. If opening the business on a Sunday is important to grow the business, check if the municipal bylaws will allow you to do this.

Rent Payment

Obviously, the amount of rent you are going to pay is a critical factor in determining whether the location is attractive. Many small business bankruptcies are due to excessive rental payments. Ask yourself how the proposed rent figures as a percentage of your anticipated sales. Is the rent within industry averages as a percentage of sales? Rental costs in excess of industry averages can be justified only if the location allows for higher mark-ups or other benefits that offset the higher cost.

Leasing

Most businesses will start life in leased premises as few small business owners have the financial resources to consider buying a building and property. Even if you do have the resources, the decision to buy rather than lease space should be made only after considerable discussion with your accountant and lawyer.

A lease represents your right to carry on business in a particular location. While you may have rented living space before, renting a space to conduct business requires some different considerations. Leasing provides flexible options that can minimize the risk. The following outline discusses some of the main advantages and disadvantages of leasing from the perspective of both the tenant (lessee) and landlord (lessor). From a negotiating viewpoint, it is helpful to understand both parties' point of view.

> Rental costs in excess of industry averages can be justified only if the location allows for higher mark-ups or other benefits that offset the higher cost.

Advantages

Tenant

1. Capital is not required to purchase the property, thereby freeing up capital for other business purposes.
2. Lease payments are generally 100% tax deductible as an expense.
3. It is generally easier to sell the business in the future if no real property is involved.
4. It may be possible to negotiate an option to purchase the building and land at the end of the lease. In this case, the advantage is the chance to acquire the land and building

when the tenant can afford it, assuming it would be a financial or business advantage to do so. In an option-to-buy situation, it is common to have a predetermined fixed price with a time limit within which to exercise the option. There may be an adjustment formula for inflation (cost-of-living index).

5. It may be possible to negotiate a lease with a variable monthly lease payment based on seasonal cash flow income of the tenant. The total annual rent would be fixed.

6. Protections can be built in to minimize personal and business financial risk, as discussed in this chapter's "Minimizing Personal and Business Risk" section.

Landlord

1. During the course of the lease, the tenant may pay more rent than would be paid if the property was purchased and, at the end of the lease, the landlord still owns the property.

2. The tenant improvements made to the premises become the landlord's property at the end of the lease, unless there is a written agreement to the contrary.

3. The landlord is able to obtain the tax advantage of owning the property by deducting depreciation on the building.

4. The landlord is taxed on a capital gains basis if the appreciated property is ever sold.

5. The tenant may be responsible for all maintenance and repairs on the space being rented, as well as all or part of the taxes. If this provision is stipulated in the lease document, it minimizes the financial outlay and therefore risk on the part of the landlord.

Disadvantages

Tenant

1. In some situations, the tenant cannot depreciate improvements made on the lease property in terms of tax deductions.

2. When the lease expires, the value of the potential of the business (goodwill) will not be of financial benefit to the tenant unless the landlord agrees to renew the lease. Having a renewal option in the lease can offset this.

3. The tenant does not reap the extra benefit of appreciation of the value of the property, even though the increased value may be directly related to the presence of the tenant. Any capital gain in the property value accrues to the benefit of the landlord.

4. It may be more difficult for the tenant to borrow money with leased premises, if there are no assets to pledge as collateral other than the lease agreement.

5. The total cash expended by the tenant in rental payments may be greater, over the term of the lease, than if payments were made for principal and interest on the purchase of the property.

6. Improvements made to the property by the tenant at the tenant's own expense are totally lost to the tenant upon termination of the lease. The landlord automatically assumes legal title to all improvements done to the property, unless there was an

agreement in the lease allowing the tenant to remove certain improvements upon termination of the lease. Improvement costs can sometimes be substantial, especially if the tenant is the first tenant in a new building.

Landlord

1. It is sometimes difficult to find financially capable and responsible tenants willing to lease at the rental rate required, or desired, to debt service the expenses, and provide a return on the investment to the landlord.

2. Leases are only as reliable as the tenants who sign them. Some tenants will break the lease at the earliest opportunity if it appears that the business is not going to be viable. Statistically, the high failure rate of small business means a large percentage of tenants will go out of business before the end of the term of the lease.

3. There is a risk of loss of continuity of cash flow if the tenant leaves, thereby creating debt servicing problems as well as empty space. The empty space could possibly deter other tenants from coming into the building.

4. Even a very credit-worthy tenant may get into financial difficulties at some point during the term of the lease. This would leave the landlord with rent collection or eviction problems, as well as possible litigation to recover the balance outstanding under the lease.

5. The landlord may incur sizeable expenses or difficulty in re-leasing the space at the termination of the lease. The tenant may have made specialized improvements to the rented space for the specific needs of the business, which are unsuitable to anyone else. The landlord may therefore have to incur the expense of extensive reconstruction to attract a new tenant.

Types of Leases

To obtain a leasing arrangement suitable to your business needs, you should be aware of the options available. The following types of leases are the most common ones. The name used to describe each lease may vary in your region, but the concept behind the description is the same.

Ground Lease

A buyer may purchase a building or business property without actually purchasing the land under it. The land may be leased separately on a long-term lease basis (for example, 99 years). By purchasing a building and leasing the underlying land, the financial outlay of capital for the land is eliminated and yet the benefit of its use can be obtained. The cost of leasing the land can also be written off as a tax-deductible expense.

Net Lease

In a net lease situation, the tenant pays a flat rate, which is all-inclusive of heat, light, water, taxes, common area use, ground maintenance, building repairs and other such costs.

Net Lease plus Taxes

A net lease plus taxes agreement is similar to the net lease, except that there is an agreed-upon extra expense for taxes. Any taxes over and above the base tax rate are passed on to the tenant totally or partially, depending on what is negotiated. The extra cost for taxes would normally be passed on annually, after the tax assessment has been obtained and paid by the landlord.

Triple Net Lease

In a triple net lease situation, the base rent is a certain price (for example, $10 per square foot of area rented), but the tenant is responsible for paying a proportionate share of all the extra charges incurred by the landlord. These are normally outlined in the lease agreement. (These extra costs or operating expenses could add up to the equivalent of another $6 or $7 per square foot, for example. The total monthly rental outlay would therefore be approximately $16 per square foot.) The operating costs may fluctuate each year based on taxes, maintenance, insurance, administrative and management costs. When one refers to a cost per square foot for lease space, it is quoted on an annual basis. To calculate the monthly rent, you multiply the square footage of the premises by the cost per square foot, and divide by 12.

Index Lease

An index lease is one in which the rent varies based on a formula of costs incurred by the landlord. For instance, the lease may vary every year based on the cost-of-living index to account for inflation.

Variable Lease

A variable lease is one in which the annual rent is agreed upon in terms of how it is calculated, but the monthly rent may vary depending on the seasonal nature of the cash flow of the business. For example, there could be a very low or no-rent period of three or four months because business activity is slow. The rent for the remaining months of the year would be high, to compensate for the period when the business was unable to pay rent.

Graduated Lease

A graduated lease requires an increase in rental payment every month for a specified period of time. This is usually done to assist a business in its first year of start-up, so that the monthly payments are related to the increase in cash flow and revenue of the business. At the end of the graduated period, the rental payments by the tenant would then be at a fixed rate, usually as in a net or triple net lease.

Percentage Lease

There are several types of percentage leases. In one type, the landlord obtains no minimum rent, but simply a percentage of the total monthly sales of the business. The landlord attempts to determine the tenant's potential revenue and bases the percentage on that amount. The percentage for rent could vary depending on the volume of sales. For example, it could be set at a higher percentage for a lower volume of sales, and at a lower percentage for a higher volume. The tenant would have to calculate whether or not the base percentage could be too difficult for the business to pay, assuming that the gross revenues are obtained.

The other variation is that the landlord calculates a minimum rent based on the tenant's potential revenues, but the rent paid is based on actual revenues. In other words, it is a percentage of the gross monthly revenue of the business. In this example, the landlord is able to budget on a minimum guaranteed rent until such time as the tenant pays a higher rent because the revenues justify it. In this type of lease, the landlord requires very tight accounting and reporting controls.

Another type of arrangement is for the percentage to be based on net profit. This type of arrangement has to be defined very carefully in the lease. The most common way is for the profit to be calculated before depreciation and/or interest and income taxes. There is usually a limit on the owner's salary; otherwise the owner could inflate the salary paid out as a management fee or to relatives in order to increase expenses so that there is no net profit. The landlord also frequently requires that the tenant spend a minimum amount of money on advertising so that sales and net profit are generated. Another provision frequently found is that the landlord requires a minimum amount spent for maintenance, so that the premises are kept in good repair and condition.

> The relationship with the landlord in a percentage lease is almost that of a partner, because the landlord has very tight controls on reporting and expenditure of monies by the business and the systems for keeping track of cash and giving out receipts.

The percentage lease is commonly used in the renting of retail stores in shopping centres. The landlord therefore obtains the same benefit that the tenant obtains in terms of the large traffic volume going through the shopping centre, which the landlord has established.

When dealing with shopping centre leases, be extremely careful that you obtain competent professional advice from your lawyer and accountant before committing yourself. The relationship with the landlord in a percentage lease is almost that of a partner, because the landlord has very tight controls on reporting and expenditure of monies by the business and the systems for keeping track of cash and giving out receipts. As the success of the tenant's business may only be partially due to the location, it would be prudent to try to negotiate a fixed maximum dollar amount that the landlord would be entitled to receive under the lease.

Legal Aspects of a Lease

The lease document is a contract and, like any other contract, it is legally binding and enforceable. The terms of the lease contract and all the rights that you and the landlord have under that contract will affect your business profit, your business survival and the ability to sell your business at some point in the future. For these reasons, it is important that you thoroughly search out the ideal location for your business, carefully review the terms of the lease, and then discuss the offer to lease or formal lease with your lawyer and accountant before signing any documents. Once you have committed yourself, it could be quite difficult — or even impossible — to get out of the lease without severe financial consequences and litigation. That is why you require professional assistance to help you in negotiating the terms of the lease customized to your specific needs.

As leases are prepared by lawyers for landlords, they tend to be one-sided. In other words, the lease requires commitments and obligations on the part of the tenant and restricts the tenant in many ways, but does not have the equivalent balance in terms of responsibility on the part of the landlord. For this reason, you need to have your lawyer protect your interests by attempting to renegotiate the terms of the lease to be more equitable and balanced, and in accordance with your budget and the degree of risk that you are prepared to accept.

> The terms of the lease contract and all the rights that you and the landlord have under that contract will affect your business profit, your business survival and the ability to sell your business at some point in the future.

Oral or Written

If you are intending to rent premises on a month-to-month basis, you may not need or be required to sign a lease. If you are operating a business with that degree of uncertainty in terms of your tenure at that location, you are probably not too concerned about your long-term rights or options at that location. Normally, on a month-to-month lease, either party can give the other party one month's notice to vacate. The goodwill component may be minimal if you were to sell your business, unless you had an attractive long-term lease in place.

The landlord may prefer to sign a month-to-month lease because the property is due to be torn down or construction work is to be done that limits the appropriateness of a long-term lease. To protect yourself fully, you should insist on a written lease. For the terms of the lease to be enforceable, it has to be in writing in most jurisdictions in Canada.

The landlord usually insists that a lease be in writing to fully protect the landlord's interests and to be sure of the duration of cash flow from the rental. The landlord's bank may require proof of lease documentation in order to finance the landlord. Any potential purchaser of the landlord's building and land will want to take a look at the nature and quality of the leases and tenants in determining the purchase price.

Offer to Lease

The first step to take when you are considering a space to lease is to present an offer to lease. Most landlords have property management agents, real estate agents or other sales personnel employed to solicit offers to lease. In other cases, you may be dealing directly with the landlord without an agent involved. When an agent is involved, there is generally a commission paid to the agent by the landlord, which can vary considerably. For example, the agent may receive 10% of the gross base rent in the first year of a three-year lease or 15% in the first year of a five-year lease or 10% on the first two years of a five-year lease. Keep in mind that the landlord's agent is acting for and on behalf of the interests of the landlord, and has an incentive to have you sign the offer to lease in terms of making a commission. The longer the lease term that you sign, the higher the commission that the agent receives. For example, if you are proposing a two-year lease with two renewable options of two years each for a total of a six-year lease, you might meet some resistance from the agent, who would otherwise try to encourage you to sign a flat five- or six-year lease because the commission would be higher.

Offer to lease forms vary considerably in format and content. Make sure that your offer to lease has escape clauses. These are conditions that have to be met to your satisfaction before you have a binding and acceptable offer.

Be certain that you have a copy of the formal lease to review before you submit your offer to lease. The formal lease document should be attached to your offer to lease as a schedule. Be wary of an offer to lease that states that a "standard lease document'" will be required to be signed without that document being given to you in advance. Leases vary widely in their content and terms, and very rarely are any two leases the same.

The offer to lease sets out the specific terms between the parties that are to be modified in the formal lease document: the length of the lease term, the rental terms, the use of the premises, the names of the parties, the description of the property involved, the frequency of rental payments, the renewal options if any, and any other special and unique terms or changes to the lease. Obviously your lawyer will need to review the formal lease in order to properly advise you and suggest modifications to be specified in the offer to lease. The offer to lease would include a reference to the formal lease and the modifications, including additions and deletions that have been noted on the lease document. Therefore, when the landlord is reviewing the offer to lease, the complete package is available for consideration. After it has been submitted, it may be difficult or impossible to negotiate further changes. If you find an alternate location that you prefer, or the terms of the other location are more favourable to you, it is important that your lawyer notify the agent immediately in writing that the offer has been withdrawn. This is assuming that it has not yet been accepted.

> Be wary of an offer to lease that states that a "standard lease document" will be required to be signed without that document being given to you in advance.

The offer to lease ideally should be in the name of a corporate entity rather than your personal name. If you have paid a low deposit at the time of the offer, it minimizes your financial risk if you need to get out of the contract. If you have included various subject conditions in the offer to lease that have to be met by the landlord or yourself, and the conditions are not met, then you get your deposit back. In this regard, you may put a provision in the offer to lease that if the offer is accepted, you will increase the deposit to the amount of the first and last month's rent, or other arrangements that you might negotiate. Ask for the deposit to be held in an account with interest accruing in your favour. The landlord may accept the offer as presented, or come back with a suggested compromise. You may prefer to have your lawyer or accountant act for you in negotiating the terms of the lease. Often business owners are unable to remain objective when they are caught up in the enthusiasm and excitement of making such a major business decision.

Be particularly cautious if you are making an offer to lease on a building that is currently under construction. It is common for delays to occur in construction, and even though the lease you may sign has a specific date for occupancy, there is always a provision in the lease that gives the landlord an out in terms of legal liability if delays occur. A description of clauses to consider in your offer and some helpful negotiation techniques and pitfalls to avoid are included, below.

REAL LIFE

If It Does Not Feel Right — Walk Away

Martine had made an offer to purchase Central Printers from its owner Felice. As the building in which the business was located was about to be demolished, Martine would have to find a suitable new location from which to operate the business. Because of the pending demolition and the need to relocate the business, Martine's lawyer had inserted a clause in the letter of intent to purchase the business that as a condition of completing the sale, Martine had to find a new location that was acceptable to her. As the majority of the business consisted of printing corporate brochures and annual reports for larger companies the premises did not need to be located in an area with high pedestrian traffic; however, it did need to be within a certain radius of the downtown core to remain in close proximity to the client base.

Martine saw a new building that was in her target area, so she contacted the landlord to see what kind of space was available. One of the street-level units was around 3,000 square feet, which was ideal for the business, so Martine made a written offer to lease the premises, subject to the satisfactory completion of the purchase of Central Printers. As part of her offer, Martine asked for the landlord to provide the equivalent of $10 per square foot ($30,000) as a tenant improvement allowance. The landlord made a counter-offer in which he deleted the tenant improvement allowance and included a requirement for Martine to personally guarantee the entire 5-year term of the lease. The landlord's position was that as this was an extremely nice building and he should have no problem leasing the space, he did not see the need to contribute towards the cost of leasehold improvements.

Martine discussed this with the landlord as she felt it was unreasonable for the landlord not to contribute to the cost of leasehold improvements and yet want the tenant to personally guarantee the entire term of the lease, which amounted to around $54,000. She explained that if for some reason the business failed and she was unable to pay the rent, the landlord would be able to take possession of the premises, have the benefit of around $30,000 in leasehold improvement and Martine would still be personally liable for the balance of the lease. Plus, if the landlord felt the building was so desirable, he should have no problem re-leasing the space if Martine was to default on the lease, especially with $30,000 of improvements that Martine had paid for.

Because Martine really liked this particular space she almost agreed to the landlord's terms, but at the last minute she decided to think about it overnight. Although Martine was disappointed, the following day she told the landlord that she would not be taking the space as she thought the landlord's demands were unreasonable. Martine continued her search and within a week found premises in the same general area with leasehold improvements already in place that were almost ideal for her business. The lease rate was comparable to the other building but she was not required to provide a personal guarantee.

Formal Lease

Once your offer to lease has been accepted, you now have to sign a formal lease. It is very rare to see any two leases that are exactly the same. Some leases are simple ones prepared by the landlord and may be only a few pages in length. For use as the formal lease, the landlord may purchase from a stationery supplier a commercial lease document that has approximately four to six pages. On the other hand, the landlord may have a lawyer prepare a document, which could be anywhere from 10 pages to 100 pages in length. Shopping centre leases and leases prepared by major Canadian real estate companies or national property management companies tend to be over 40 pages. Attached to the formal lease document would be various schedules, including a sketch or map of the exact location that is being leased, or construction plans if you are making changes to a location in the process of being built. There are other documents that might be attached to the lease, which set out the terms between the parties.

There are many different terms in a lease depending on the sophistication of the landlord and whether you are leasing from a shopping centre or not. A description of the key terms that might be found in a lease will be discussed in "Key Terms of a Lease," below.

Impact of Government Legislation

Even though you may have a written lease setting out the terms of your relationship, there is government legislation that affects a landlord-tenant relationship. You should be aware of the following legislation.

Municipal Legislation

Each community will have municipal legislation dealing with businesses in the form of bylaws that affect zoning requirements. These bylaws regulate the types of businesses that can be operated in various areas throughout the city. Health and safety regulations could have a bearing on the type of business that you intend to operate.

Provincial Legislation

The provinces may have different titles and content in the following legislation, but the underlying purpose is the same:

1. *Commercial Tenancy Act.* This legislation governs the relationship between the landlord and tenant, whether a lease is signed or not. Certain provisions of this Act can be waived in the lease, but the Act provides rights and remedies to both the landlord and tenant.

2. *Short Form of Leases Act.* Some leases that are very short (a few pages in length) refer to the fact that the lease is to be governed by the *Short Form of Leases Act.* This saves the landlord from drawing up a lengthy lease, because the essential terms of the landlord-tenant relationship would be governed by that Act.

3. *Rent Distress Act.* In the event that a tenant fails to pay the rent when it is due, the landlord is entitled to restrain — in other words, lock-up the premises — until such time as the rent arrears are paid. There are other protections for both the landlord and tenant, which are set out in the Act.

4. *Real Estate Act.* The *Real Estate Act* covers factors such as the registering of a lease by the tenant or landlord in the Land Titles Office or the equivalent, depending on the province.

Federal Legislation

The federal *Bankruptcy and Insolvency Act* sets out provisions when a landlord or tenant is petitioned into bankruptcy or voluntarily declares bankruptcy.

Key Terms of a Lease

There are many key terms or clauses in a lease that you should be aware of to avoid pitfalls in your negotiating. Not all are included, and the sequence may vary. Shopping centre leases or leases prepared by major property management companies tend to be very extensive, and have many more terms than outlined below.

Rent Clause

The rent clause may appear to be an obvious one but it has to be clear for your protection exactly how the rent is calculated and when it is due and payable. (See "Types of Leases," above.) You will need to know when the rent has to be paid. For example, if you are responsible for taxes and maintenance costs, are they payable once a year when the landlord calculates what their costs have been for that year, or does the landlord forecast operational expenses on a monthly basis and you have to make that payment every month? In this latter example, you could request that the landlord put those funds in a separate interest-bearing account. If there is a deficiency, you would have to pay the difference at that time; if there is an excess, it would either be returned to you or credited towards the running account for the next budget period.

There could also be provision for extra charges that the landlord would have the right to change arbitrarily every year. For example, in a shopping centre complex there could be a provision for an administrative and promotion fee that is paid to the landlord for administering and promoting the mall. A clause in the lease might say that the landlord is entitled to increase its administrative fees from time to time as the landlord so wishes. This would be an open-ended clause that could limit your ability to budget carefully in terms of trying to calculate the exact rent over the period of a year.

Commencement Date Clause

This is the date on which you would be responsible for commencing your rent payments. It may not necessarily be the same date that you take possession of the premises. In other words, the landlord may have allowed you a rent-free period.

If you are leasing premises that are being constructed, the occupancy date may not be specific or accurate because of possible delays in completing the premises. You could have expended a lot of money ordering inventory and equipment (for example, if you are opening a clothing store), to find that you have to wait three or six months longer before you can move in. The fine print of most leases states that if there is any delay in construction, the landlord is not responsible. There could be many reasons for the delay, for example, lack of proper financing, construction management problems, or simply unrealistic projections on the part of the landlord. You might be in a position, because of the terms of the lease, that you do not have any legal recourse against the landlord. Therefore, in terms of financial commitments that you make, be particularly cautious about relying on good faith that the landlord's proposed date of completion of the building and occupancy is accurate.

> If you ignore the use clause and offer a service or product that is not included, then you could be deemed to be in breach of the lease.

Use Clause

This is the provision in the lease that sets out exactly what your business intends to use the premises for. It is to your advantage to have the use description as broad as possible, in case you may want to expand the range of products or services that you offer through your business. A too-restrictive use clause could limit your profits and impair your business survival. Once the use clause has been agreed on, the landlord may not be prepared to modify that provision at some later point. If you ignore the use clause and offer a service or product that is not included, then you could be deemed to be in breach of the lease. Depending on the terms of the lease, there could be resultant legal and financial problems.

Non-Competition Clause

The non-competition clause is inserted in the lease to protect the lessee from a competitor coming into the premises and causing the lessee's business to suffer. For example, a dentist might want to have a clause in the lease stating that no other dentist could rent office space in the building during the term of the lease. If your jewellery store had a non-competition clause, and a gift store in the building started to sell jewellery to compete with you, you could ask the landlord to invoke the non-competition clause. On the other hand, if the gift store's use was very broad, the gift store could argue that there was no restriction in its lease in the type of product that it sold as far as jewellery was concerned. You can see why the use clause issue and the non-competition clause are interrelated and very important.

Demolition/Construction Clause

There could be a clause in the lease that allows the landlord to give short-term notice (for example, six months) to the tenant to leave the premises. This could happen even if you have a 10-year lease. The landlord could arbitrarily give this notice if there is a clause allowing it to do so to demolish the building or make substantial structural changes. Be extremely cautious in signing any lease that has such a clause; in effect, you just have a short-term lease. You would have great difficulty selling your business to any other buyer because of the high risk. What buyer would be prepared to pay for leasehold improvements or goodwill that had been developed over many years if the lease could be terminated within six months? In practical terms, the landlord may never invoke the demolition/construction clause but the risk is always there for any potential buyer.

Acceleration Clause

The landlord may have a provision in the lease that in the event of your default on the terms of the lease, the full face amount of the lease could be accelerated and you could be sued for that amount. In other words, if you had a five-year lease at $1,000 per month, the face amount of the lease would be $60,000 over the term. If you are one year into the lease and breach the lease, the landlord could attempt to sue you for $48,000 with an acceleration clause. In reality, though, the landlord would have an obligation in law to minimize its losses by immediately attempting to re-rent the premises if you have breached the lease and departed.

Default Clause

There are many provisions throughout the lease that set out the basis on which the landlord can deem you to be in default. One obvious ground for default would be failure on your part to pay rent. There could be other grounds: using the premises outside the terms of the lease, going into bankruptcy, failing to have the required insurance on the premises, failure to keep your business open during the hours required by the shopping mall, failing to maintain your premises, subletting without permission, among others.

If default occurs, generally there is a time period within which you have to remedy the default after you have been given notice (for example, three days or one week or one month). If you fail to remedy the default within the time required, other legal and financial actions could occur, including eviction from the premises.

Penalty Clause

The penalty clause provision may or may not be in the lease. It generally sets out that if you are in default of any of the terms of the lease, a three-month penalty is imposed on you in addition to the other rights and remedies that the landlord may have against you. If you are paying $1,000 per month, then you would have to pay a three-month penalty of $3,000. This is built in as an incentive for the tenant not to breach the terms of the lease. A penalty clause can be broad in terms of what constitutes a penalty, or limited to the terms specified.

Entry Clause

The entry clause provision sets out the basis on which the landlord can enter your premises. Obviously, the landlord can enter in situations such as fire, leaking water pipes causing damage, and other reasons relating to safety and limiting damages, but there are other instances where the landlord may enter. The subject of entry is a key one in terms of the legal rights of the tenant. For example, if the tenant had paid rent until the end of January but moved out on January 20, and the landlord entered the premises to show the premises to a prospective tenant on January 25, the tenant could claim that the landlord had terminated the lease. If there were four years left on the lease, this could be a substantial loss to the landlord if the space remained vacant for the next four years. This example shows why the landlord would want to make sure that the entry clause in the lease allows the landlord to enter in certain circumstances without limiting the landlord's future legal options against the tenant.

Assignment Clause

The assignment clause is normally combined with the subletting clause. It may state that the tenant is unable to assign the lease under any circumstances, or that an assignment may be acceptable with the prior written consent of the landlord, such consent not to be unreasonably withheld. In this example, the landlord has the right to investigate the creditworthiness of any prospective assignee. If the landlord believes that the assignee is not a good risk, the landlord can refuse to approve the assignment. In that event, the tenant would have to find a new purchaser of the business, continue operating, or breach the contract and leave the premises.

Another type of assignment clause to be wary of is one that states that if the tenant requests the landlord to assign (or sublet) the premises, the landlord has the right to immediately, or 30 days thereafter, deem the lease to be terminated. The reason that a landlord may want to insert this provision is to give the landlord the option, if rental rates have increased since the commencement of the lease, to attempt to renegotiate the terms of the lease. For example, assume that the tenant is two years into a five-year lease and paying $10 per square foot. The prevailing rate due to market demand in the area is now $20 per square foot in the premises. The tenant could sell the business at a very attractive profit because of the immense savings to the prospective buyer in terms of rental. On the other hand, the landlord may not be prepared to accept the assignment and could immediately declare the lease to be at an end unless the prevailing rate of $20 per square foot was renegotiated into the lease. Naturally, this would have a serious effect on the ability of the tenant to sell the business at all, or at the price for which the tenant was hoping.

Subletting Clause

The subletting clause relates to the tenant subletting a portion of the space to a third party. There could be an economic downturn or other circumstances that require the tenant to save on overhead and expenses. One way to do this would be to rent part of the leased space to another business to reduce expenses and increase cash flow. The normal provision in the lease is that the landlord would permit subletting but only with the prior written consent of the landlord. This enables the landlord to do a check of the prospective subtenant in terms of the type of business that it intends to operate. It is possible that the subtenant might be contravening various non-competition clauses in the master lease between the landlord and other tenants. The sublease clause may be an important one to consider in relation to a potential purchaser of the business, or for the survival of the business if downsizing is required at some future point.

> It is normally a stipulation in the lease that the landlord obtains proof of insurance coverage and proof that the premium has been paid.

Improvement/Fixture Clause

The improvement/fixture clause sets out the provision that all improvements and fixtures on the premises shall be deemed to belong to the landlord. Upon installation, they immediately become part of the building, and cannot be removed without the landlord's prior written consent. Depending on the type of business that you have, you could be putting in expensive fixtures and improvements that you would like to take away with you at the end of the lease term. If this is the situation, you should negotiate very toughly at the outset on this point and specify the exact fixtures and improvements that you want to take away at the end of the lease.

The landlord may be concerned about damages that could occur to the premises if a tenant tries to remove improvements and fixtures. The landlord may therefore require a provision in the lease that any structural or cosmetic damage that may occur to the premises as a consequence of your removal of the specified fixtures or improvements shall be repaired at your cost. On balance, you may feel that this is a fair stipulation.

Utilities

The utility provision sets out the expenses for which the tenant is responsible, such as electricity, water, telephone, sewage, garbage removal or any other matters under these categories. The tenant may be responsible to pay a portion of the cost or all of the cost, depending on the circumstances. You should find out from the landlord what the average rates would be, and then modify those rates based on your anticipated utilities usage.

Insurance

Most leases have a clause stating that the tenant is responsible for maintaining various types of insurance and the specified minimum amount of coverage for each of those types of insurance. For example, there could be a requirement for a minimum $1,000,000 general liability coverage. It is normally a stipulation in the lease that the landlord obtains proof of insurance coverage and proof that the premium has been paid.

Maintenance and Repairs

In some leases, the landlord is responsible for all maintenance and repairs to do with the building and surrounding area such as parking and landscaping. In other leases, the landlord wants to pass on to the tenants virtually all the maintenance and repair costs. This is usually done on a percentage basis, proportional to the amount of square footage that the tenant occupies.

If the tenant is responsible for these extra costs, it is important that the tenant have an estimate of the past costs and projected costs over the next number of years. For example, perhaps the landlord needs to completely re-roof all the premises or repair the parking lot because of numerous potholes, or completely repaint the premises inside and outside. You might feel it is unfair for the landlord to pass on to the tenant all these costs that should otherwise be borne by the landlord. The time to negotiate the maintenance and repair costs to your liking is at the very outset, before anything is signed.

Security Deposit

Depending on the length of the lease, the landlord may ask for the last one, two, or three months' rent as a security deposit for any damage caused by the tenant. When an offer to lease is made, it is also common to have the landlord request the first month's rent, although technically that is not a security deposit.

Make sure that you try to negotiate with the landlord a provision in the contract that interest is to run to the favour of the tenant for the security deposit monies. If your rent was $2,500 per month and you paid two months' rent as security deposit, that is $5,000. If the lease is a five-year term and you negotiated a flat rate of 10% per year on the security deposit, you would have an additional $2,500 to your credit by the end of the lease term. If you negotiated that the security deposit monies bear interest at the bank prime rate, which is variable, then you could take advantage of the changing rate of interest. You could also attempt to negotiate with the landlord that the security deposit monies bear interest at the bank prime rate and that interest be compounded. This would earn you even more money by the end of the term of the lease. Many tenants overlook the interest provision on their deposit money.

> The time to negotiate the maintenance and repair costs to your liking is at the very outset, before anything is signed.

Guarantees

If the lease is in the name of a proprietorship or a partnership, the owners are automatically personally liable for the full amount of debts or liabilities of that partnership, including any liabilities due to a breach of the lease. For this reason, many people incorporate a company before signing a lease with the landlord. The landlord may request a personal guarantee or a guarantee from another company of a corporate lease. However, you should always try to negotiate out of the guarantee provision. Some suggestions for doing this are covered in the "Minimizing Personal and Business Risk" section.

Promotion and Administrative Cost Clause

In shopping malls, it is common to have a provision that the tenant pays a portion of the landlord's administrative and promotional costs. The tenant should be aware of what these costs have been in the past and what they might be in the future by speaking with the landlord and other tenants. It could turn out that the extra costs incurred would be greater than the amount that the tenant was budgeting for and therefore the location would not be a viable one. It could also turn out that the amount that the landlord wants is unfair in relative terms compared to other shopping-centre landlords.

Renewal Clause

You may want to negotiate an option to renew the lease for a further term or terms upon the expiry of the present lease. Some option-to-renew provisions include: fixing a ceiling on the amount of the rent increase if the option were renewed, having the rent increase based on a cost-of-living index or having the rent increase negotiated between the parties and if an agreement cannot be reached, then an arbitrator under a provincial arbitration statute could be utilized to make a decision.

Holdover Clause

There should be a clause in the lease that gives the terms if the tenant stays on the premises beyond the termination date of the lease. Normally it states that the tenant shall remain on a month-to-month basis after the lease has terminated and on the same rental terms. On a month-to-month lease, either the landlord or tenant can give each other one month's notice.

Option to Purchase

If the tenant wishes at some point to purchase the premises, then this provision should be negotiated at the outset and clearly stated in the lease. Do not rely on the landlord's oral promise that you would have an option on the property and the terms of that option. The purchase price should be specified, or a formula for calculating the purchase price, and a stipulated period of time during which the option will be held open. This clause also protects the tenant from someone else buying the property for the duration of the option period. The landlord may require an additional payment for this option, which could be a flat sum payment at the outset of the lease, or a nominal amount paid every month over the term of the lease. The extra charge may or may not be applied against the eventual property purchase. The tenant may also negotiate a provision that allows the option of applying a percentage of the monthly rent payments towards the down payment or purchase price of the property if the tenant elects to exercise the option.

Minimizing Personal and Business Risk

There is always a potentially high degree of personal and business risk in signing a lease. The location may turn out to be a poor one; competition may start to affect the business; or health, marital, or partnership problems may impair the business operation. For these reasons and many more, it is vital that precautions be built into the lease to minimize risk as much as possible.

Many small business owners are not aware of the wide range of protections that can be negotiated into a lease. Here are some common, effective techniques to discuss with your lawyer when negotiating the offer to lease.

Incorporate

It is wise to incorporate in any business situation that involves high risk. A long-term lease obviously involves potential risk. Statistically, approximately 75% of small businesses fail within three years of start-up. For these reasons, incorporating a company and signing the lease under the corporate name would be a prudent consideration.

Penalty Clause

You may wish to negotiate a three-month penalty as the total amount of damages that the landlord would expect from the tenant in the event that the lease is breached. The landlord may require that the three-month penalty be paid in advance and represent the last three months of the term of the lease or the penalty, whichever comes first. Again, make sure that you ask that the funds go into an interest-bearing account with compound interest to the favour of the tenant.

The tenant could budget as part of the start-up costs the downside risk as being three months' rent and have that money put aside by giving it to the landlord under the terms of the lease. In this example, no other security would be given to the landlord and the landlord would have no further recourse against the tenant if the tenant left before the term of the lease.

Alternatively, it may be negotiated that in the event the tenant breached the terms of the lease, the tenant would pay a penalty of three months' rent, and the penalty would represent the full amount that the tenant would be responsible for. No penalty deposit would be paid in advance.

Another form of penalty provision could be that the amount of the penalty be decreased based on the length of time that the tenant remained in the premises under the terms of the lease. For example, in a five-year lease, the clause might state that if the lease is terminated with four or more years left on it, there would be a five-month penalty; with three to four years left in the lease, it would be a four-month penalty; with two to three years, a three-month penalty; with one to two years, a two-month penalty; and with under one year left on the lease, it would be a one-month penalty.

> Many small business owners are not aware of the wide range of protections that can be negotiated into a lease.

Short-term Lease with Options to Renew

To minimize the risk associated with signing a long-term lease, you may instead decide to have the initial lease period relatively short. By the end of the short-term lease, you would be in a better position to decide whether it is viable to remain in the leased premises for a longer period of time. For example, rather than signing a five-year lease, it might be prudent to negotiate a one-year lease with two renewable two-year options. If you wanted a seven-year lease, you might negotiate a two-year lease with two renewable options for two years and three years.

This type of structure would enable you to stay for the full period of time if desired, but with limited time interval commitments. A provision could be negotiated that there would be no increase in rent at the time of the first option, but that there could be an increase in rent at the time of the second option if the landlord so elects. The clause would then set out the amount of the increase, or a formula under which it would be calculated, if any rent increase were to occur.

No Personal Guarantee

For a corporate lease, it is not uncommon for a landlord to request a personal guarantee or guarantees by the directors. While approximately 50% of landlords might request a personal guarantee, the majority of those could be persuaded to waive this request through effective negotiating techniques. The most direct approach is to state that unless the personal guarantee provision is removed, other premises will be leased elsewhere that do not require a personal guarantee.

Another approach is to limit the extent of the personal guarantees. You may negotiate a provision that the personal guarantee automatically expires at the end of the first year of the lease. This clause could state that in the event that the tenant terminates the lease before the end of the year, the personal guarantor shall be responsible for the balance of the first year's rent. From the perspective of the landlord, the first year is probably the highest risk with a new tenant. The landlord would be protected in that the tenant would remain or be responsible for at least one year's rent.

If a personal guarantee is given, it could be on condition that the guarantee be limited to a fixed amount, such as a maximum of three months' rent. Whenever a lease is terminated, landlords are required in law to exert their best efforts to locate another tenant. If a landlord is unable to re-rent the premises immediately, the personal guarantor would only have to pay up to but not more than three months' rent.

If your attempts to avoid giving a personal guarantee have been unsuccessful, your next step would be to minimize the overall risk and exposure. Wherever possible, do not agree to provide more than one guarantor. In the case of default, the landlord would be entitled to sue both you and the second guarantor for the full amount outstanding on the lease.

Free or Reduced Rent

Often a landlord is willing to offer a free-rent period or reduced rental payments as an incentive to rent the premises. This is often the case when the space has been vacant for some time. Try to structure the rent payments in the first year to limit the financial outlay as much as possible. Following are some suggestions.

1. Request graduated or reduced rental payments. Have the rental payments start at a low rate and to graduate up to the higher amount every month over a period of the first

year or two. The aggregate amount may be less than the normal annual aggregate rent for the subsequent years of the lease.

2. Negotiate from one to six months' free rent. The amount of free rent will depend on the length of the lease, the improvements the tenant is paying for, the type of business (if it enhances the image of the building) and other factors. Although the landlord may not agree to have the first six months rent free, the landlord may agree to six months' free rent staggered throughout the term of the lease, for example, the sixth, twelfth and eighteenth month.

3. Try to have the landlord pay for all the costs of renovations up to an agreed maximum. It depends on the circumstances as to how much the landlord would be prepared to pay. For example, the landlord might be desperate to have a good tenant in the building, to draw in other prospective tenants as well as customers. The tenant might agree to a 10-year lease on the basis that the landlord pays $50,000 for improvements. Everything depends on the circumstances and your negotiating leverage.

4. Request that the first year of maintenance charges be waived. In the case of a triple net lease, the operating expenses over and above the base rent could be considerable. In this example, request that the first year is a net lease with a flat rate, with the triple net lease feature commencing in the second year. There would be no carrying forward of the triple net extras from the first year to subsequent years.

Construction Allowances

If you are going into premises that are being newly constructed, provisions may be negotiated with the landlord to save you renovation expenses. The provision may state that the landlord would pay to have all the leasehold improvements done that you require, as a condition of signing the lease. It would be less expensive for the landlord to pay for such costs if the improvements were being done at the same time that the landlord is paying for the overall construction of the building.

Lease Assignment

You should be careful to remove your personal liability and risk before selling your business and assigning the lease to a buyer. Otherwise, in the event that the buyer defaults on the terms of the lease, the landlord has the right to sue not only the buyer as the assignee, but also your company as the assignor. Ask the landlord to remove your personal guarantee — assuming you gave one — at the time that the lease is assigned. Be certain this agreement is in writing and signed by the landlord. The landlord can obtain personal guarantees from the buyer of the business if desired.

If the landlord will not release your company from the lease, then incorporate a new company for any future business purposes, and transfer any assets to the new company. If the landlord refuses to release the personal guarantee on your original lease, and therefore you have ongoing potential exposure if the new buyer defaults on the lease, then arrange with the buyer to negotiate a completely new lease with the landlord. This may involve the buyer having to pay more rent and you may have to reduce the purchase price accordingly. The key point is to have your personal name released from any future liability exposure.

Negotiating a Lease

In most situations, the tenant does not negotiate directly with the landlord. Normally the landlord hires staff or a sales agent in the form of a realtor or property management company to advertise and negotiate the rental of the business premises. Landlords and sales agents tend to be sophisticated in terms of the negotiating process and effective sales techniques. Therefore, the small business owner is often at a disadvantage in terms of this type of business experience.

> Landlords and sales agents tend to be sophisticated in terms of the negotiating process and effective sales techniques.

When you are negotiating a lease, there are various strategies and tactics that you should consider. As in any negotiation, it is important to understand the needs of the other side. The sales agent's motivations include earning a commission and satisfying the landlord so that ongoing business can be obtained. As the sales agent is acting for and on behalf of the landlord, it is therefore prudent not to disclose to the sales agent any information that could impair your negotiating position. Being overly enthusiastic about the location may reduce your negotiating stance. In other words, try to keep the sales agent guessing as to whether or not you are planning to select that location.

In the case of a landlord, there are several needs the landlord could have that would provide incentive for a deal to be made along the lines that you are proposing. Some of these needs may include the following:

1. **The landlord wants occupancy to attract new tenants.** The more tenants in the building, the easier it will be for the landlord to attract other tenants into the building. It implies stability and traffic flow, and these are important factors to any tenant as well as to the landlord. If a location is newly opened or soon to be opened, you should have better negotiating leverage in terms of being one of the first tenants to sign up for the building.

2. **The landlord needs cash flow to debt service the bank loan.** A landlord has to account to the bank in terms of generating the cash flow to pay the mortgage. The more vacant space in the premises, the less cash flow and therefore the more pressure the landlord is under from the bank. The landlord may be motivated to rent the space and therefore may be more flexible in negotiating the lease. It may take the immediate cash flow pressure off the landlord, even though there is a risk that the tenant may not be around a year later.

3. **Full occupancy enhances the selling price of the building.** If the landlord intends to sell the building, a prospective buyer would find it far more attractive and the selling price would be accordingly higher if the tenancy of the building was at full

occupancy. In other words, there is a direct financial benefit to the landlord to be flexible in negotiations with the prospective tenant if it helps fill up the building.

4. **Bank financing more accessible.** If the landlord wishes to borrow money on the building to invest in other buildings or for other business reasons, the bank will lend money to the landlord based on the amount of cash flow being generated by the tenants in the building. Therefore, this may provide incentive for flexibility on the landlord's part.

5. **Competition.** In order to maintain maximum occupancy and remain competitive in lease costs, a landlord has to be flexible in negotiating leases.

When negotiating it is helpful to understand the context in which the landlord is operating. In many situations you are doing the landlord a favour by becoming a tenant, not the other way around. Adopting this viewpoint in negotiations will help you to balance an otherwise one-sided lease arrangement.

Steps in Negotiating a Lease

- Thoroughly understand leasing terms and concepts. Speak to your accountant and lawyer for clarification of your questions or concerns.
- Determine your overall criteria regarding the ideal location, the amount of money you are prepared to spend and other factors.
- Thoroughly research potential locations and short-list them to three locations, if at all possible. Any one of these locations should be acceptable to you. Prepare a list of your questions and concerns that are to be answered by the landlord or the landlord's representative.
- Obtain all documents required to assess the three locations. This includes a copy of the lease, building plans if the building is being constructed and other information that your lawyer or accountant may request of you.
- Review the documentation yourself and determine your priority in terms of your preference of location.
- Set up a meeting with your lawyer and accountant and discuss the prospective premises.
- Decide on your negotiating position regarding terms after your consultation with your professional advisors.
- Decide whether you are going to do the negotiating or have your lawyer do the negotiating on your behalf. If it appears tactically advantageous for you to do the negotiating, then make sure your game plan is well-thought-out in advance. If you involve your lawyer, it is common for the other side to involve its lawyer in the negotiating stage, especially in the case of negotiating legal terms in the agreement.
- Submit your offer to lease in detail with the formal lease attached, with any suggested modifications.
- Advise the agent that you are seriously considering other premises and if they are not serious about agreeing with your terms, then you will have no alternative but to take

your business elsewhere. If you say this, make sure that you mean it, and would be prepared, if necessary, to walk away from the deal.

- Put pressure on the agent and the landlord in terms of placing a deadline on accepting the offer to lease. The deadline could be two or three days, or longer, depending on the circumstances. A major Canadian property management company or landlord may require the documents to be approved at head office and this could take a longer period of time. In general, the offer should not be open for any longer than a week, the shorter the better. Placing a deadline implies to the landlord that you are serious about going elsewhere if agreement cannot be reached.

- If the landlord does not accept the offer, or if a counter-offer is made to you and you are not in agreement with it, then try the next location on your priority list. This approach will eventually get you the location and lease terms that you want. Do not hesitate to use your accountant and lawyer to assist with lease negotiations. This money will be well-spent, and you will have peace of mind knowing that your decision is based on expert advice.

> Do not hesitate to use your accountant and lawyer to assist with lease negotiations. This money will be well-spent, and you will have peace of mind knowing that your decision is based on expert advice.

The location of your business is critical to its success. There are many different types of locations. Some may be suitable for a viable business and some may not. Other considerations are the quality of the building and the nature of the relationship with the landlord. The terms of your lease and how effectively you negotiate it will make a big difference in your future profit picture. You also need flexible options if the location does not work out for you, you do not need the space, or if you have health or partnership problems and want to get out of the lease. There are various types of leases to consider. Obtain an experienced business lawyer to assist you in negotiations and in checking all the terms of the lease. This is money well-spent for peace of mind.

(14)

CLOSING THE SALE

Drafting the Purchase and Sale Agreement

After all the conditions contained in the letter of intent have been satisfied and signed off on, the next step is to have your lawyer prepare the first draft of the purchase and sale agreement. A sample asset purchase agreement is provided in Appendix 14.1. Customarily, the buyer has the right to control the drafting of the closing documents. It is short-sighted for the buyer to have the seller's lawyer draft the agreement in order for the buyer to save on legal fees. It is typical for the first draft to reflect the needs and concerns of the party whose lawyers produce the draft. Although this bias is natural, every effort should be made to keep the first draft as fair as possible to both sides. This will help keep the negotiation process shorter and less expensive. If the draft is too one-sided it can also destroy any trust and rapport that has been developed between the buyer and seller, and the deal could be jeopardized.

The purchase and sale agreement is probably one of the most important legal documents you will ever sign. A carefully constructed agreement can be your best insurance policy for preventing any future problems. Obviously, there is no such thing as a standard agreement as each situation is different and the agreement will have its own set of considerations. The agreement will also look different, depending on whether you are buying the shares or assets of the business. The agreement is likely to be a lengthy, complicated document, plus there will be a number of other documents that will be attached as schedules to the agreement. You should review the agreement carefully with your lawyer to ensure that you fully understand the implications of whatever is included in the agreement.

> If the draft is too one-sided it can also destroy any trust and rapport that has been developed between the buyer and seller, and the deal could be jeopardized.

You will have to live with the consequences once the agreement has been executed. Do not be rushed or pressured when it comes time to execute the agreement. Take all the time you need to read everything thoroughly and question anything you do not understand before you put your signature on the dotted line.

Take all the time you need to read everything thoroughly and question anything you do not understand before you put your signature on the dotted line.

Structure of the Purchase and Sale Agreement

Whether they relate to the purchase and sale of assets or shares, the agreements are structurally very similar. The conceptual difference is that a purchase of shares is considered an acquisition of the target company "warts and all." In other words, the buyer, while entitled to all of the company's benefits, is also subject to all of its liabilities, whether existing, conditional, disclosed or undisclosed. In an asset purchase situation, the buyer is only subject to those liabilities that in some way are attached to the assets being acquired.

Typically, purchase and sale agreements cover the following topics:

1. **Identification of the buyer and seller.**
2. **Purchase and sale.** This section sets out all the assets included in the sale, for example, premises, inventories, equipment, furniture, prepaid expenses, customer lists, cash, accounts receivable, business records, intellectual property, licence rights and supply contracts. It also lists any items that are excluded from the sale (for example, cash and bank balances, and income tax refunds), liabilities the buyer will assume and those liabilities the seller will retain.
3. **Purchase price and terms of payment.** This section states the purchase price and terms of payment, how the balance of the purchase price is to be paid (for example, bank draft or certified cheque) and the allocation of the purchase price. The agreement may also have provisions for a holdback to be applied against any claims based on any breach of the vendor's representations and warranties and if so, it will require a certain amount of money to be paid into trust and held on the terms and subject to the conditions of an escrow agreement. It also describes any other financing arrangements such as vendor financing. If the seller is providing some of the financing, there will be other documents to sign such as a promissory note. A sample promissory note is included at Appendix 14.2.

   If a business is sold by way of an asset sale, rather than a share sale, the assets sold are subject to GST, which should be added to the purchase price. This can be avoided if both the seller and buyer of the business are GST registrants and file certain documentation at the time of the sale, which has the net effect of waiving the requirement of both charging and remitting GST in the course of the sale of a business. It is essential, however, that both buyer and seller be registered with the GST program and that the documents be filed in order to take advantage of this exception. If, on the other hand, the business sale takes place by way of a sale of corporate shares, as opposed to assets, no GST is payable on account of the price of the shares.
4. **Vendor's representations and warranties.** In this section, the seller confirms that the information provided to the buyer with respect to the material information about the business is true and accurate (for example, licences, regulatory approvals, financial records, tax matters and environmental issues). If problems are discovered with any of

the vendor's representations during the due diligence process they should be addressed candidly and completely prior to execution of the agreement. This is a very important section as the content of the vendor's representations affects the price that the buyer is willing to pay for the business.

5. **Purchaser's representations and warranties.** These claims assure the vendor of the purchaser's ability to complete the transaction.

6. **Vendor's covenants.** This defines the obligations of vendors with respect to their conduct during the period between the signing and the closing (for example, the vendor must conduct business in the normal manner). There could be several days, weeks or even months between signing the documents and actually closing the deal and taking over the business. Consequently, it is important that the agreement contains specific provisions regarding such matters as prices, inventory levels and employees. This section will also include the requirement for the vendor to execute a non-competition agreement in a form that is attached to the agreement.

7. **Purchaser's covenants.** This section typically includes a requirement for the buyer to maintain confidentiality prior to closing and to offer employment to current employees of the business.

8. **Vendor's conditions of closing.** This section lists issues that must be completed by the purchaser prior to closing. The breach or non-fulfillment of a condition by one party will give the other party the unilateral right to terminate the transaction without necessarily releasing the first party from liability for breach of contract or even misrepresentation.

9. **Purchaser's conditions of closing.** This section lists issues that must be completed by the vendor prior to closing.

10. **Indemnification by the vendor.** The indemnity consists of essentially two parts — an indemnity for damages suffered by the buyer (supplementary indemnity) and an indemnity against liabilities incurred by the purchaser to third parties (third party indemnity) arising out of circumstances set out in this section relating to items that may be discovered after the closing.

11. **Closing arrangements.** Date, time, location and documentation to be delivered.

12. **General provisions.**

13. **Schedules to the agreement.** There are a number of schedules attached to the agreement that are incorporated into the agreement by reference. These schedules may include financial statements, employee agreements, material contracts, licence rights, lists of machinery, equipment and furniture, and lease agreements.

The Closing

Once both parties have agreed on the language of the purchase agreement, both parties will sign it. The agreement will state the date at which the final transfer of ownership and possession of the business will occur, and when the seller will receive his or her funds. The closing is the point in time at which all the parties sign all necessary documents.

Once an agreement is made with the vendor, the next step is to prepare and sign all the necessary documentation to protect your interests. This would include the purchase and sale agreement. This document is prepared by your lawyer to protect your interests. It is common for the purchaser's lawyer to negotiate with the vendor's lawyer. Once all the legal paperwork is done, the closing occurs, money changes hands and you are the proud owner of your new business.

Appendix 14.1
Sample Asset Purchase Agreement

THIS AGREEMENT made the 26th day of June 2002

BETWEEN: XYZ Inc., a corporation incorporated
under the laws of the Province of British Columbia,

(the "Purchaser")

AND: ABBCC Inc., a corporation incorporated
under the laws of the Province of British Columbia

(the "Vendor")

1. SUBJECT MATTER

1.01 The Purchaser agrees to buy and the Vendor agrees to sell to the Purchaser as a going concern all the undertaking and assets owned by the Vendor in connection with the printing business carried on as Quick Printers at 95 Toronto St., Richmond, British Columbia ("the business") including, without limiting the generality of the foregoing:

(a) the furniture, fixtures and equipment more particularly described in Schedule A (the "equipment");

(b) all saleable stock in trade ("the stock in trade");

(c) all useable parts and supplies ("the parts and supplies");

(d) all leasehold interest in the lease held by the Vendor from WWW Holdings Inc. ("the lease");

(e) the goodwill of the business together with the exclusive right to the Purchaser to represent itself as carrying on business in succession to the Vendor and to use the business style of the business and variations in the business to be carried on by the Purchaser ("the goodwill").

The following assets are expressly excluded from the purchase and sale:

(a) cash on hand or on deposit, and

(b) accounts receivable.

2. PURCHASE PRICE

2.01 The purchase price payable for the undertaking and assets agreed to be bought and sold is the total of the amounts computed and allocated as follows:

(a) for the equipment — $200,000;

(b) for the stock in trade, its direct cost to the Vendor;

(c) for the parts and supplies, their direct cost to the Vendor;

(d) for the goodwill — $50,000;

(e) for all other assets agreed to be bought and sold — $1.00.

2.02 The purchase price for the stock in trade shall be established by an inventory taken and valued after close of business on the day before the day of closing. The Vendor shall produce evidence satisfactory to the Purchaser of the direct cost to the Vendor of items included in stock in trade. The Purchaser may exclude from the purchase and sale any items, which the Purchaser reasonably considers unsaleable by reason of defect in quality or in respect of which the Purchaser is not reasonably satisfied as to proof of direct cost.

2.03 The purchase price for the parts and supplies shall be established by an inventory taken and valued after close of business on the day before the day of closing. The Vendor shall produce evidence satisfactory to the Purchaser of the direct cost to the Vendor of items included in the parts and supplies. The Purchaser may exclude from the purchase and sale any items, which the Purchaser reasonably considers unuseable or in respect of which the Purchaser is not reasonably satisfied as to proof of direct cost.

3. TERMS OF PAYMENT

3.01 The Vendor acknowledges receiving a cheque for $10,000 from the Purchaser on execution of this agreement to be held as a deposit by the Vendor on account of the purchase price of the undertaking and assets agreed to be bought and sold and as security for the Purchaser's due performance of this agreement.

3.02 The balance of the purchase price for the undertaking and assets agreed to be bought and sold shall be paid, subject to adjustments, by certified cheque on closing.

3.03 The balance of the purchase price due on closing shall be specially adjusted for all prepaid and assumed operating expenses of the business including but not limited to rent and utilities.

4. CONDITIONS, REPRESENTATIONS AND WARRANTIES

4.01 In addition to anything else in this agreement, the following are conditions of completing this agreement in favour of the Purchaser:

(a) that the Purchaser obtain financing on terms satisfactory to it to complete the purchase;

(b) that the carrying on of the business at its present location is not prohibited by land use restrictions;

(c) that the lessor of the lease consents to its assignment to the Purchaser;

(d) that the Purchaser obtain all the permits and licences required for it to carry on the business;

(e) that the Vendor supply or deliver on closing all of the closing documents.

4.02 The following representations and warranties are made and given by the Vendor to the Purchaser and expressly survive the closing of this agreement. The representations are true as of the date of this agreement and will be true as of the date of closing when they shall continue as warranties according to their terms. At the option of the Purchaser, the representations and warranties may be treated as conditions of the closing of this agreement in favour of the Purchaser. However, the closing of this agreement shall not operate as a waiver or otherwise result in a merger to deprive the Purchaser of the right to sue the Vendor for breach of warranty in respect of any matter warranted, whether or not ascertained by the Purchaser prior to closing:

(a) the Vendor is a resident of Canada within the meaning of the Income Tax Act of Canada;

(b) the Vendor owns and has the right to sell the items listed in Schedule A;

(c) the assets agreed to be bought and sold are sold free and clear of all liens, encumbrances and charges;

(d) the equipment is in good operating condition;

(e) the undertaking and assets agreed to be bought and sold will not be adversely affected in any material respect in any way, whether by the Vendor or by any other person or cause whatsoever, up to closing and the Vendor will carry on business as usual until closing and not do anything before or after closing to prejudice the goodwill;

(f) the financial statements for the business produced by the Vendor and appended as Schedule B are fair and accurate, and prepared in accordance with generally accepted accounting principles.

(g) the lease is in good standing and the Vendor has fulfilled all of its obligations under the lease;

(h) the Vendor has made full and fair disclosure in all material respects of any matter that could reasonably be expected to affect the Purchaser's decision to purchase the undertaking and assets agreed to be bought and sold on the terms set out in this agreement;

(i) the Vendor will execute such assignments, consents, clearances or assurances after closing, prepared at the Purchaser's expense, as the Purchaser considers necessary or desirable to assure the Purchaser of the proper and effective completion of this agreement.

5. RISK

5.01 The risk of loss or damage to the undertaking and assets agreed to be bought and sold remains with the Vendor until closing.

5.02 In the event of loss or damage to the tangible assets agreed to be bought and sold prior to closing, at the option of the Purchaser, the replacement cost of the assets lost or damaged or any of them may be deducted from the total purchase price otherwise payable by the Purchaser under this agreement and the corresponding lost or damaged assets shall be excluded from the purchase and sale.

6. SALES TAXES

6.01 The Purchaser shall pay any and all sales taxes payable in respect of the purchase and sale of assets pursuant to this agreement.

6.02 The Vendor shall pay all sales taxes payable or collectible in connection with carrying on the business up to closing and obtain and supply the Purchaser with satisfactory proof of payment within a reasonable time of closing.

7. NON-COMPETITION

7.01 The Vendor covenants with the Purchaser that, in consideration of the closing of this agreement, the Vendor will not operate a printing business or in any way aid and assist any other person to operate such a business in the Greater Vancouver area for a period of two (2) years from the date of closing.

8. BULK SALES

8.01 This agreement shall be completed and the Vendor agrees to comply with any applicable laws governing the sale in bulk of the stock in trade or of any of the other assets pursuant to this agreement.

9. CLOSING DOCUMENTS

9.01 The Vendor shall deliver to the Purchaser, in registrable form where applicable, the following closing documents ("the closing documents"), prepared or obtained at the Vendor's expense, on or before closing:

(a) duplicate, properly executed Bills of Sale of the equipment, stock in trade and parts and supplies together with evidence satisfactory to the Purchaser that the sale complies with any laws governing the sale in bulk of the stock in trade or of the sale of any of the other assets pursuant to this agreement;

(b) a statutory declaration that the Vendor is a resident of Canada within the meaning of the Income Tax Act of Canada as of the date of closing;

(c) all records and financial data, including but not limited to any lists of customers and suppliers, relevant to the continuation of the business by the Purchaser;

(d) a duly executed notice in proper form revoking any registration of the style of the business under any business name registration law;

(e) an executed assignment of the lease to the Purchaser endorsed with the lessor's consent to the assignment;

(f) such other assignments, consents, clearances or assurances as the Purchaser reasonably considers necessary or desirable to assure the Purchaser of the proper and effective completion of this agreement.

11. CLOSING DATE

11.01 The purchase and sale in this agreement shall close on the 31st day of August, 2002.

12. MISCELLANEOUS

12.01 In this agreement, the singular includes the plural and the masculine includes the feminine and neuter and vice versa unless the context otherwise requires.

12.02 The capitalized headings in this agreement are only for convenience of reference and do not form part of or affect the interpretation of this agreement.

12.03 If any provision or part of any provision in this agreement is void for any reason, it shall be severed without affecting the validity of the balance of the agreement.

12.04 Time is of the essence of this agreement.

12.05 There are no representations, warranties, conditions, terms or collateral contracts affecting the transaction contemplated in this agreement except as set out in this agreement.

12.06 This agreement binds and benefits the parties and their respective heirs, executors, administrators, personal representatives, successors and assignees.

12.07 This agreement is governed by the laws of the Province of British Columbia.

13. ACCEPTANCE

13.01 This agreement executed on behalf of the Purchaser constitutes an offer to purchase, which can only be accepted by the Vendor by return of at least one originally accepted copy of agreement to the Purchaser on or before the 15th day of July, 2002 failing which the offer becomes null and void. If this offer becomes null and void or is validly revoked before acceptance or this agreement is not completed by the Purchaser for any valid reason, any deposit tendered with it on behalf of the Purchaser shall be returned without penalty or interest.

IN WITNESS WHEREOF this Agreement has been executed by the parties.

XYZ Inc.
[the Purchaser]

By: _____

Name: _____

Title: _____

ABBCC Inc.
[the Vendor]

By: _____

Name: _____

Title: _____

SIGNED,
SEALED AND DELIVERED
in the presence of:

_____

Witness

Appendix 14.2
Sample Promissory Note

$48,000.00   Due in instalments

FOR VALUE RECEIVED the undersigned promises to pay to or to the order of George Vendor Holdings Ltd., at 100 – Ontario Drive, Winnipeg, Manitoba, the principal amount of forty eight thousand dollars ($48,000.00) in lawful money of Canada, payable in equal monthly instalments at principal of one thousand dollars ($1,000.00) each on the 1st day of each month commencing on the 1st day of January, 2003 up to and including the 1st day of December, 2004, or until such principal amount outstanding has been paid, and to pay interest on the 1st day of each month commencing on the 1st day of January, 2003 at that variable rate per annum which is equal to two (2%) percentage points above the Prime Bank Rate, adjusted immediately without notice on each change in the Prime Bank Rate, calculated monthly not in advance, on the principal amount from time to time remaining unpaid. Payments received shall be applied firstly in payment of unpaid accrued interest and the balance if any in reduction of principal.

In this promissory note the "Prime Bank Rate" means the commercial lending rate of interest expressed as an annual rate quoted or published by the Bank of Montreal as the reference rate of interest from time to time (commonly known as "prime") for the purpose of determining the rate of interest that it charges to its commercial customers for loans in Canadian funds. At the date hereof the "Prime Bank Rate" is four percent (4%).

Upon default in payment of any payment when due hereunder, the entire unpaid balance of the principal amount and accrued interest shall become immediately due and payable without notice or demand and the undersigned covenants to pay interest thereon and on subsequent overdue interest at the rate aforesaid, both before and after judgment, until paid in full. The covenants to pay interest shall not merge on the taking of a judgment or judgments with respect to any of the obligations herein stipulated for.

The Borrower hereby waives demand and presentment for payment, notice of non-payment, protest, notice of protest, notice of dishonour, bringing of suit and diligence in taking any action.

DATED at Winnipeg in the province of Manitoba, this 31st day of December, 2002.

Per: _____
         [Authorized Signing Officer]

(15)

UNDER NEW OWNERSHIP

What Do You Do Now?

Congratulations, all the documents have been executed, the money has been paid, the keys have been handed over and you are now the official owner of the business. You have a number of employees who will be looking to you for direction and wondering what their new boss will be like. You may have had the opportunity to work in the business for a while, so you are not going in completely cold. You may have entered into an agreement with the seller to stay on for a period of time until you learn the ropes. On the other hand, you may have been working at your job until the day you took over the business, the seller left town the day the money changed hands, and you are completely on your own. You are feeling a little excited and a little nervous. In fact, you might be downright scared, especially if you have never run your own business. Regardless, reality has set in and the buck stops with you. So, what do you do now?

If It Ain't Broke — Don't Fix It

Yes, the old adage is true: if it ain't broke — don't fix it. However, if you are faced with serious problems involving your customers, employees or suppliers you have no alternative but to take remedial action. You may have come into the business with some preconceptions about what needed to be done but the best thing you can do is to maintain the status quo until you learn to manage the business and understand the critical interdependencies in the business. Certainly you may have to make some minor decisions but you should avoid making any major changes until you learn the routines and the culture of the business and are fully aware of the implications of any decisions you might make.

One thing is for certain — there will be surprises. Some of them may be pleasant surprises and others may not be so pleasant. Expect them and do not overreact to them. If you encounter problems, you can usually find someone to help. Do not overlook the employees to help you solve a problem, as they can be a valuable resource. Also, the seller will be motivated to help you, especially if the seller provided some of the financing to buy the business or has been retained on a management contract.

Focus on the Critical Factors

Every business has at least three — and never more than six — critical factors that determine the long-term profitability of the business. You should attempt to identify the critical factors in your business as early as possible and focus attention, attitude and atmosphere on those critical factors. The critical factors vary from business to business but generally include such areas as cash flow, cost of goods, sales revenues, wastage, productivity, inventory controls, quality control, customer service, employee satisfaction, operating expenses and delivery times. Introduce some simple controls that will enable you to monitor performance in the critical areas.

> You should attempt to identify the critical factors in your business as early as possible and focus attention, attitude and atmosphere on those critical factors.

Strategic Planning

One of the most valuable exercises you can do is to carry out a strategic planning session as early as possible. There are a number of rules to follow that will allow you to get the most out of such a session.

1. All key decision-makers must be involved in the session.
2. Set aside sufficient time to complete the strategic planning in one session.
3. Choose a location outside of the business.
4. There can be no interruptions.
5. Start by establishing one-year goals for the company. The goals must be understandable, measurable, realistic and agreed upon by everyone in attendance. The easiest way to set the company's goals is to pose the question "Where do we want to be one year from today?" In other words, if you were all sitting around the same table in exactly one year what would the company look like? Do not deal with any obstacles to achieving your goals at this point in the process, just focus on getting consensus. Do not rush this section of the process. It may take time to get everyone going in the same direction, but it is a very valuable exercise and can be critical to the success of your strategic plan.
6. Once the goals have been established, you can identify the obstacles that will prevent you from achieving your goals. Do not try and find ways of overcoming the obstacles at this point, just identify them.
7. The next step is to find ways of overcoming the obstacles to achieving your goals. You will find that as you remove one obstacle you will find solutions for two or three as the obstacles generally involve the same things, for example, money, people and communication.

8. Once you have completed items 5, 6 and 7 above, you need to establish a strategic plan to achieve your goals. The strategic plan should only focus on what you need to do in the next 30, 60 and 90 days in order to reach your year-end goals. Put down on paper who needs to do what and by when. In other words, every task must be designated to one or more people.

9. Review the strategic plan every 30 days to see if you are on track and extend the plan for a further 30 days. If not, you will have to make some adjustments if you want to meet your year-end goals.

Employees are Your Biggest Asset

Items such as buildings and equipment may have a high capital cost but the most valuable asset of any business is its employees. Consequently, you should focus your initial efforts on your people. Get to know them and understand their skills and knowledge. You should arrange to get all the employees together at one time and have the seller introduce you as the new owner. Depending on the type of business and the location, this can be done either on or off the premises. If you choose to do it off-site at a venue such as a local hotel, keep it reasonably brief and do not allow too much alcohol or the meeting may deteriorate quickly and you may not get the result for which you are looking.

In these situations, honesty is the best policy. Prior to closing you may have had the opportunity to assess the employee situation and you may have arranged for the seller to terminate those whom you did not wish to retain. It is important to understand that nothing creates anxiety faster than uncertainty. Consequently, your goal should be to reassure the employees that you will not be making any decisions until you have had the opportunity to fully assess the situation. Under no circumstances should you guarantee that every employee's job is guaranteed.

Customers

Depending on the type of business, you should personally visit at least 10 of your major customers. If the business is retail-oriented and the business is fairly evenly distributed over the customer base you should do a random sampling of your customers to obtain feedback. A simple way to get good feedback is to ask them just two questions: How are we doing and how can we do it better?

Suppliers

It is easy to overlook the importance of suppliers to the success of your business. Meet important suppliers personally and try to make them part of your team.

Retaining the Previous Owner through the Transition

You may have entered into a management contract with the seller to provide the seller's personal services during the period of transition. Such an arrangement can be very helpful to ease into the business, but it also has some drawbacks. First, the employees may feel an allegiance to the previous owner and find it difficult to communicate directly with you while the old boss is still in the picture. Secondly, there could be other dynamics such as a personality conflict between you and the previous owner or you may simply find it difficult to operate or implement changes while the previous owner is still involved. Any agreement between the seller and buyer with respect to the seller providing post-sale personal service should include a provision for the buyer to terminate the agreement earlier at the buyer's option. If the agreement is for the seller to provide personal services for a three-month period of transition, you may feel at the end of two months that you have received all you can from the previous owner or you may find — for various reasons — that it would be easier to operate the business without the seller being around. If that should prove to be the case, you need to be able to terminate the agreement earlier without any animosity. A sample management contract is included at Appendix 15.1.

REAL LIFE

Understand Critical Interdependencies

Nadine had been a sales manager for 10 years, but had never run her own business before she purchased Regional Wholesalers Inc. Nadine was anxious to improve the business and thought she should make changes quickly in order to prove to the employees that she was the boss and was not afraid to make changes in order to improve the business.

The first significant change that Nadine made was to terminate Key Importers, who had been a supplier to the business for more than 12 years. Unfortunately, Nadine made this change without consulting any of the key employees and was unaware that the president of Key Importers was the brother-in-law of Ahmed, who was president of one of the company's biggest customers, Local Suppliers Inc. Nadine had simply looked at the price that Regional Wholesalers was paying for the products they purchased from Key Importers, without taking into consideration the payment terms and delivery times that they provided, or the fact that one of her major customers had referred Regional Wholesalers to the business in the first place. In other words, she had failed to look at the total picture or consult with her employees, who could have warned her of the consequences of carrying out such a drastic action. Local Suppliers Inc. was one of Nadine's biggest customers. In fact, it accounted for almost 25% of her business. The loss of a customer of this size was devastating on her business. Nadine attempted to meet with Ahmed, the President of Local Suppliers Inc., to discuss the situation but Ahmed refused to meet with her. Nadine learned a hard lesson and from that moment on she consulted with her key employees and other business advisors before making any major business decisions.

After you have taken over the business, you have a lot of management challenges and decision-making ahead of you. You need to have a clear vision of what your first steps will be. Your employees, customers and suppliers may have expectations, anticipation and trepidation during the transition period. It is common to have the previous owner assist in the transition for the sake of continuity. The previous owner may also assist in the learning curve that your new acquisition presents. However, in certain situations, once the sale is made it is not always possible or desirable to involve the previous owner. Every situation is different.

Appendix 15.1
Sample Management Agreement

THIS AGREEMENT made as of the 1st day of December, 2002.

BETWEEN: ABC LIMITED
            (hereinafter called "the employer")

                                                OF THE FIRST PART

AND: JOHN SMITH
            (hereinafter called "the employee")

                                                OF THE SECOND PART

   WHEREAS the employer and the employee have agreed to enter into an employment relationship for their mutual benefit and are desirous of setting out terms and conditions thereof, this agreement witnesses that the parties agree as follows:

1. Employment

(a) The employee represents to the employer that the employee has the required skills and experience to perform the duties and exercise the responsibilities required of the employee as a marketing manager. In particular, the employee represents that he will be able to undertake a senior responsibility for sales and marketing, training, supervision, planning and budgeting. In carrying out these duties and responsibilities, the employee shall comply with all lawful and reasonable instructions as may from time to time be given by superiors or those representing the employer.

(b) In consideration for the employee's agreement hereto and the employee's performance in accordance herewith the employer employs the employee.

(c) The effective performance of the employee's duties requires the highest level of integrity and the employer's complete confidence in the employee's relationship with other employees of the employer and with all persons dealt with by the employee in the course of employment.

(d) It is understood and agreed to by the employee that the employer reserves the right to change the employee's assignments, duties and reporting relationships. In particular, it is understood and agreed to that the employer plans, in its discretion, to involve the employee in national sales matters with a view to his being able, if so directed, to assume full responsibility for national sales.

2. Exclusive Service

(a) During the term of employment the employee shall well and faithfully serve the employer and shall not, during the term, be employed or engaged in any capacity promoting, undertaking or carrying out any other business.

(b) The employee is employed on a full-time basis for the employer and it is understood that the hours of work involved will vary and be irregular and are those required to meet the objectives of the employment.

3. Confidential Information

(a) The employee acknowledges that as Marketing Manager, and in such other position as he may from time to time be appointed to, the employee will acquire information about certain matters and things that are confidential to the employer, and which information is the exclusive property of the employer, including:

  (i) customer lists;

  (ii) pricing policies;

  (iii) list of suppliers.

(b) The employee acknowledges such information as referred to in clause 3(a) above could be used to the detriment of the employer. Accordingly, the employee undertakes to treat confidentially all such information and agrees not to disclose same to any third party either during or after the term of employment.

(c) The employee acknowledges that, without prejudice to any and all rights of the employer, an injunction is the only effective remedy to protect the employer's rights and property as set out in clauses 3(a) and 3(b).

4. Noncompetition

(a) The employee acknowledges that as Marketing Manager for the employer he will gain a knowledge of, and a close working relationship with, the employer's customers, which would injure the employer if made available to a competitor or if used for competitive purposes. The employee therefore agrees that, for a period of six (6) months from the termination of employment pursuant to this agreement for any reasons or cause, the employee will not be employed by another employer directly or indirectly engaged in a business which is in competition with the employer, in a position where the duties are the same or similar to those duties performed for the other employer pursuant to this agreement.

5. Remuneration and Benefits

(a) In consideration of the employee's undertaking and the performance of the obligations contained herein the employer shall pay and grant the following salary and benefits:

  (i) a salary of $100,000 per annum, payable in arrears in equal biweekly instalments, subject to an annual review to be on or about January 1, 2004;

  (ii) such other benefit program as is made generally available by the employer from time to time pursuant to the provisions thereof;

  (iii) the reimbursement of any expenses authorized and incurred pursuant to the employee's employment in accordance with the employer's generally established practice as applied from time to time;

  (iv) an automobile allowance to $1,500 per month plus reimbursement for gas and repair expenses generated by use of the automobile on behalf of the employer. The employee shall insure said automobile at his expense in an amount satisfactory to the employer and shall produce proof of same to the employer when requested to do so;

(v) an annual bonus in the absolute discretion of the employer which bonus may not be given at all in any year.

6. Termination

(a) This agreement may be terminated in the following manner in the specified circumstances:

   (i) by the employee upon the giving of not less than one (1) month's notice to the employer;

   (ii) by the employer upon the giving of not less than two (2) month's notice to the employee, in which case the employee shall be free to seek other employment;

   (iii) by the employer, at its option, for cause including:

      (A) a material breach of the provisions of this agreement including the policies attached hereto;

      (B) conviction of the employee of a criminal offence punishable by indictment where such cause is not prohibited by law;

      (C) alcoholism or drug addiction of the employee;

      (D) the absence of the employee from the performance of his duties for any reason, other than for authorized vacation, for a period in excess of 40 working days total in any six-month period;

     or

   (iv) by the employee for cause including a material breach of this agreement.

(b) The giving of notice or the payment of severance pay by the employer to the employee upon termination shall not prevent the employer from alleging cause for said termination.

(c) The employee authorizes the employer to deduct from any payment due to the employee at any time, including from a termination payment, any amounts owed to the employer by reason of purchases, advances or loans, or in recompense for damage to or loss of the employer's property save only that this provision shall be applied so as not to conflict with any applicable legislation.

7. Severability. In the event that any provision herein or part thereof shall be deemed void or invalid by a court of competent jurisdiction, the remaining provisions, or parts thereof, shall be and remain in full force and effect.

8. Entire Agreement. This agreement constitutes the entire agreement between the parties hereto with respect to the employment of the employee, and any and all previous agreements, written or oral, express or implied between the parties hereto or on their behalf relating to the employment of the employee by the employer are hereby terminated and cancelled and each of the parties hereto hereby releases and forever discharges the other of and from all manner of actions, causes of action, claims, demands whatsoever under or in respect of any such agreement.

9. Notices

(a) Any notice required or permitted to be given to the employee shall be sufficiently given if delivered to the employee personally or if mailed by registered mail to the employee's address last known to the employer.

(b) Any notice required or permitted to be given to the employer shall be sufficiently given if delivered to President, ABC Limited personally or if mailed by registered mail to the employer's head office at its address last known to the employee.

(c) Any notice given by mail shall be deemed to have been given forty-eight (48) hours after the time it is posted.

IN WITNESS WHERE the parties have duly executed this agreement this 1st day of December 2002, in the city of Oshawa in the province of Ontario.

_____   _____

ABC Limited   John Smith
(Authorized Signatory)   (Signature)

(16)

SELLING YOUR BUSINESS

Introduction

Although the focus of this book has been on the business buyer, we have included this chapter for those interested in selling their business. The selling of a business is not an everyday event. For most people, it is a once-in-a-lifetime experience. Obviously, many people wishing to sell their business may have bought it in the first place (unless they are selling a business that they started on their own), therefore they are already aware of most of the procedures involved in the process. However, their involvement has been from the buyer's perspective rather than from the seller's prospective. Consequently, the seller may not be familiar with some aspects of the sale such as finding a buyer, preparing the business for sale, how to get the best price, seller financing, timing of the sale or using a broker.

> The consequences involved in selling the business are generally greater and can have a longer lasting impact than any business decisions previously made.

Look Within

Before making the decision to sell, business owners should fully evaluate and understand their motivation for selling their business. The first step is to ask, "Why do I want to sell the business?" The honest answer to this question will influence a number of factors, including the timing of the sale. The consequences involved in selling the business are generally greater and can have a longer lasting impact than any business decisions previously made, including buying the business in the first place. As the end result can be devastating or rewarding — financially and emotionally —sellers owe it to themselves, their families and their employees to use an informed approach in bringing about a successful sale and in obtaining the highest possible value for the business.

Selling the business may be the most difficult decision that a business owner ever has to make. Some business owners agonize over the situation without ever making the decision to sell, while others wait too long to sell. Indecision or lack of proper planning and preparation can prove to be very costly. In most situations, it is better to sell the business sooner rather than later, provided that the sale is not forced.

Forced Sale of a Business

The keys to selling the business on the best terms and conditions are planning, preparation and presentation; these things cannot be achieved if you are in a panic to sell the business. By failing to prepare for the eventual sale of the business, the business owner allows the end game to be determined by external forces. As is the case with the sale of almost anything, if you are in a position where you are forced to sell, you are almost guaranteed to receive the lowest price and the worst possible terms. There are a number of reasons that can lead to the forced sale of a business.

> In most situations, it is better to sell the business sooner rather than later, provided that the sale is not forced.

- **Emotional reasons:** the business owner is burned-out, bored, wants to devote time, energy and money on other business interests, or simply does not want the stress of running a business anymore.
- **Personal problems:** there has been poor health, divorce or a death in the family.
- **Lack of operating or expansion capital:** the owner has used up all financial resources, accounts receivable are too high or uncollectible, suppliers are refusing to supply inventory until their accounts are current, a major piece of equipment has to be replaced, or creditors are making demands for repayment.

Other Reasons

If the business owner is motivated to sell for one of the following reasons, time is usually on the owner's side and there is adequate time to prepare for the sale in order to obtain the highest price and the best possible terms for the business.

- **Change in lifestyle:** the business owner may want to change lifestyle from the long hours involved in running a business to a more laid-back lifestyle or the owner wishes to retire.
- **Personal economics:** the business owner may want to liquidate or diversify money that is currently tied up in the business. In this situation, the owner may still desire to participate in the business under a management contract with a new owner.

Alternatives to Selling

Before you make a final decision to sell your business, you should consider some of the alternatives. If you are selling the business because of certain problems, you may be able to solve the problem rather than resort to selling the business. For example, if you are contemplating selling because of stress or burnout, you could delegate some of your workload or take on a partner, although taking on a partner may be a short-term solution but a long-term problem. Another solution is to sell part of your business. Or you could cut back on the number of clients, reduce the number of products or services you offer, or reduce the size of the geographic area you service. Sometimes business owners take on too many obligations outside of the business, such as service in the community and association leadership, which can become overwhelming. Examine if some of these activities could be curtailed.

> By failing to prepare for the eventual sale of the business, the business owner allows the end game to be determined by external forces.

If the problem is financial, you usually have two options: get more or need less. Selling a part of your business or bringing in a partner can reduce workload and generate extra capital. It may be possible to sell unwanted assets to raise cash, or you could consider selling some items of equipment and leasing them back. Reducing the amount of money you require generally means improving the efficiency of your business or refinancing some of your loans to reduce the amount of the payments. Regardless of the problem, you should carefully explore all options before selling the business.

Consider the Impact on your Business

In contemplating the sale of your business you have to consider that when the news gets out that your business is on the market, there may be an impact. News of the sale has the potential to disrupt your relationships with your customers, employees, suppliers, landlord and bankers, and to damage your business. Unfortunately, if you are going to sell the business, you have no alternative but to let people know that it is for sale.

It is important to carry on business as usual. As the selling process could take a year or longer, you cannot allow yourself to be distracted, but must remain focused on the day-to-day demands of business so that you have a healthy business at the end of the process, regardless of whether the business sells or not.

> As the selling process could take a year or longer . . . remain focused on the day-to-day demands of business so that you have a healthy business at the end of the process, regardless of whether the business sells or not.

Tax Considerations

Before you put the business on the market, you should discuss the tax implications thoroughly with your accountant. Obviously, you want to receive the highest amount possible from the sale of the business. The federal government's retention of the $500,000 small business capital gains deduction is a strong incentive for shareholders to sell company shares rather than business assets. This is one of the few tax shelters available to small business and could be reduced or eliminated at any time. The basis of the program is that if an owner sells the shares of a business, the owner could be exempt from tax up to

$500,000 of the capital gain on the sale. The maximum amount of exemption is $500,000, assuming that the $100,000 personal tax portion of the $500,000 has not been used in the past.

There are two levels of taxation when a company sells assets. In the first instance, the company receives the proceeds and is responsible for the payment of applicable taxes at the time the sale closes. Once the taxes have been paid, the company distributes the funds to its shareholders, which as individuals are subject to normal income tax considerations. On the other hand, if an individual receives money from the sale of shares, there is only one level of taxation.

Allocation of the Purchase Price

If the deal is structured as an asset purchase, then once the purchase price has been agreed on, it will be necessary to allocate the purchase price among the various assets of the business (for example, land, buildings, equipment, patents, inventory and goodwill) for tax purposes. As your goal is to minimize tax liability in the year of the sale, you will be motivated to allocate the purchase price so that it will result in no taxable income. If the deal involves the transfer of land, you will want as much of the purchase price to be allocated to that particular asset as land is not depreciable. Consequently, the sale of land could result in a capital gain, which is subject to more favourable tax treatment.

> If the deal involves the transfer of land, you will want as much of the purchase price to be allocated to that particular asset as land is not depreciable.

Buildings depreciate at a lower rate than other assets and consequently any recaptured capital cost allowance will be relatively small. The buyer usually wants a relatively low value allocated to land and buildings and higher values allocated to other depreciable assets, allowing the buyer to take advantage of higher capital cost allowances and make it possible for the buyer to write off the purchase price faster.

As there is the possibility of an increased recapture of capital costs allowance for assets such as machinery and other equipment, your goal should be to allocate lower values to these assets. If higher values are allocated to these types of assets, higher tax liability can result for the seller as recaptures of capital cost allowance are treated as income.

As the seller, you always want the lowest amount allocated to inventory, as it is treated as ordinary business income, which means that the sale proceeds from inventory are treated as ordinary income and taxed accordingly.

Allocation of the purchase price is a complex process because both parties have conflicting needs, making it extremely important to have experienced and competent professional advisors to advise you on the best way to structure the deal and to guide you through the negotiation process. It is possible to structure the deal so that taxes are minimized, or possibly avoided altogether, however, this requires both buyer and seller working in cooperation.

Exemption from GST

If both the purchaser and the seller are:

- registered for purposes of GST;
- the purchased assets comprise all, or substantially all, of the property used in the business, and
- the business is a commercial activity (as defined in the governing legislation),

then both parties can file an election pursuant to section 167(1) of the *Excise Tax Act* (Canada) to exempt the sale of the assets from GST.

Providing Vendor Financing

Pros

Providing some level of financing for the buyer may be the only way to sell the business, as banks have fairly strict lending criteria for acquisition loans and may not be willing to give the buyer all or any of the financing. In fact, the majority of small- and medium-sized businesses are purchased with a significant portion of the purchase price financed by the owner. You may be motivated to provide financing if you feel it is necessary to get the price you want for the business or have confidence in the buyer, or because of your tax situation.

Cons

When you provide financing to the buyer, you essentially retain many of the risks associated with continued ownership of the business, yet you effectively give up control of its management. To some degree, this means that the buyer's ability to repay you will depend on the future success of the business without you having influence over the business. If the buyer mismanages the business and is unable to make payments on your financing, you may have no other recourse than to foreclose on the note and repossess the business.

> When you provide financing to the buyer, you essentially retain many of the risks associated with continued ownership of the business, yet you effectively give up control of its management.

Mechanics of Vendor Financing

The simplest method of providing vendor financing is to have the buyer make a down payment and carry back a note or mortgage for the balance of the purchase price. Try to get as big a down payment as possible. The assets of the business usually secure the note. Depending on a number of factors including the size of the loan, the value of the assets and the buyer's business experience, you could require the buyer to put up a personal residence as additional collateral or to personally guarantee the loan.

The payment schedule, interest rate, loan period or any other terms can be adjusted to reflect your needs and the buyer's financial situation. The interest rate charged on the note normally varies with the prime rate and is usually less than the interest rate charged by banks for business loans.

In some situations, sellers may require the buyer to take out a life insurance policy with the seller as beneficiary, so that the loan will be paid off if the buyer dies. In addition, the purchase and sale agreement may restrict the new owner's sale of assets, acquisitions and expansions until the note is paid off, and provide for the seller to be provided with regular financial statements so the seller can keep track of the business's financial health.

In most cases, financing provided by the seller will be for a relatively short term, although the loan will be amortized over a much longer payment schedule to keep the payments to a manageable amount. At the end of the term (for example, five years), there will still be a substantial portion of principal remaining and the buyer is usually required to obtain outside financing to pay off the balance of the loan. The basic philosophy is that at that point, the business will have a solid track record and it will be easier for the buyer to obtain bank financing.

If the buyer has obtained primary financing from a bank, the buyer may ask you to take back subordinated debt for the balance of the purchase price. In this situation, you will be second in line if the buyer defaults on the primary loan to the bank. In addition, the bank will probably have secured the loan against all or most of the hard assets of the business and the buyer's personal residence, leaving you with little or no collateral as security for the loan. If you agree to provide this level of financing, you should demand a higher interest rate.

Obviously, you will need to do a thorough check of the buyer's background — including a credit check — before you finalize any such financing arrangements.

Earn-Outs

An earn-out is often used in situations where there is disagreement between the parties about how much the business is actually worth. An earn-out is essentially an agreement in which a minimum purchase price is agreed upon, with a provision that the seller will be entitled to more money if the business reaches certain financial goals in the future. Such goals should be stated in terms of percentages of gross sales or revenues, rather than net revenues, because expenses are relatively easy to manipulate, which can result in a distortion of net revenues.

An earn-out can be calculated as a percentage of sales, gross profit, net profit or other figure. It is not uncommon to establish a floor or ceiling for the earn-out. Earn-outs do not preclude the payment of a portion of the purchase price in cash or instalment notes, rather, they are normally paid in addition to other forms of payment. Because the payment of money to the seller under the provisions of the earn-out is predicated on the performance of the business, it is important that the seller continue to operate the business through the period of the earn-out.

If you do use an earn-out, it is important to state in the purchase and sale agreement who is responsible for reviewing the books and verifying the business's performance. If you agree to an earn-out, you may wish to consider entering an employment or consulting relationship

> Obviously, you will need to do a thorough check of the buyer's background — including a credit check — before you finalize any such financing arrangements.

with the buyer so that you can monitor the performance of the business and ensure that the buyer is doing everything necessary to reach the stated goals.

Preparing to Sell the Business

Get Your Books in Order

Preparation can increase the price received and make a deal easier to structure. Have professionally prepared statements if you do not already have them. The financial statements should be no older than 90 days. If they are too stale-dated, the information may not be relevant to the potential buyer. If the size of your company warrants, have audited statements prepared.

Although buyers generally conduct their own verification as part of their pre-purchase investigation, their level of concern will be reduced if you have complete and professionally prepared statements. As most closely held businesses are not required to have their books audited and consequently have no reason to incur what is a significant expense, unaudited statements are usually acceptable to the majority of buyers. It is possible that the buyer will ask you to agree to have up-to-date financial statements prepared by an independent accountant as a condition of closing the sale.

> Preparation can increase the price received and make a deal easier to structure.

The majority of privately held businesses operate in a manner designed to minimize the seller's tax liability. Unfortunately, this creates a conflict as the same operating techniques and accounting practices that minimize tax liability also minimize the value of a business. Although it is possible to reconstruct financial statements to reflect the actual operating performance of the business, it may result in the owner having to pay back income taxes and penalties. Consequently, in order to make the necessary changes to the accounting practices to reflect a three- to five-year track record of maximum profits, any plan to sell a business should be made years in advance of the actual sale, which is not always feasible.

Your desire to maximize personal wealth by understating earnings may have to be replaced with the desire to increase the value of the company. Items may have to be capitalized rather than expensed. Salaries, bonuses and redundant personnel may have to be trimmed. You may need to reduce expenses in the areas of travel, entertainment and charitable donations. Discretionary expenses should be decreased or made clearly identifiable.

Spruce up the Business

The business should be clean, the inventory current and the equipment in good working order.

Prepare a Valuation Report

A valuation report or appraisal should be prepared as it eliminates guesswork and the painful trial and error method of pricing on which so many owners rely. Place a reasonable price on your business, as an inflated figure either turns off or slows down potential buyers. Set price and terms for your company that you can defend with confidence and credibility.

Review Your Lease

If you are operating the business from leased space, you should review your lease to ensure that you have sufficient time remaining that will make the sale attractive to a purchaser. If not, negotiate with the landlord for the additional time before you start marketing the business.

Obtain an Appraisal on Your Real Estate

If you own your real estate, consider having it appraised, unless you have a fairly recent appraisal. You may find your building alone is worth more than if the business and real estate were sold together.

Packaging the Business

A business presentation package should be prepared. All facets of the business should be addressed in this document. They include:
- a history of the business;
- a description of how the business operates;
- a description of the facilities;
- a discussion of suppliers;
- a review of marketing practices;
- a description of the competition;
- a review of personnel, including an organizational chart, description of job responsibilities, rates of pay and willingness of key employees to stay on after the sale;
- identification of the owners;
- explanation of insurance coverage;
- discussion of any pending legal matters or contingent liabilities; and
- financial statements for the past three to five years.

Prepare Yourself for After the Sale

A very important factor that is often overlooked is to decide what you will do after the sale of your business. In other words, your plan should include what you are going to do with your time, how you will invest the proceeds of the sale, and how you plan to make a living after the business is sold. If you are planning to retire, you must ensure that you have set aside sufficient funds to finance your retirement, as the sale of few businesses will generate the dollars required to allow for a comfortable retirement.

> Place a reasonable price on your business, as an inflated figure either turns off or slows down potential buyers.

If you will be in a position where you will need to generate cash flow and have failed to identify an opportunity that will allow you to do this, you may end up depleting the proceeds you derived from the sale of the business. If your plan is to take a few months to have a break and decide on your next course of action, this too has to be factored into your financial planning. If the business has consumed all of your time, you should consider developing some outside interests or you may end up with too much time on your hands.

Finding Buyers

Using a Business Broker

Most business owners use the services of a business broker because they do not have the time or knowledge to market the business properly. The key is to search out the successful business brokers and to ignore the rest. Seek out a broker who is familiar with your area of business. Investigate the broker's reputation in the marketplace before you deal with them.

A business broker will usually require the exclusive right to sell the business for a period of six months or more. In addition to selling the business, the broker will also perform some tangible services, such as preparing a presentation package for prospective buyers and a valuation report. Typically, business brokers charge a fee based on a percentage of the purchase price, although they may also require a retainer in addition to the success fee. In almost all situations, the seller pays the broker's fees. Fees for the sale of companies selling for less than $1 million typically range from 8% to 12%, with some minimum amount of commission provided. For sales in excess of $1million, a sliding scale based on the Lehman formula — or some similar formula — is often used with the commission rate dropping for each incremental $1 million in price. The sliding scale used in the Lehman formula is:

- 5% of the first $1 million
- 4% of the second $1 million
- 3% of the third $1 million
- 2% of the fourth $1 million
- 1% of the fifth million and over

Services provided by an experienced broker can include:

1. **A business valuation.** A business valuation may be provided by the business broker or by a professional specializing in business valuation (for example, accountant or business appraiser).
2. **A marketing package.** A marketing package or confidential business offering should be created that will best display your business to prospective buyers. The seller should always review and approve the presentation before it is distributed.
3. **Confidentiality/Non-Disclosure Agreement.** All prospective buyers must sign a confidentiality/non-disclosure agreement. A broker can provide such an agreement and have every prospect execute it at the appropriate time.
4. **Screening prospective buyers.** Screening and qualification is required to make sure that only those individuals or companies with the requisite skills and financial ability

to purchase are shown your company. This will save you a lot of time, as you will only be dealing with qualified prospects. As brokers are a third party to the transaction, it is often easier for them to ask the prospect the necessary qualifying questions than it is for the seller.

5. **Negotiating the sale.** The broker normally conducts the negotiations on behalf of the seller, although it is possible for the seller to be personally involved in the negotiations. A good broker understands the art of negotiation and can be a valuable asset in this stage of the sale. It is important that the respective roles of the seller and broker are clearly defined in the negotiation process.

6. **Generating leads.** The broker is responsible for generating leads for prospective buyers. A good business broker invests as much time cultivating a stable of prospects as trying to sell a business. Consequently, the broker may already have prospects that fit your buyer profile. A broker will also advertise the business in newspapers or trade publications at their expense.

Using a Realtor

Realtors will list your business on the multiple listing service. In rural areas that cannot support a full-time business broker, most business owners go through realtors. Search out a realtor who specializes in commercial real estate and not the realtor who just does it as a sideline.

Marketing the Business Yourself

If you elect to market the business yourself, without the use of any intermediaries, you will need to consider the following.

Generating Leads

There are a number of ways to generate leads. The more leads you generate, the higher the chances of closing a sale quickly and on good terms and conditions. Therefore, you should employ as many lead generation strategies as possible.

Print Advertising

Business opportunity classified ads are a viable way to advertise a business for sale. The larger local newspapers are the best source of such ads for small- and medium-sized businesses. Business opportunity ads, whether for small or large businesses, usually describe the business in several short phrases, keeping its identity anonymous, and list a phone number to call or post office box for reply. The ad should be worded to demonstrate the business's best qualities, (both financial and non-financial) and many include a qualifying statement describing the kind of cash investment or experience required.

There are some publications that specialize in the sale of commercial real estate, franchises and business opportunities such as *Western Investor*, which covers British Columbia, Alberta, Saskatchewan and Manitoba. If your industry has a trade publication, you may wish to advertise there, as you are exposing your business to people who already understand the industry and may be looking to make an acquisition.

Networking

The more people that know you are selling your business, the greater your chance of finding a buyer.

Your suppliers, accountant, banker, lawyer or trade association, often may be aware of potential buyers. Every industry has a trade association and trade association publications can do a good job of communicating the sale of a business. If you think a buyer is likely to come from the same industry, contact the trade association's publications department to see if classified advertising is permitted.

Negotiating the Sale

Negotiating in the emotional atmosphere that surrounds every business transfer requires skill and experience. Most individuals find it difficult to handle the negotiations effectively, as emotion and ego get in the way of the process. Consequently, most use an intermediary such as a business broker to handle negotiations on their behalf. If you are working with an intermediary, make sure you clearly understand your respective roles and responsibilities during the negotiation process.

> Before you commence negotiations, decide on which items are important to you and be prepared to trade-off the less essential ones.

During the negotiation process, you may receive offers that are well below your expectations or that contain terms that are simply unacceptable. Remember it is not personal — it is just business. Maintain your composure and respond with a counter-offer that you consider acceptable, rather than letting emotions get the best of you. Before you commence negotiations, decide on which items are important to you and be prepared to trade-off the less essential ones.

It is imperative that your lawyer review any documents before you sign them.

Executing a Confidentiality/Non-Disclosure Agreement

At some point during the due diligence process, you should require the buyer to sign a confidentiality/non-disclosure agreement that legally binds the buyer from disclosing any information about your business. See Appendix 10.2 for a sample confidentiality/non-disclosure agreement. Whenever you buy a business, you should also be considering your exit timing and strategy. For example, are you intending to pass the business on to your children, to eventually sell it, or to wind down and only work part-time and hire a manager to run the business? It is helpful to consider what your long-term intentions are at the very beginning. There are various triggering events to the selling of a business. One of the questions you will try to find out when you consider buying the business, is why it is for sale.

Preparing to sell your business also involves the following considerations: taxes, the pros and cons of providing vendor financing, various steps to follow to get your business and documentation in shape, and how to package the business to make it attractive. Sale preparation includes determining where you might find prospective buyers, negotiating the sale, and executing all the documentation; basically, the flip-side of the purchasing process.

Now that you have completed this guide, you should have a very realistic and practical understanding of the process, as well as tips and strategies to accomplish your goals. This will provide you with the confidence needed to make the decisions that are right for you.

We wish you good luck, best wishes and a satisfying and profitable adventure in your own business.

GLOSSARY

Accounts payable: The outstanding bills of a firm; money that a firm owes its suppliers for goods and services purchased for the operation of the business. Accounts payables are included on the balance sheet under current liabilities.

Accounts receivable: The money that is owed to a firm by its customers for goods or services they have purchased from it. Accounts receivable are included on the balance sheet under current assets.

Acid test: An accounting ratio used for measuring the amount of liquid assets (cash on hand and anything that can be easily and quickly turned into cash) a company has on hand for meeting its short term obligations.

Agent: Someone who legally represents someone else, and can act in that person's or company's name.

Agreement of purchase and sale: A written agreement between the owner and a purchaser for the purchase of a business on a pre-determined price and terms.

AGS: Annual gross sales.

Allocation of purchase price: In an asset sale, the purchase price must be allocated to certain assets with the balance being applied to goodwill.

Amortization: A long-term expense calculated on a monthly or periodic cost basis.

ANP: Annual net profit.

Arbitration: The resolution of a dispute between two parties by an impartial third party. Used in commercial disputes when direct negotiations fail. The arbitrator's decision may or may not be final, depending on the nature of the contract. Each province has legislation covering arbitration, which sets out procedures.

Arm's length: Refers to a transaction between two or more unrelated companies or individuals.

Articles of incorporation: A legal document filed with the provincial and/or federal government that sets forth the purposes and/or regulations for a corporation. These papers must be approved by the provincial and/or federal government before a corporation legally exists and is allowed to do business.

Assets: The valuable resources or property rights owned by an individual or business enterprise. Tangible assets include cash, inventory, land and buildings. Intangible assets include patents and goodwill.

Asset sale: Purchase of certain assets and/or liabilities leaving the seller the remainder as well as the corporate entity.

Audit: A check of an organization's financial statements by someone whose independence of the organization and professional qualifications creates faith in the person's judgment. An audit testifies to the honesty and accuracy of the organization's records. Professionally qualified accountants perform audits.

Bad debts: Money owed to a business that the business cannot collect.

Balance sheet: An itemized statement listing the total assets and total liabilities of a business in order to portray its net worth at a given moment in time.

Bankruptcy: The financial and legal position of a person or corporation unable to pay debts. A legal bankrupt must transfer control of any remaining assets to a trustee in bankruptcy. Governed by the federal *Bankruptcy and Insolvency Act.*

Blended payments: Equal payments consisting of both a principal and an interest component, paid each month during the term of the mortgage. The principal portion increases each month, while the interest portion decreases, but the total monthly payment does not change.

Board of directors: Representatives elected by the shareholders to direct the affairs of a company.

Book value: Also know as "net worth," this is the figure obtained by deducting all the liabilities from all of the assets.

Breakup value: The estimated value of a business after its operations are stopped and the assets sold and the liabilities paid off. The breakup value is usually less than the going concern value.

Broker: Someone who brings a potential buyer and a potential seller together, in return for a fee or commission charged to one, the other, or both, for example, business, franchise or insurance brokers.

Business expense: The expense of producing and/or selling a product, which can be deducted from gross income to arrive at net income for taxation purposes.

Buy-sell agreement: See "Shotgun agreement."

Capital: The amounts of money owner(s) have invested in the business (including profits that are not taken out).

Capital cost allowance: The amount of tax relief that the Canada Customs and Revenue Agency allows for depreciation, for example, wear and tear on capital property. This would include an asset that has a useful but diminishing life over time (car, equipment, furniture, etc.). Different assets have different amounts of annual depreciation, for example, ranging from 4% to 100%.

Capital gain: A gain that is earned on the sale of an asset or a gain deemed to be realized on the death of an individual, as if the asset had been sold on the date of death (for example, deemed disposition). The difference between a capital property's fair market value and its adjusted cost base — essentially, what you have made on the investment.

Capital loss: A loss experienced on the sale of an asset or loss deemed to be experienced on the death of an individual, as if the asset had been sold on the date of death.

Capitalization: A company's total ownership and borrowed capital. Ownership capital includes stock and paid-in surplus; borrowed capital includes bank debt, bonds, etc.

Capitalization factor: The conversion of income into value as part of the valuation process by the application of a capitalization factor (any multiplier or divisor used to convert income to value).

Cash flow: Profit before income tax, depreciation, interest and owner compensation, and benefits.

Cash position: See "Liabilities."

Chattel mortgage: A charge over goods or equipment of a movable nature, as opposed to real estate. This document must be registered with the provincial government.

Collateral: Assets placed by a borrower as security on a loan to protect the interests of the lender. Bank loans are often collateralized or secured by a company's accounts receivables, inventory, and/or equipment.

Collateral security: See "Security."

Collection period: The average number of days it takes a company to collect receivables.

Common law: The precedents established by previous court decisions, which have all the force of written statutes unless Parliament passes a law to the contrary.

Common stock: Securities that represent ownership in a corporation and carry voting privileges.

Conditional sale: A sale made but not final until certain acts or events take place.

Conditions: The limits written into an agreement between a borrower and lender. The limits specify exactly what each party is expected to do in exchange for the benefits each will receive.

CCRA: Canada Customs and Revenue Agency (formerly Revenue Canada).

Consignment: Sale of goods through a third party whereby ownership of the goods remain in the name of the supplier until the goods have been sold, at which time the seller is indebted to the supplier.

Contingencies: Performance is dependent on the successful outcome of a named event (for example, verification of tax returns).

Continuing power of attorney: A power of attorney that contains a continuing or enduring clause so that it will remain effective even if you become mentally incapable.

Contract: An agreement regarding mutual responsibilities between two or more parties. In business law, a contract exists when there has been a meeting of minds, whether the contract is written or oral. However, a contract should be clear and in written form to protect your interests.

Corporation: A business comprised of one or more individuals treated by the law as a separate legal entity. Liability is limited to the assets of the corporation. See "Limited company."

Co-signers: Joint signers of a loan agreement, pledging to meet the obligations in case of default. When you ask someone to co-sign a note, you are asking the person to fully assume a debt with you if you cannot pay it back. The co-signer guarantees the loan will be paid back, and the lender can take legal action against them if they refuse to pay.

Cost of goods sold: Generally includes amount of goods and labour for service or delivery.

Covenant: A promise or legal arrangement you make when getting a loan. You must adhere to these covenants for your loan to remain in good standing.

Covenant not to compete: Agreement that the seller will not compete with the buyer for so many years within a certain area.

Credit bureau: A business whose product is information, which it sells, on the credit transactions and relevant personal information of individual people, as well as companies.

Creditor: Person to whom money is due.

Current ratio: Comparison of current assets to current liabilities (assets divided by liabilities).

Debenture: A formal legal document provided as security for a loan. It has the practical effect of being a mortgage on the corporation. Only a corporation can issue a debenture.

Debt: Money that must be paid back to someone else, sometimes with interest.

Deemed realization: A transfer of assets, which for tax purposes, is considered a sale by the CCRA, although no cash or other consideration may be involved.

Demand loan: A loan that must be repaid whenever the lender chooses.

Depreciation: Loss in value of a fixed asset due to wear and tear or obsolescence (which cannot be repaired by normal repairs).

Depreciable capital assets: Assets such as buildings and equipment, the purchase price of which will be written off as deductions for income tax purposes in the form of annual capital cost allowances (also know as depreciation) over a period of time.

Due diligence: Process of evaluating the business for purchase within a set amount of time.

EBIT: Earnings before interest and taxes.

EBITA: Earnings before interest, taxes and amortization.

EBITDA: Earnings before interest, taxes, depreciation and amortization.

Equity: See "Book value."

Equity capital/financing: All money invested in a business in exchange for ownership (shares). Venture capital is equity provided by outside investors. Equity does not have to be repaid on a specific date and there are no interest charges, although dividends are normally paid from time to time.

Escrow: Held by a third party until all conditions are met.

Fair market value: The price at which a willing seller is prepared to sell to a willing purchaser in an open market.

Financial statements: Documents that show your financial situation. Two major statements are needed to cover the information necessary to run a business and get financing: income statement and balance sheet.

Fiscal year: An accounting cycle of 12 months that could start at any point during a calendar year.

Foreclose: To sell or cause to be sold a property, when the owner fails to meet mortgage, tax or other debt payments on it. The courts must approve foreclosure.

Form of business organization: The legal structure that is established and registered with the appropriate level(s) of government in order to carry on a business. The three most common forms are proprietorships, partnerships and limited companies.

Franchisee: The person (or firm) who has purchased a franchise and is responsible for managing the business.

Franchising: A way of starting a business whereby an already established firm supplies the product, trademark, techniques, materials and expertise, and sets standards in exchange for purchase price and ongoing benefit.

Franchisor: The person (or firm) granting a franchise.

Generally accepted accounting procedures (GAAP): This is the term used to describe the basis on which financial statements are normally prepared. This is codified in the *Handbook of the Canadian Institute of Chartered Accountants*.

Good faith: An unspoken attitude of honesty and serious intention between two or more parties.

Goodwill: The difference between the total value of the business and the hard assets.

Gross profit: Income from sales less cost of goods sold — before overhead, general and administrative expenses.

Guarantee: A promise to pay, which could be a corporate guarantee or a personal guarantee.

Holding company: A company that exists to buy and own a majority of shares in other companies, thus to control them.

Income splitting: A tax planning device frequently available to business owners where total tax paid by the company and the shareholders can be minimized. Splitting can refer to splitting between salaries and dividends, husband and wife salaries, or other such arrangements.

Intellectual property: Knowledge and information that can be legally owned, as defined by laws governing copyright, trademarks, patents, industrial design and royalty obligations.

Joint and several liability: A legal term meaning that each (general) partner is fully liable for all the debts of the partnership and the partner's personal assets may be required to pay off debts incurred by another partner.

Key personnel insurance: Special insurance available on the lives of the principal active shareholders in a company. Can be used to fund buy-sell agreements as well as to provide funds to continue the company in the event of one manager's death. The name the policies are registered in, as well as who pays the premiums, can have important tax implications. Therefore, obtain tax advice in advance.

Lease: A contract in which the owner of a piece of property gives the exclusive use of it to someone else, in exchange for a stated sum of money, for the duration of a specified time.

Leasehold improvement: Renovation and other improvements made to the business premises. These become the property of the landlord.

Lessee: The tenant (or person) who signs a lease to get temporary use of space.

Lessor: The company (or person) providing temporary use of space in return for rental payments.

Letter of intent: Non-binding intent to purchase and intent to sell.

Leveraged buy-out: To complete the financing in the purchase of a company, the purchaser borrows against its unused borrowing capacity — usually based on the company's market value of its assets rather than on the book value.

Liabilities: All the debts of a business. Liabilities include short-term or current liabilities such as accounts payable, income taxes due, the amount of long-term debt that must be paid within 12 months; and long-term liabilities such as long-term debts and deferred income taxes. On a balance sheet, liabilities are subtracted from assets, what remains is the shareholder's equity or ownership in the business.

Lien: A charge placed over an asset by such parties as (1) the seller of that asset or (2) in the case of construction or repairs, by the person who carries out the work. The lien holder may take possession until the asset or work is paid for in full. Liens must be registered under the various provincial laws in order to be protected and enforceable.

Limited company: A separate legal entity that is owned by shareholders for the purpose of carrying on business. Assets and liabilities of owners (shareholders) are separate from the company. Can be private or public, as well as provincial or federal. Also called incorporated company or corporation.

Limited liability: The legal protection accorded shareholders of an incorporated company whereby the owner's financial liability is limited to the amount of the owner's share ownership, except where the owner owes money to the company or has assumed additional liabilities, for example, personally guaranteeing its debts.

Limited partnership: A legal partnership where certain owners assume responsibility only up to the amount of their investment. Investors who put up money for a business venture without being directly involved in its operation are not held responsible for the debts of the other partners beyond the possible loss of money they have invested.

Line of credit: A negotiated agreement with a bank, subject to periodic review, whereby the borrower is permitted to draw upon additional funds up to a specified limit at a certain rate of interest, for example, prime rate plus 2%.

Liquidate: To settle a debt or to convert to cash.

Liquidity: A term used to describe the solvency of a business and which has special reference to the degree of readiness in which assets can be converted into cash without a loss. If a firm's current assets cannot be converted into cash to meet current liabilities, the firm is said to be illiquid. A frequent measurement of liquidity is the quick or acid test ratio.

Lis pendens: A notice which can be registered on the title of a piece of property and which shows that the property is subject to a forthcoming lawsuit. The property cannot be transferred to another owner while the *lis pendens* is on title.

Long-term liabilities: Debts that will not be paid off within one year.

Majority owners: The owners of a majority of the stock (shares) in a corporation.

Markup: The amount added to cost to arrive at a retail price (expenses plus desired profit).

Medium-term financing: Loans or other credit on which the principal does not have to be repaid for three to five years.

MGS: Monthly gross sales.

Mortgagee: An individual or institutional lender that holds a mortgage on property as security for a loan.

Mortgagor: A person who offers a mortgage on property in exchange for cash consideration.

Negative covenant: An undertaking not to do certain things. It is frequently argued that negative covenants are preferable to positive covenants because it is easier to establish if something which was not to have been done has in fact been done, rather than vice versa. The breaking of a covenant usually constitutes a default, which in turn gives rise to certain specified remedies that can be taken by the security holder.

Net lease: Signifies a property lease where a lessee or tenant is responsible for all costs such as taxes, heat, light, power, insurance and maintenance.

Net profit: The difference between total income and total expenses.

Net worth: See "Book value."

Non-depreciable capital property: Assets, such as land, that are not subject to depreciation.

Non-disclosure agreement: Agreement from buyer that the buyer will not divulge information about the business or that the business is for sale. The agreement stipulates that the buyer will not talk to employees, customers, suppliers or anyone not directly involved in sale (such as, lawyer or accountant).

Non-recurring item: Income or expense arising from a cause not likely to exist in future years.

Offer to purchase: A formal, legal agreement, which offers a certain price for a specified real property. The offer may be firm (no conditions attached) or conditional (certain conditions must be fulfilled). Once the offer is accepted, it becomes an agreement of purchase and sale.

Owner's equity: See "Capital."

Partner: One of the owners of an unincorporated business.

Partnership: A legal business relationship of two or more people or companies who share responsibilities, resources, profits and liabilities. An agreement in writing is essential, detailing the nature of the relationship. Each province has legislation governing this type of business structure.

Payables: Trade or other liabilities that are due. One of the basic records kept by a bookkeeper is accounts payable.

Personal guarantee: A personal promise made by an individual on behalf of a personal or corporate borrower to repay a debt if the borrower fails to repay as agreed.

Power of attorney: A written document by which you grant to someone the authority to act on your behalf on various matters. A power of attorney is different from a will, which provides for the orderly distribution of your estate after your death; the former terminates upon your death. There are different types of powers of attorney dealing with specific or general financial or health issues.

Preferred creditor: A creditor who must be paid after secured creditors and before unsecured creditors in the event of a business failure under the *Bankruptcy and Insolvency Act.*

Pro forma: A projection or estimate of what may result in the future from actions in the present. A *pro forma* financial statement is one that shows how the actual operations of the business will turn out if certain assumptions are realized.

Profit: The excess of the selling price over all costs and expenses incurred in making the sale. Gross profit is the profit before corporate income taxes. Net profit is the final profit of the firm after all deductions have been made.

Proprietorship: See "Sole proprietorship."

Prorate: To spread equally over a period of time.

Recapture of capital cost allowance: The recovery of amounts previously written off as capital cost allowances. For example, when an asset is sold for more than its undepreciated book value. Recovered amounts are treated as income for tax purposes.

Receivables: Money owing to a company from those who were extended credit.

Receivership: The control of a business and its assets by a receiver (usually a chartered accountant). This person is appointed by the creditor under the term of a debenture and remains in control until the debts are paid or the business and/or assets are sold.

Residual value: Estimated scrap value of a tangible asset.

Retained earnings: Those profits that are kept in a corporation and not distributed as dividends.

Return on investment (ROI): The determination of the profit to be accrued from a capital investment. Where the investment risk is high, the expected ROI should also be high, in relation to other forms of investment such as Canada Savings Bonds, real estate or bank deposits. The higher the risk, the higher the expected return.

Secured: Protected or guaranteed. A secured loan makes the lender better protected, by having the debtor place something of value as collateral as a guarantee of repayment, for example, a chattel mortgage or debenture.

Securities: Negotiable instruments, such as stocks and bonds.

Security: Assets(s) belonging to the business or to you personally, which are pledged to the bank in support of a loan and which can be sold in the event you do not repay your loan. In the case of term loans, the property, (for example, land, buildings, equipment) being purchased with the loan usually forms the security for the loan.

Service business: Firm dealing in non-merchandising activities.

Shareholders' equity: See "Capital."

Shotgun agreement: An agreement between partners that gives either party the right to offer to buy all of the other's shares in the event of a disagreement. The offer states a price that can be accepted or rejected. If the other party refuses the bid, the party must buy the offeror's shares at the offeror's offering price.

Simple interest: Interest on the principal only as compared to compound interest.

Small business: A firm with 20 or fewer employees. This is the definition used in Statistics Canada's monthly employment survey. According to the federal and various provincial governments, a small business is any manufacturing firm with fewer than 100 employees or, in any other sector, a firm with fewer than 50 employees. Using either definition, small business accounts for 80% to 90% of all businesses in Canada.

Sole proprietorship: A business owned by one person. Personal and business assets and liabilities are not considered separate legal entities.

Subject clauses: Conditions that have to be met or escape options in an offer to purchase and sell, allowing the potential buyer or seller to back out if the deal starts to look unsatisfactory.

Subordinated debt: An obligation where one lender has agreed in writing to rank behind another in claiming an asset. The lender will receive his or her capital back only after the other has been fully paid out. A bank will often insist that shareholder loans be subordinated to the obligations to the bank.

Subrogation: See "Subordinated debt."

Taxable income: Gross income minus both exemptions and personal deductions.

Term loan: A loan intended for medium- or long-term financing to supply cash to purchase fixed assets, such as machinery, land or buildings, or to renovate business premises.

Terms of sale: The conditions concerning payment for a purchase.

Trade credit: The credit terms offered by suppliers (no interest is charged until after the due date).

Trademark: A name, symbol or other mark that identifies a product to customers, and is legally owned by its manufacturer or inventor.

Trust account: A separate account in which a lawyer holds funds until the transaction closes.

Turnkey operation: A project such as setting up a business or an office in which all work is done by a contractor and handed over in working order to the owner.

Turnover: The rate at which an asset, such as inventory, is replaced within a given time period.

Venture capital: An individual or institution that provides high risk debt or equity capital unavailable from traditional sources for the growth (or in some instances, seed funding) of small businesses at any stage before the business goes public.

Winding up: The legal procedures of closing down a limited company.

Working capital: Surplus liquid cash used to finance ongoing operations of the business.

SOURCES OF FURTHER INFORMATION

As a fledgling small business owner, or a potential one, you may feel overwhelmed by the amount of information that you need to know. Many entrepreneurs do not know where to access the most current and practical information easily, effectively and inexpensively. The next best thing to knowing something, is knowing where to find it.

The following information should assist you in that search. It contains the names of key business and trade publications, directories, handbooks and magazines. It also lists Canadian publications that are primarily free of charge, although a few are sold at a nominal cost. Information is included about the main business and trade associations in Canada, as well as some of the courses, seminars, consulting and counselling services that are available. A lack of knowledge is a frequent cause of business failure in Canada. Refer to "Web sites of Interest," for Web sites of many of the organizations below, as well as many other excellent information sources.

Associations

Business and trade associations provide an excellent means of staying current on legislation, market factors and trends affecting your industry. Other benefits of belonging to an association include access to free or nominal-cost publications, regular meetings, conferences, seminars, trade fairs, newsletters, contacts and assistance to new business owners. There are usually national, provincial and local associations or chapters. Two directories to help you locate them are *Directory of Associations in Canada* (Micromedia) and *Encyclopedia of Associations* (Gale Research Company). The latter includes Canadian, American and international associations. In addition, check your Yellow Pages under "Associations." Here are some of the main small business associations.

Canadian Chamber of Commerce

The Canadian Chamber of Commerce, with offices in Ottawa, Toronto and Montreal, has a small business committee and an active body that lobbies the federal government on various issues. Check with your local chamber of commerce or board of trade regarding membership benefits.

Canadian Council of Better Business Bureaus

Businesses may join at the national or local division. With 17 offices throughout Canada, local divisions assist businesses with various services, including arbitration of customer complaints.

Canadian Federation of Independent Business (CFIB)

With offices in major Canadian cities and over 80,000 members nationally, this is the largest political action group for small- and medium-sized businesses in Canada. The CFIB provides services and library access for members only.

Canadian Organization of Small Business (COSB)

The COSB represents independent business by lobbying government and provides services for members only.

Consulting/Counselling Services

Many sources of free or low-cost counselling are available. To gain the most benefit from the assistance you receive, be certain to prepare a list of specific questions in advance. Here are some of the sources to explore:

Business Development Bank of Canada (BDC)

Regarding raising financing, the BDC can provide advice, a financial matchmaking service, database services and other forms of assistance. Check your phone book for a BDC office.

Community Colleges/Institutes of Technology

Many commerce or business management departments have clinics set up for the public to provide small business assistance, staffed by students with guidance from their instructors.

Community Futures

In many smaller communities, there are community futures offices. These provide counselling and other assistance to those starting small business ventures.

Local Economic Development Commission

Many communities have an economic development department or enterprise development centre that provides free advice and counselling to prospective and existing small business owners. They can also assist you in cutting through government bureaucracy and provide you with information on current government funding assistance procedures, local community initiatives or incentives, as well as statistical information and future growth trends in the community.

Provincial Government Small Business Ministries

All provincial governments have a free counselling program that provides small business assistance ranging from start-up to management and financing. You can obtain the advice in person or over the telephone via a toll-free small business hotline. Many provinces also have an excellent business resource library, which includes videotapes and computer-based business information and analyses. For provincial contact addresses and phone numbers, refer to "Web sites of Interest."

Universities

The students of business schools of many universities provide a low-cost or free consulting service to small business owners. The students benefit through practical "real world" business experience. Backup assistance is provided by their instructors to ensure that quality service is given to the business owner. Assistance provided can include preparation of a business plan, market research study, feasibility study and financial analysis.

Courses and Seminars

Courses and seminars are rich sources of information. Contact the closest office of the following institutions or companies to be put on their mailing list for upcoming business offerings.

Business Development Bank of Canada (BDC)

The BDC offers a wide range of small business seminars, including such topics as tax tips, understanding financial statements, conducting a market survey, retailing, credit and collection, raising financing, motivating employees and time management.

Community Colleges/Institutes of Technology

Extensive course offerings of one- and two-day programs relating to small business management can be found at community colleges and institutes of technology. Generally, seminar leaders are experts with practical "real world" experience. These institutions also have a full selection of daytime and evening business management courses leading to a certificate in Business Administration. Some courses are transferable for credit toward a university degree.

Dun & Bradstreet

Dun and Bradstreet offers a wide selection of practical education programs relating to areas of small business management, such as sales, telemarketing and credit and collection.

Provincial Governments

Most provincial government ministries that deal with small businesses offer seminars on an ongoing basis.

School Boards

Generally offer 10- to 12-week evening adult education courses and condensed one-day Saturday programs on a range of small business management topics.

Universities

Universities may offer non-credit continuing education courses of a one- or two-day duration on business start-ups or specialized subject areas, such as marketing professional services, employee relations, etc.

Federal Government

Business Development Bank of Canada (BDC)

800 Victoria Square
5 Place Ville Marie
Montreal, Quebec H3B 5E7
(514) 283-5904
(888) 463-6232 (toll-free)
www.bdc.ca
BDC is a federal Crown corporation that can be contacted for information on small business management seminars, clinics, financing, financial matchmaking, do-it-yourself kits, publications and government programs (federal, provincial and municipal).

Foreign Affairs and International Trade Canada

125 Sussex Dr.
Ottawa, Ontario K1A 0G2
(613) 996-9134
(800) 267-8376 (toll-free)
www.dfait-maeci.gc.ca
Foreign Affairs and International Trade Canada is an excellent and comprehensive information source of all federal government programs, services, assistance and financial support for the novice or experienced exporter. This is also the contact for information relating to imports.

Industry Canada

235 Queen St.
Ottawa, Ontario K1A 0H5
(613) 995-8900
www.ic.gc.ca

Contact Industry Canada for information on matters relating to federal incorporation, trade-marks, trade names, copyright, patent, industrial design, bankruptcy, consumer protection legislation, federal government assistance and incentive programs for small business and publications. Industry Canada has district offices in major cities throughout Canada and a superb Web site.

Public Works and Government Services Canada
11 Laurier St.
Ottawa, Ontario K1A 0S5
(800) O-CANADA (toll-free)
www.pwgsc.gc.ca
Public Works offers information on how to sell products or services to federal government and Crown corporations as well as statistical information and publications. Public Works operates the computerized "open bidding service" system accessible by potential suppliers with offices in major cities throughout Canada.

Statistics Canada
Customer Inquiries
Tunney's Pasture
Ottawa, Ontario K1A 0T6
(613) 951-8116
(800) 263-1136 (toll-free)
www.statcan.ca
Contact Statistics Canada for information and statistics on geographic, demographic and other population characteristics for small business planning and decision-making. You can access publications and computer data. Statistics Canada has offices in major cities throughout Canada.

Free or Low-Cost Publications
These publications are either free of charge or sold at a nominal cost. Request a detailed list of the publications available from the following sources.

Federal Government
The following outline highlights some of the information available from these sources. Refer to the government Web site: www.strategis.gc.ca for additional information.

Business Development Bank of Canada
See section on banks.

Canada Customs and Revenue Agency
- income tax and small business
- employer's kit

- Goods and Services Tax
- interpretation bulletins
- information circulars
- pamphlets, leaflets, guides and forms
- Thinking About Importing? What You Should Know
- Customs Commercial System: Questions and Answers
- numerous other publications on importing and related taxes

Foreign Affairs and International Trade Canada
- export information kit
- directory of Canadian foreign trade representatives and Canadian consulates abroad guide for Canadian exporters series (covers several countries in the world and various states or regions in the United States)

Industry Canada
- trademarks, copyright, industrial design, and patents
- bankruptcy
- consumer protection
- federal incorporation
- material on financial assistance programs and application procedures
- directory of courses and other informational material relating to recreation, tourism, and hospitality market surveys

Public Works and Government Services Canada
- information kit
- supplier's guide
- series of pamphlets on subjects such as: tendering, buying government surplus, marketing your products and services, late or delayed bids, profit policy, unsolicited proposals, and payment on contracts
- numerous other publications on importing and related taxes

Statistics Canada
- Catalogue of all publications.

Provincial Governments
Many excellent publications are available, most free of charge. You can request publications from provinces outside of your own.

Municipal Governments
Contact the city hall in your community to obtain information on licensing requirements and local bylaws. Also, inquire at your local economic development commission and Chamber

of Commerce for pamphlets and other assistance they can provide. Many communities have excellent information and support services for people considering starting up a small business, including incubator centres. Your community may also have a business development centre or Community Futures Program. These are frequently funded in part by the federal government to stimulate business enterprise.

Accounting Firms

The major accounting firms with branches across Canada have numerous publications that are helpful to your small business success. In most cases, they are free of charge and cover a wide range of subject areas. Contact the librarian of the accounting office nearest you to ask for an updated list of publications. The firms are listed in the Yellow Pages of your telephone directory under "Accountants — Chartered." The primary national and international firms are as follows. Some of their Web sites are noted in "Web sites of Interest."

- BDO Dunwoody
- Deloitte & Touche
- Ernst & Young
- KPMG
- PricewaterhouseCoopers

Banks

For copies of small business publications, contact the Canadian Bankers Association or the commercial branch of any of the chartered banks listed below.

- Canadian Bankers Association
  2 First Canadian Place
  Toronto, Ontario
  M5X 1E1
  www.cba.ca
- Bank of Montreal
- Canadian Imperial Bank of Commerce
- Business Development Bank of Canada
- Royal Bank of Canada
- TD Canada Trust
- Bank of Nova Scotia

Dial-A-Law

Several provinces throughout Canada have a free service providing taped information about small business law matters, as well as other areas of law. The program is normally sponsored by the Canadian Bar Association in conjunction with the provincial law society. The tapes are approximately 10 minutes in length and cover a wide range of topics. In some provinces, transcripts of the tapes are available free or at a nominal cost. Call the lawyer referral service in your province to request further information.

Miscellaneous Publications
The following associations or organizations have various publications available:
- Canadian Franchise Association
- Canadian Chamber of Commerce
- Credit Institute of Canada
- Canadian Institute of Chartered Accountants
- Canadian Manufacturers' and Exporters
- Canadian Restaurant and Foodservices Association
- Canadian Securities Institute
- Dun & Bradstreet of Canada
- Canadian Council for International Business
- Investment Dealers Association of Canada
- any board of trade

Magazines
Magazines are an important means of keeping current on trends, ideas, opportunities and legislation. There are many excellent magazines available at the public library and local newsstand, tailored to the needs of small- and medium-sized businesses. There are also national, provincial and local business publications in Canada that might interest you. In addition, there are many American publications that provide fresh ideas, trends and perspectives that can stimulate your imagination. Your subscription costs are tax deductible as a business expense. A partial listing of suggested national publications follows:

Canadian Business
777 Bay St.
5th Floor
Toronto, Ontario
M5W 1A7

Entrepreneur
2445 McCabe Way
Irvine, California
92614

Inc
38 Commercial Wharf
Boston, Massachusetts 02110

Income Opportunities
380 Lexington Ave.
New York, N.Y. 10017

Profit
777 Bay St.
5th Floor
Toronto, Ontario
M5W 1A7

Small Business Opportunities®
1115 Broadway
New York, N.Y. 10010

Networking Organizations

Many major cities have venture or enterprise clubs or forums. The purpose of such groups is to provide networking, business opportunities and education programs in an informal setting, designed for investors and those looking for investment.

Provincial and Federal Governments — Small Business

For information on provincial and federal small business assistance and match-making programs, free counselling, seminars, publications, small business reference material, selling goods or services, provincial governments and management assistance programs, refer to the Canada Business Services Centre Web site, in "Web sites of Interest." It will list the provincial and territorial offices.

Recommended Books

Here are some helpful guides, authored or co-authored by Douglas Gray

- *The Complete Canadian Small Business Guide*, 3rd ed. (McGraw-Hill Ryerson)
- *The Canadian Small Business Legal Advisor* (McGraw-Hill Ryerson)
- *So You Want to Buy a Franchise* (McGraw-Hill Ryerson)
- *The Canadian Guide to Will and Estate Planning*, 2nd ed. (McGraw-Hill Ryerson)
- *Marketing Your Product*, 2nd ed. (Self-Counsel Press)
- *Start and Run a Profitable Consulting Business*, 6th ed. (Self-Counsel Press)
- *Start and Run a Profitable Business Using Your Computer* (Self-Counsel Press)

WEB SITES OF INTEREST

Family Business
Canadian Association of Family Enterprise   www.cafeuc.org
Canadian Enterprise Development Group Inc.   www.smallbiz.ca
Family Firm Institute   www.ffi.org

Financial and Stock Market Information
Bloomberg Financial News   www.bloomberg.com
Canadian Business Magazine   www.canadianbusiness.com
IE:Money — Personal Finance   www.iemoney.com
Sedar (database information filed with regulatory   www.sedar.com
     agencies by public companies and mutual funds)
Yahoo Finance   http://finance.yahoo.com

Financial Institutions
Canadian Imperial Bank of Commerce   www.cibc.com
Bank of Montreal   www.mbanx.com
Bank of Nova Scotia   www.scotiabank.ca
Royal Bank of Canada   www.royalbank.com
TD Bank Financial Group   www.td.com

Financial Planning
Canadian Association of Financial Planners   www.cafp.org
Financial Planners Standards Council of Canada   www.cfp-ca.org
Microsoft Money   www.msn.ca

Franchising

Canadian Enterprise Development Group Inc.   www.smallbiz.ca
Canadian Franchise Association   www.cfa.ca
Canadian Franchise Information   www.franchise101.com
International Franchise Association   www.franchise.org

Home Based Business

Canadian Enterprise Development Group Inc.   www.smallbiz.ca
Homeworks   www.homeworks.com

Insurance

Canadian Life and Health Insurance Association   www.clhia.ca
Insurance Bureau of Canada   www.ibc.ca

Provincial Government Departments

Government of Alberta   www.gov.ab.ca
Government of British Columbia   www.gov.bc.ca
Government of Manitoba   www.gov.mb.ca
Government of New Brunswick   www.gov.nb.ca
Government of Newfoundland   www.gov.nf.ca
Government of Nova Scotia   www.gov.ns.ca
Government of Ontario   www.gov.on.ca
Government of Prince Edward Island   www.gov.pe.ca
Government of Quebec   www.gouv.qc.ca
Government of Saskatchewan   www.gov.sk.ca

News Publications

Canwest Global   www.canada.com
National Post   www.nationalpost.com
The Globe and Mail   www.globeandmail.com
Toronto Star   www.torontostar.com

Small Business Information

Association of Collegiate Entrepreneurs   www.acecanada.ca
Business Development Bank of Canada   www.bdc.ca
Canadian Business Service Centres   www.cbsc.org
Canadian Enterprise Development Group Inc.   www.smallbiz.ca
Canadian Federation of Independent Business   www.cfib.ca
CanadaOne   www.canadaone.com
Canadian Small Business Information   www.strategis.ic.gc.ca
ENTERWeb (Enterprise Development Worldwide)   www.enterweb.org

Entre World   www.entreworld.org
Export Development Canada   www.edc.ca
Inc. Magazine   www.inc.com
Industry Canada business and consumer site   www.commercecan.ic.gc.ca
Interactive business planner   www.cbsc.org/ibp
Pan Canadian Community Futures Network   www.communityfutures.ca
Profit Guide   www.profitguide.com
Statistics Canada   www.statcan.ca
The Idea Café   www.ideacafe.com
U.S. Small Business Administration   www.sba.gov

Tax Information

BDO Dunwoody Accounting Firm   www.bdo.ca
Deloitte & Touche Accounting Firm   www.deloitte.ca
Ernst & Young Accounting Firm   www.ey.com/global/gcr.nsf/
                                                        canada/tax_welcome
Internal Revenue Service (IRS) — U.S.   www.irs.ustreas.gov
KPMG Accounting Firm   www.kpmg.ca
PricewaterhouseCoopers Accounting Firm   www.pwcglobal.com
Revenue Canada (taxation and customs)   www.revcan.ca

Will and Estate Planning

Canadian Retirement Planning Institute Inc.   www.estateplanning.ca

INDEX

A

Acceleration clause, 158
Accountant, 19
Accounting firms, 217
Accounts receivable turnover ratio, 78–79
Accrual accounting, 80–81
Acid-test ratio, 76
Advertising, 52
Advisors. *See* Professional advisors
Appraisal, 195–196
Arthur Wishart Act (Franchise Disclosure), 2000, 54
Asset purchase, 89, 192
Asset purchase agreement, 173–177
Assets, 72
Assignment clause, 159
Assignment of lease, 159, 165–166
Associations, 211–212

B

Balance sheet, 71–73, 82–83
Balance sheet ratio analysis, 76–77
Bank financing, 120–121
Bank loan proposal letter, 134–135
BDC, 212, 213, 214
Book valuation method, 95
Books, 219
Business brokers, 21, 50–51, 197–198
Business Development Bank of Canada (BDC), 212, 213, 214
Business due diligence, 100
Business immigrants, 7
Business loan application, 136–138
Business plan, 123, 125–132
Business presentation package, 196
Buying a business
    advantages/disadvantages, 35–36
    asset purchase, 89
    available cash, 41
    cash flow, 40–41
    closing the sale, 169–178
    contacting owners directly, 49–50
    financing, 117–144. *See also* Financing
    investigation process, 99–108
    lease, 147–168. *See also* Lease
    location, 38–39, 145–147
    looking for a business, 50–52
    negotiation process, 109–116
    opportunities for growth, 41
    purchase and sale agreement, 169–171
    share purchase, 88–89
    size of business, 40
    starting a business, compared, 36–37
    taxes, 87–88
    timing, 48
    valuation of business, 91–97
    where to look, 48–49
Buying a business checklist, 42–45

C

Canada Business Corporations Act (CBCA), **24**
Canada Business Services Centre Web site, **219**
Canadian Bankers Association, **217**
Canadian Business, **218**
Canadian Chamber of Commerce, **212**
Canadian Council of Better Business Bureaus, **212**
Canadian Federation of Independent Business (CFIB), **212**
Canadian Guide to Will and Estate Planning, The, **219**
Canadian Organization of Small Business (COSB), **212**
Canadian Small Business Legal Advisor, The, **219**
Capitalization of earnings, 95–96
Capitalization rate, 95
Case studies. *See* Real life
Cash-basis accounting, 80
Cash flow, 77
CBCA, 24
CFIB, 212
Checklists
    buying a business, 42–45
    due diligence, 105–106
    franchise agreement terms, 68–70
    franchise assessment, 64–67
    partnership agreement, 30–34
    personal cost-of-living budget, 13–14
    personal net worth, 11–12
    projected financial needs, 15
    sources of financing, 139–144
Closing the sale, 169–178
Collateral, 120
Commencement date clause, 157
Commercial Tenancy Act, 156
Community futures offices, 212
Comparable sales, 95
Complete Canadian Small Business Guide, The, **219**
Confidentiality/non-disclosure agreement, 104, 107–108, 199
Construction allowances, 165
Consulting/counselling services, 212–213
Corporate refugees, 6–7
Corporation, 23–25, 163
COSB, 212
Cost of goods sold, 74
Courses/seminars, 213–214
Critical factors, 180
Current assets, 72
Current liabilities, 72
Current ratio, 76
Customers, 181

D

Debt financing, 117
Debt/worth ratio, 77
Default clause, 158
Definitions (glossary), 201–209
Demolition/construction clause, 158

Deposit, 114, 161
Dial-a-Law, 217
Directory of Associations in Canada, 211
Distress liquidation value, 96
Drive-by traffic, 145
Due diligence, 99–100, 105–106
Due diligence checklist, 105–106
Dun & Bradstreet, 213

E
Earn-out, 119–120, 194
Employees, 181
Encyclopedia of Associations, 211
Entrepreneur, 218
Entrepreneurship, 1–15
    acceptable of risk, 2
    family support, 2
    financial comfort level, 8–10
    forms (checklists), 11–15
    personal inventory, 3–7
    untouchables, 3
Entry clause, 159
Equity financing, 118
Examples. *See* Samples

F
Fair market value, 91–92
Family support, 2, 118
Feedback, 6
Financial comfort level, 8–10
Financial ratios. *See* Ratio analysis
Financial statements, 71–85
    balance sheet, 71–73
    evaluating, 73–75
    income statement, 73
    ratio analysis, 75–79. *See also* Ratio analysis
    reliability, 79–81
Financing, 117–144
    banks, 120–121
    checklist, 139–144
    earn-out, 119–120
    family and friends, 118
    loan proposal, 122–123
    partnership, 119
    personal equity, 118
    samples, 125–138
    seller, 119–120
    Small Business Loans Act, 121
Fire sale price, 96
Fixed assets, 72
Forces sale of business, 190
Foreign Affairs and International Trade Canada, 214
Form of business organization. *See* Legal structure
Formal lease, 155
Forms. *See* Checklists
Franchise, 54
Franchise agreement, 62–63, 68–70
Franchise agreements terms checklist, 68–70
Franchise assessment checklist, 64–67
Franchisee, 54
Franchising, 53–70
    checklists, 64–70
    competitive, 58

    critical factors, 57–59
    definitions, 54
    disclosure requirements, 54–55
    entrepreneurial opportunity, 58
    fees, 61
    franchise agreement, 62–63
    investigate, 55–57
    legislation, 54
    product/service, 57–58
    pros/cons, 59–61
Franchisor, 54
Free/low-cost publications, 215–217

G
Glossary, 201–209
Goal orientation, 6
Goods and services tax (GST), 87–88, 192–193
Graduated lease, 150
Gross margin ratio, 77
Gross profit, 77
Gross revenues, 74
Ground lease, 149
GST, 87–88, 192–193

H
Harmonized sales tax (HST), 88
Hidden business market, 48
Holdover clause, 162
Hours of operation, 147
HST, 88

I
Immigrants, 7
Improvement/fixture clause, 160
Inc, 218
Income capitalization, 95
Income Opportunities, 218
Income statement, 73, 84–85
Income statement ratio analysis, 77–78
Index lease, 150
Industry Canada, 214–215
Information sources. *See* Sources of information
Insurance agent, 21
Intangible assets, 72
Internet web sites, 220–222
Inventory turnover ratio, 78
Investigation process, 99–108

K
Knowledge, 4

L
Land transfer tax, 88
Lawyer, 19
Lawyer referral service, 217
Lease, 147–168
    acceleration clause, 158
    advantages/disadvantages, 147–149
    assignment, 159, 165–166
    assignment clause, 159
    commencement date clause, 157
    construction allowances, 165
    default clause, 158

demolition/construction clause, 158
entry clause, 159
formal, 155
free/reduced rent, 164–165
guarantees, 161, 164
holdover clause, 162
improvement/fixture clause, 160
insurance, 160
key terms, 156–162
legal aspects, 151–154
legislation, 155–156
maintenance and repairs, 160–161
negotiation, 166–168
non-competition clause, 157
offer to lease, 152–154
option to purchase, 162
penalty clause, 158, 163
promotion and administrative cost clause,
        161–162
renewal clause, 162
rent clause, 156
risk, 162–166
security deposit, 161
subletting clause, 159–160
types, 149–151
use clause, 157
utilities, 160
Legal due diligence, 100
Legal structure, 23–34
    agreements, 28
    corporation, 23–25
    partnership, 26–27
    partnership agreement checklist, 30–34
    sole proprietorship, 25–26
Letter of intent, 112–116
Leverage ratio, 77
Liabilities, 72
Liquidation value, 96
Liquidity ratios, 76–77
Loan/financing proposal outline, 133
Loan proposal, 122–123
Local economic development commission, 212–213
Location, 145–147
Long-term liabilities, 72

M
Magazines, 218
Management contract, 182, 184–187
Management ratios, 78–79
Marketing Your Product, 219
Mental traits, 5–6
Month-to-month lease, 162

N
Negotiation process, 109–116
Net lease, 149
Net lease plus taxes, 150
Net profit, 75
Net profit margin ratio, 78
Net worth, 9–14
Networking, 52
Networking organizations, 219
Newspaper ads, 52

No-shop agreement, 114
Non-competition clause, 157
Non-disclosure agreement, 104, 107–108
Notes to financial statements, 75

O
Offer to lease, 152–154
Operating expenses, 75
Option to purchase, 162
Orderly liquidation value, 96

P
Partnership, 26–27
Partnership agreement checklist, 30–34
Penalty clause, 158, 163
Percentage lease, 150–151
Personal cost-of-living budget checklist, 13–14
Personal financial statement, 9–14
Personal guarantees, 161, 164
Personal inventory, 3–7
Personal net worth checklist, 11–12
Physical traits, 5
Professional advisors, 17–21
    accountant, 19
    business broker, 21, 50–51
    insurance agent, 21
    lawyer, 19
Profit, 218
Profit and loss statement, 73
Projected financial needs checklists, 15
Promissory note, 178
Promotion and administrative cost clause, 161–162
Property purchase tax, 88
Provincial/federal small business assistance, 219
Provincial government small business ministries, 213
Provincial sales tax (PST), 88
Public Works and Government Services Canada, 215
Purchase and sale agreement, 169–171

Q
Quick ratio, 76

R
Ratio analysis, 75–79
    liquidity ratios, 76–77
    management ratios, 78–79
    state of income ratios, 77–78
Real Estate Act, 156
Real life
    agreements, 28
    business broker, 51–52
    critical interdependencies, 182
    franchise, 56
    home equity, 123–124
    investigation process, 103–104
    lawyer, 20–21
    lease, 154–155
    Murphy's law, 39–40
    partnership, 27
    valuation of business, 93–94
Realtors, 52, 198
Remedial action, 179
Renewal clause, 162

Rent clause, 156
Rent Distress Act, 156
Resourcefulness, 6
Return on assets, 79
Return on investment (ROI), 79
Revenues, 74
ROI, 79
Rule of two-thirds, 8

S
Samples
    asset purchase agreement, 173–177
    balance sheet, 82–83
    bank loan proposal letter, 134–135
    business loan application, 136–138
    business plan outline, 125–132
    income statement, 84–85
    letter of intent, 115–116
    loan/financing proposal outline, 133
    management agreement, 184–187
    non-disclosure agreement, 107–108
    promissory note, 178
Secured loan, 120
Security deposit, 161
Self-determination, 6
Seller financing, 119–120
Selling your business, 189–200
    alternatives to selling, 190–191
    finding buyers, 197–199
    forced sale of business, 190
    negotiating, 199
    non-disclosure agreement, 199
    packaging the business, 196
    preparation, 195–196
    self-assessment, 189
    taxes, 191–193
    valuation report, 195–196
    vendor financing, 193–195
Share purchase, 88–89
Shareholders' equity, 72–73
Shopping centre, 146
Short Form of Leases Act, 156
Skills, 4
Small business capital gains deduction, 88
Small Business Loans Act, 121
Small Business Opportunities, 218
Small business publications, 217
So You Want to Buy a Franchise, 219
Sole proprietorship, 25–26
Sources of financing checklists, 139–144
Sources of information, 211–219
    associations, 211–212
    books, 219
    consulting/counselling services, 212–213
    courses/seminars, 213–214
    federal government, 214–215
    free/low-cost publications, 215–217
    magazines, 218
    miscellaneous publications, 218
    networking organizations, 219
    small business assistance, 219

Start and Run a Profitable Business Using Your Computer, 219
Start and Run a Profitable Consulting Business, 219
Starting a business, 36–37
Statement of financial position, 71
Statistics Canada, 215
Strategic planning, 180–181
Subletting clause, 159–160
Suppliers, 181
Surprises, 179

T
Taxes
    buying, 87–88
    selling, 191–193
Traits, 4–6
Triple net lease, 150

U
Unaudited statements, 80
Unencumbered capital, 10
Untouchables, 3
Use clause, 157

V
Valuation of business, 91–97
Valuation report, 195–196
Variable lease, 150
Vendor financing, 190
Versatility, 6
Vignettes. *See* Real life

W
Walk-by traffic, 145
Web sites, 220–222
Western Investor, 52
Working capital, 77

ABOUT THE AUTHORS

Douglas Gray, LL.B.

Douglas Gray is a Vancouver-based expert on small business. Formerly a practicing lawyer, he is now a consultant, speaker, columnist and author/co-author of 20 best-selling business and personal finance books. Among these titles is Canada's most popular and comprehensive business book, *The Complete Canadian Small Business Guide*, 3rd edition. His books include eleven titles on small business, six on real estate and three on retirement and estate planning issues. Some of his business books are published in up to nine foreign languages.

Douglas has given seminars to over 250,000 people nationally and internationally in his various areas of expertise. He is the President of the Canadian Enterprise Development Group Inc.

He is a regular expert contributor on business and personal finance issues for various Internet sites and Microsoft and Quicken CD-ROMs, as well as magazines and newspapers. He is frequently interviewed by the media as an authority on business and personal finance matters.

Through his law practice, Douglas assisted numerous clients in negotiating the buying and selling of businesses, as well as providing the necessary legal protections.

Douglas lives in Vancouver. His Web site is: www.smallbiz.ca.

Norman P. Friend

Norman Friend is Chief Executive Officer of Noro Licensing Strategies, Inc., which owns the Canadian master license rights for the Amato Gelato Cafe™ franchise. Their Web site is www.amatogelato.ca.

Widely recognized as an expert in expansion strategies, franchise development, marketing plans and franchisee recruitment, Norman is the co-author of *The Complete Canadian Franchise Guide* and *So You Want to Buy a Franchise*, both published by McGraw-Hill Ryerson. He has contributed numerous articles on business and franchising to national publications and is regularly interviewed by the media. An accomplished professional public speaker, he has presented numerous seminars and keynote talks to business organizations, universities, colleges, professional associations and financial institutions throughout North America.

Norman has personally negotiated the sale of over 200 businesses, including single unit franchises, established businesses, franchise networks, sub-franchises and International master licenses ranging from $7,000 to $2 million.

Norman resides in Vancouver. His Web site is: www.amatogelato.ca.

Other Best-Selling Books by Douglas Gray

Small Business Titles

The Complete Canadian Small Business Guide (with Diana Gray), 3rd edition

So You Want To Buy a Franchise (with Norman Friend)

Home Inc.: The Canadian Home-Based Business Guide (with Diana Gray), 2nd edition

The Canadian Small Business Legal Advisor

Start and Run a Profitable Consulting Business, 6th edition

Start and Run a Profitable Business Using Your Computer

Have You Got What It Takes?: The Entrepreneur's Complete Self-Assessment Guide, 3rd edition

Marketing Your Product (with Donald Cyr), 3rd edition

Real Estate Titles

Canadian Home Buying Made Easy: The Streetsmart Guide for First-Time Home Buyers, 2nd edition

Condo Buying Made Easy: The Canadian Guide to Apartment and Townhouse Condos, Co-ops and Timeshares, 2nd edition

Mortgages Made Easy

Mortgage Payment Tables Made Easy

Making Money in Real Estate

Personal Finance/Retirement Planning Titles

The Canadian Guide to Will and Estate Planning (with John Budd), 2nd edition

The Canadian Snowbird Guide: Everything You Need to Know About Living Part-time in the USA and Mexico, 3rd edition

Risk-Free Retirement

Other Best-Selling Books by Norman Friend

Small Business Titles

So You Want To Buy a Franchise (with Douglas Gray)

Reader Feedback and Author Seminars

If you would like to give feedback on the contents of this book or suggestions for future revisions, or would like further information about seminars and consulting services available provided by the authors, please contact:

Canadian Enterprise Development Group Inc.
#300 – 3665 Kingsway
Vancouver, B.C. V5R 5W2
Tel: 604-436-9311
Fax: 604-436-9155
E-mail: seminars@smallbiz.ca
Web site: www.smallbiz.ca